SENTINEL

EXPOSING THE REAL CHE GUEVARA

Humberto Fontova fled Cuba in 1961, at the age of seven, with his family. He is a journalist who resides in the New Orleans area. Fontova holds a B.A. in political science from the University of New Orleans and a master's degree in Latin American studies from Tulane University. He is a frequent commentator on both English- and Spanish-language media and is the author of four books, including *Fidel: Hollywood's Favorite Tyrant.*

EXPOSING THE REAL

CHE GUEVARA

AND THE USEFUL IDIOTS WHO IDOLIZE HIM

Humberto Fontova

Sentinel

SENTINEL
Published by the Penguin Group
Penguin Group (USA) Inc., 375 Hudson Street,
New York, New York 10014, U.S.A.
Penguin Group (Canada), 90 Eglinton Avenue East, Suite 700,
Toronto, Ontario, Canada M4P 2Y3 (a division of Pearson Penguin Canada Inc.)
Penguin Books Ltd, 80 Strand, London WC2R 0RL, England
Penguin Ireland, 25 St Stephen's Green, Dublin 2, Ireland (a division of Penguin Books Ltd)
Penguin Group (Australia), 250 Camberwell Road, Camberwell,
Victoria 3124, Australia (a division of Pearson Australia Group Pty Ltd)
Penguin Books India Pvt Ltd, 11 Community Centre,
Panchsheel Park, New Delhi – 110 017, India
Penguin Group (NZ), 67 Apollo Drive, Rosedale, North Shore 0632, New Zealand
(a division of Pearson New Zealand Ltd)
Penguin Books (South Africa) (Pty) Ltd, 24 Sturdee Avenue,
Rosebank, Johannesburg 2196, South Africa

Penguin Books Ltd, Registered Offices:
80 Strand, London WC2R 0RL, England

First published in the United States of America by Sentinel, a member of Penguin Group (USA) Inc. 2007
This paperback edition published 2008

3 5 7 9 10 8 6 4 2

Copyright © Humberto Fontova, 2007
All rights reserved

Insert credits: Joaquin Sanjenis, courtesy of Ricardo Nuñez-Protuondo: p. 1; AP/Wide World Photos / Jose Goita; p. 2 top; AP/Wide World Photos / Amy Sancetta: p. 2 bottom; AP/Wide World Photos / Dario Lopez-Mills: p. 3 top; AP/Wide World Photos / Chris Pizello: p. 3 bottom; startraksphoto.com / Bill Davila: p. 4 top; AP/Wide World Photos / Keystone / Laurent Gilleron: p. 4 bottom; AP/Wide World Photos / Joe Caveretta: p. 5; Emilio Izquierdo Jr. / photographer unknown: p. 6 top and bottom; Barbara Rangel / photographer unknown: p. 7; Felix Rodriquez / photographer unknown: p. 8; Enrique Encinosa / photographer unknown: p. 9 top and bottom and p. 10.

THE LIBRARY OF CONGRESS HAS CATALOGED THE HARDCOVER EDITION AS FOLLOWS:

Fontova, Humberto.
Exposing the real Che Guevara : and the useful idiots who idolize him / Humberto Fontova.
p.   cm.
ISBN 978-1-59523-027-0 (hc.)
ISBN 978-1-59523-052-2 (pbk.)
1. Guevara, Ernesto, 1928–1967.   2. Guerrillas—Latin America.   3. Revolutionaries—Latin America.
I. Title.
F2849.22.G85F66   2007
355.4'25092—dc22
2006035721

Printed in the United States of America
Set in Adobe Garamond
Designed by Spring Hoteling

Contents

PREFACE

"These Cubans seem to not have slept a wink since they grabbed their assets and headed for Florida," Michael Moore writes in his book *Downsize This!*

Some Cubans certainly "grabbed assets," but not those who headed for Florida. Michael Moore might have profited from witnessing the scenes at Havana's Rancho Boyeros airport in 1961 as tens of thousands of Cubans "headed for Florida" and "assets were grabbed."

My eight-year-old sister, Patricia, my five-year-old brother, Ricky, and this writer, then seven years old, watched as a scowling *miliciana* jerked my mother's earrings from her ears. "These belong to *La Revolución!*" the woman snapped, and then turned toward my sister. "That, too!" and she reached for the little crucifix around Patricia's neck, pulling it roughly over her head. My mother, Esther, winced and glowered, but she'd been lining up the paperwork for our flight to freedom for a year. She wasn't about to botch it now.

For millions of Cubans, being able to leave your homeland utterly penniless and with the clothes on your back for an uncertain future in a foreign country was (and is today) considered the equivalent of winning the lottery. My mother, a college professor, bore the minor larceny stoically. My father, standing beside her, had just emptied his pockets for another guard as his face hardened. Humberto Senior was an architect. That look (we knew so well) of an imminent eruption was manifesting. Suddenly, uniformed men surrounded Humberto. "*Señor,* you're coming with us."

"To where?" my mother gasped.

"You! Keep your mouth shut!" snapped the *miliciana.* And Humberto was dragged off. "Then we're not leaving!" said my mother as she tried to follow him. "If you can't leave, we're not leaving!" She started to choke up.

My father stopped and turned around as the men grabbed his arms. "You *are* leaving," he said. "Whatever happens to me—I don't want you and the children growing up in a communist country!" It would be a few weeks before Castro admitted he was a Marxist-Leninist. At the word "communist," my father's police escort bristled and jerked him forward.

"We're not leaving!" yelled my mother.

"You are!" yelled my father over his shoulder as he disappeared through the doors. As the doors snapped shut my mom finally broke down. Her shoulders heaved and her hands rose to wipe the tears, but her arms were promptly pulled down by the white-knuckled clutches of her terrified children's little hands. So again my mom composed herself.

"Papi will be out in a minute," she smiled at us while wiping the tears. "He forgot to sign some papers."

Two hours later everyone was lining to board the flight for Miami. But Papi had not emerged from those doors. The agonized look returned to mother's face. It was time for a decision. Cuba's prisons were filled to suffocation at the time. Firing squads were working triple shifts. But her husband had made himself very clear.

"Let's go!" she stood and blurted. "Come on, kids. Time to go on our trip! Papi will meet us later . . ." she gasped and her shoulders started heaving again. Her children's white-knuckled clutches returned to her hands, and we joined that heartsick procession to the big plane, a Lockheed Constellation.

Seeing the big plane, climbing aboard, and hearing the engines crank up excited me, and for a few minutes I forgot about my dad.

"*Volveremos!*" yelled a man a few seats in front of us. Others picked up the cry. Doug MacArthur's famous "I shall return" had been picked up by Cubans, but in the plural. South Florida was alive with exile paramilitary groups, and no one expected that during the height of the Cold War the United States would acquiesce in a Soviet client state ninety miles from its border. The man who started the chant fully expected to be back soon, carbine in hand.

But it was mostly women and children who filled that huge plane, and soon their gasps, sniffles, and sobs were competing with the shouts and the engine noise.

We landed in Miami and somehow found our way to a cousin's little apartment. These relatives had left a few months earlier. From their crowded little kitchen Mom quickly dialed the operator for a call to our grandmother, still in Cuba. The connection went through and she immediately asked about my father. There was a light pause. She frowned, and then she dropped the receiver and fell to the floor.

Her frightened children got to her first. "*Qué pasa!*" Patricia wailed. Our mother was not moving. While one aunt took her in her arms, another picked up the phone, raised it to hear, and somehow made herself heard over the din in that kitchen. Aunt Nena was nodding with the phone pressed to her ear. "Ayy no!" she finally shrieked.

My mother had fainted. Aunt Nena came close when she heard the same thing over the phone. Our father was a prisoner at El G-2 in Havana. This was the headquarters for the military police. Prisoners went to El G-2 for "questioning." From there most went to the La Cabana prison-fortress for "revolutionary justice." But many did not survive the "questioning." The Cuba Archive Project has documented hundreds of deaths at G-2 stations. This was a process that the Left is willing to call by its proper name—"death squads"—anywhere else in Latin America but Cuba.

In a few moments, my mother regained consciousness, but I cannot say she revived. Penniless and friendless in a strange new country, with three children to somehow feed, clothe, school, and raise, Esther Maria Fontova y Pelaez believed herself to be a widow.

A few months later, we were in New Orleans, where we also had relatives, with a little more room in their apartment (only three Cuban refugee families were holed up inside). From this little kitchen my mother answered the phone one morning. Her shriek brought Patricia, Ricky, and me rushing into the kitchen. But this was a shriek of joy. It was Papi on the line—and he was calling from Miami! He had gotten out.

Mom's shriek that morning still rings in our ears. Her scream the following day as Dad emerged from the plane's door at New Orleans' international airport was equally loud. The images of Mom racing across the tarmac, Papi breaking into a run as he hit the ground, and our parents embracing upon contact will never vanish, or even dim.

Today my father hunts and fishes with his children and grandchildren every weekend. Our story had a happy ending. But thousands upon thousands of Cuban families were not as fortunate. One of them was my cousin Pedro's.

That same year, 1961, Pedro was a frail, mild-mannered youth who taught catechism classes at his church in the La Vibora section of Havana. He always came home for lunch and for dinner. One night he didn't show up, and his mother became worried. After several phone calls she became frantic. People were disappearing all over Cuba in those days. She called the local priest, and he promptly joined the search. Father Velazquez was a longtime friend of Pedro, who taught religion classes in his very parish, and quickly suspected something serious. This wasn't like Pedro.

The priest called the local first-aid station and tensed when told that, yes, in fact, the body of a slim, tall youth fitting Pedro's description had been brought in. Father Velazquez hurried down to the station and had his worst fears confirmed. He quickly called my aunt with the news.

The anguished screams from my grandmother when she answered that phone and the accompanying chorus from my mother and sisters still echo in my head. My aunt was silent, however; she seemed in a daze after hearing the voice on the phone informing her that her son's—my cousin Pedro's—corpse was at the station.

Aunt Maria was a widow and her brother went instead. "He died of a heart attack," he was told by the *milicianos*, the secret police bullies trained by the subject of this book. My uncle seethed but somehow controlled himself. His nephew's body was bruised and banged up horribly. Technically, the *milicianos* were probably right. His heart did give out. This is normal under the oft-used interrogation techniques of Cuba's police and militia. Pedro, a fervent Catholic activist, often spoke against the regime during his religion classes, and word of his counter-revolutionary commentary had quickly gotten out. The regime responded in the customary manner.

Until her death in 1993 in New York, my aunt never recovered. Once at a demonstration in New York this saintly woman, a Catholic social worker in Cuba, was denounced as a "*gusana!*" (worm) and "fascist!" by jeering student demonstrators, parroting the epithets of a totalitarian regime.

If Cuban Americans strike you as too passionate, over the top, even a little crazy, there is a reason. Practically every day, we turn on our televisions or go out to the street only to see the image of the very man who trained the secret police to murder our relatives—thousands of men, women, and boys. This man committed many of these murders with his own hands. And yet we see him celebrated everywhere as the quintessence of humanity, progress, and compassion.

That man, that murderer, is Ernesto "Che" Guevara.

ACKNOWLEDGMENTS

To Cuba's Greatest Generation: the thousands of freedom-fighters who fought alone against a Soviet-lavished enemy and died forgotten in Cuba's hills or defiantly in front of firing squads. To the others among their band of brothers who suffered the longest terms of political incarceration of the twentieth century. Few heroes remain as unsung by history as these.

Cuba's Greatest Generation also includes the parents who sacrificed all to see their children grow up free. These parents, who include mine, weren't fleeing their homeland; they fled a disease ravaging it, desperate for their children to avoid the deadly infection.

Those superlong "I'd also like to thank . . ." at the Oscars usually annoy. But believe me, there was nothing annoying about the many people who helped me with this project. During every visit and every phone call at whatever hour I found them a fount of fascinating information and relentless good cheer. Considering what some of them had been through I still marvel.

Mr. Roberto Martin-Perez, for instance, qualifies along with his Cuban-American compatriots, Angel Del Fana and the late Eusebio Peñalver, as the longest-jailed political prisoners of the twentieth century. For thirty years Mr. Martin-Perez was holed up and tortured in various work camps and dungeons of Castro and Che's extensive

Cuban Gulag. Stalin let Alexander Solzhenitzyn off with less than a third the sentence Fidel and Che slapped on Mr. Martin-Perez, Del Fana, and Peñalver. But have you ever heard of them in the mainstream media? I aim to rectify such injustices with this book.

Roberto and his jailed band of brothers could have escaped much of their suffering by simply wearing the uniform of common criminals or signing the confession their communist captors constantly thrust in their faces. The demand to confess to criminality only steeled these men's resolution. They knew full well who were the genuine criminals and who needed to confess: their jailers, from the guards right up to the men at the top—Fidel and Che.

You'd never guess his background from first talking to Mr. Martin-Perez. He smiles constantly. He laughs often and loudly. His lovely wife, Miami radio legend Ninoska Perez-Castellon, was also on hand to inform, direct, and amuse me with my every inquiry. Her radio colleague, Enrique Encinosa, has written as exhaustively and authoritatively as anyone regarding the Cuban people's armed resistance to communism. Enrique's info and insights, both those contained in his books and those expounded over lunch and dinner, contributed much to this book.

In 1964, seventeen-year-old Emilio Izquierdo was rounded up at Russian machine-gunpoint and thrown in a forced labor camp with thousands of other youths. "Active in Catholic organizations," read the charge against him. The prison camp system where Emilio suffered for years had been initiated in 1961 by the man honored as "Chesucristo" in posters and museum displays. Emilio was tremendously helpful with this project.

From afar I'd always revered Mr. Mario Riveron, Mr. Felix Rodriguez, and their band of brothers in the Bay of Pigs Veterans Association. Larger than life heroes, these men put their lives on the line in the anti–Castro/Che fight from day one. Well over half of their brothers in the anti-communist resistance died in front of firing squads, often after torture. Señores Riveron and Rodriguez, along with hundreds of others, knew the odds. They volunteered anyway and stuck with the fight until the last day the United States was willing to wage it.

Later Mr. Riveron and Mr. Rodriguez had key roles in tracking down and capturing Che Guevara in Bolivia. Their Bay of Pigs brothers-in-arms, Nilo Messer, Jose Castaño, Gus Ponzoa, and Esteban Escheverria, also contributed their first-person accounts to this book. What a thrill to hear the details of these men's freedom fight firsthand. What a privilege to be allowed to record it. What an honor to now regard these men as friends.

Misters Carlos Lazo, Serafin Suarez, and Enrique Enrizo were all career officers in Cuba's Constitutional Armed Forces and all got in some licks at Che Guevara's guerrilla band. Their side of the Cuban rebellion story is rarely—if ever—heard. I'm grateful that they took the time to recount it here.

Mrs. Maria Werlau and Dr. Armando Lago labor daily and doggedly attempting to document every death caused by the Castro/Che regime. They require reliable sources and investigate them thoroughly. Their task would make Sisyphus cower, yet they persist. Their selfless and lonely project, titled The Cuba Archive, has been lauded by everyone from the *Miami Herald* to the *Wall Street Journal*. Many of their findings are featured in this book. If that wasn't enough, both Mrs. Werlau and Dr. Lago were always available to this author with additional details or to direct him to a primary source. Many, many thanks to these new friends.

Pedro Corzo of the Instituto de La Memoria Historica Cubana complements much of Mrs. Werlau and Dr. Lago's work by producing excellent documentaries. These put a face to many of these faceless murders. Mr. Corzo's films include interviews with the relatives of the murdered and with now-disenchanted associates of the murderers. His documentaries, *Guevara: Anatomia de un Mito* and *Tributo a Mi Papa* were particularly informative and moving. Manifold thanks to Mr. Pedro Corzo.

Mrs. Barbara Rangel-Rojas's childhood memories of her grandfather's televised murder could not have been easy to dredge up. I'm thankful she chose to include them in this book. The same applies to Guillermo Robaina's recounting of his heroic brother Aldo's death and Lazaro Pineiro's recounting of his father's murder and desecration by the Castroites. Mrs. Janet Ray Weininger, besides detailing her father's martyrdom during the Bay of Pigs, went well above and beyond the call of duty in helping me in every way.

Cuban scholar/researcher/public servant Salvador Diaz-Verson had Fidel and Che's number from day one. How he kept his cool while reading the *New York Times*, listening to U.S. State Department "experts," or watching Ed Murrow on CBS singing these covert communists' praises, we can only guess. Mr. Diaz-Verson's daughter, Sylvia, made all of her famous father's papers and correspondence available for this book. She also recounted little-known but fascinating details of his life. I extend heartfelt thanks to Sylvia—for the invaluable info as well as for her custom made Che T-shirts and tasty pastelitos.

Bay of Pigs vet Mr. Miguel Uria, who edits the superb Spanish-language Webzine *Guaracabuya*, enlisted as my part-time scout for this book, pointing me toward often obscure but invariably excellent primary sources. Miguel's journalistic colleague, Hugo Byrne, also came through with many spicy details.

Employing his computer wizardry, investigative zeal, and international network of Cuba contacts, Jose "El Tiburon" Cadenas of the authoritative Webzine *La Nueva Cuba* kept me well-informed on Cuba/Che news throughout the writing of this book.

Mr. Marcos Bravo had early links to Castro's July 26th Movement. As such he was in a great position to uncover much about Che Guevara's strange psychology and his often stormy relationship with his revolutionary peers. Bravo's work *Ernesto Guevara: Un Sepulcro Blanqueado* was enormously informative and our conversations filled in all the gaps. Many thanks, Señor Bravo.

Charlie Bravo (no relation to Marcos), Miguel Forcelledo, and Carmen Cartaya were all "roqueros" in their day, Cuban youth who "dug" rock music in the sixties. Today when they see a Che T-shirt on a young headbanger or on Carlos Santana and Eric Burdon, they're well past the point of rage or even annoyance. They can only laugh at the imbecility. In this book they explain why. A hearty high-five to these still rocking amigos.

Cuban-American bloggers Valentin "El Barbaro" Prieto of Babalu Blog and Henry "El Conductor" Gomez of Cuban-American Pundits kept me abreast of late-breaking news in Cuba and of scoops in Miami, the capital of the Cuban exile. From Prince Charles to Johnny Depp, no Che T-shirt–wearing celebrity escaped these attentive bloggers' notice and they knew just who to alert. Val and Henry's spirit always inspires and their blogs always inform and entertain.

So again, *un fuerte abrazo*, to all the amigos-collaborators mentioned above.

Now for the dedication. Husband authors dedicating their books to their "loving and supportive wives" has become a sappy cliche—but please hear me out.

Yes, this book is dedicated to my wife, Shirley. And for reasons well known to all our family and friends. Recently her husband was crippled and wheelchair-bound for months after a life-threatening accident, and his future looked uncertain. On top of managing a household of five and working full-time, this forced her to moonlight as nurse and physical therapist, to say nothing of the emotional stress.

Then just as her husband was (literally) getting back on his feet and the doctor's prognosis brightened—just as she kicked back, popped a cork, and was midway through a brief sigh of relief, Hurricane Katrina drew a bead on her hometown.

Her sigh was cut short as she gulped once from her wineglass and scrambled to organize her families' frantic evacuation to a neighboring state.

She returned to find her home of twenty years utterly demolished, many of her lifelong possessions gone forever, and, yet again, a very uncertain future looming. Time for another sigh, but not of relief this time.

During these minor distractions, her two sons somehow started college and her daughter graduated from same and was married. There was also the small matter, as I said, of holding down a full-time profession, as in: managing an entire department at a major bank. Banks, by the way, cannot afford the luxury of closing during crises, even (especially!) after the most destructive hurricane in American history.

How easy it might have been to throw up her hands during this madhouse of heartbreak, turmoil, and travail. How tempting the Thelma and Louise solution must have looked. What an audience her tear-drenched breakdown—her victimization by that villain, fate!—might have drawn for Oprah!

Instead, by merely allowing Calgon to "take her away" from time to time, and occasionally patronizing the product of some (moderately priced) vintners, she kept the whole thing going. And without any of the overt physical symptoms that warrant a camera close-up and teary hug by Ms. Winfrey.

When we met during spring break in 1977, I sensed I was lucky—but I had no idea just how lucky. We met when I tottered over on my platform shoes—my bell bottoms billowing and my polyester collars flapping—and beckoned her to hit the disco floor during the song "I Will Survive."

Little did I dream, as we gyrated under that flashing ball, how aptly and enduringly the song's title would define that hot disco babe's spirit. This book would have been a sheer impossibility without her faith, companionship, gumption, undying support, and multifarious talents, which include still turning heads while strutting and spinning to Gloria Gaynor's classic disco anthem—especially at a raucous French Quarter party celebrating a recent book.

So there, I think a little sappiness is called for.

INTRODUCTION

The man in *The Motorcycle Diaries*, who loved lepers as Jesus did, who forded a river at great personal risk to show his compassion for them, is the man who declared that "a revolutionary must become a *cold killing machine motivated by pure hate.*" As we shall see, he set a spirited example of this principle. This is the man who boasted that he executed from "revolutionary conviction" rather than from any "archaic bourgeois details" like judicial evidence, and who urged "atomic extermination" as the final solution for those American "hyenas" (and came hearth-thumpingly close with nuclear missiles in October 1962).

"If the nuclear missiles had remained we would have used them against the very heart of America, including New York City," Che Guevara confided to the *London Daily Worker* in November 1962. "We will march the path of victory even if it costs millions of atomic victims. . . . We must keep our hatred alive and fan it to paroxysm." This is the same man *Time* felt was worthy to be placed next to Mother Teresa.

He cofounded a regime that jailed or ran off enough of its citizens to merit comparison to the regimes of Hitler or Stalin. He declared that "individualism must disappear!" In 1959, with the help of KGB agents, Che helped found, train, and indoctrinate Cuba's secret police.

Che, whose image writhes in an undisclosed location on U.N. Global Humanitarian award winner Angelina Jolie's epidermis in the form of a tattoo, provoked one of the biggest refugee crises in the history of this hemisphere with his firing squads and prisons. On top of the two million who made it to freedom with only the clothes on their backs, an estimated eighty thousand Cubans have died of thirst, exposure, or drowning, or were ripped apart by sharks. They died attempting to flee Che Guevara and his legacy.

Ignorance, willful or otherwise, is not exactly rare on the topic of Che Guevara. Do rock stars Carlos Santana and Eric Burdon know they are plugging a regime that in the mid to late sixties rounded up *roqueros* and longhairs en masse and herded them into prison camps for forced labor under a scorching sun? Many young prisoners were severely punished for "counter-revolutionary crimes" that often involved nothing worse than listening to the Animals. When Madonna camps it up in her Che outfit, does she realize she's plugging a regime that criminalized gay sex and punished anything smacking of gay mannerisms? In the mid-sixties the crime of effeminate behavior got thousands of youths yanked from Cuba's streets and parks by secret police and dumped into prison camps. In an echo of the Auschwitz logo, between the machine gunners posted on the watchtowers, bold letters above the gate read, "Work Will Make Men Out of You."

Does Mike Tyson—who has been consistently and horribly stomped in fight after fight ever since his visit to Cuba—know that his record of defeat perfectly mimics the combat record of his tattoo idol? Do the A-list hipsters and Beautiful People at the Sundance Film Festival—do Tipper and Al Gore, do Sharon, and Meryl, and Paris—know that they stood in rapturous ovation not just for a movie, but for a movie that glorified a man who jailed or exiled most of Cuba's best writers, poets, and independent filmmakers? Who transformed Cuban cinema into a propaganda machine?

Would Robert Redford—who was required to screen the film for Che's widow, Aleida (who heads Cuba's Che Guevara Studies Center), and Fidel Castro for their approval before release—think it appropriate for Robert Ackerman, who made *The Reagans*, to have to have gone to Nancy Reagan to get her approval? We can only imagine the shrieks of outrage from the Sundance crowd—about "censorship!" and "selling out!" Might Redford have employed a bit of the lust for investigative reporting he portrayed so well in *All The President's Men* to tell the truth about Che? (Whatever happened to "talking truth to power"?)

Fortunately for Robert Redford, who lived in New York in October 1962, Nikita Khrushchev had the good sense to yank those missile launchers from the eager reach of the subsequently famous "Motorcycle Diarist," as well as from the hands of the Stalinist dictator who so kindly gave Redford final benediction on his movie. Also fortunately for Redford and all those unbearably hip Sundance attendees, none were born in Cuba and thus forced to live with their hero's totalitarian handiwork. Is Christopher Hitchens aware that one week after his selfless Che Guevara entered Havana, he stole what was probably the most luxurious house in Cuba and moved in after the rightful owner fled with his family to escape a firing squad?

Che's mansion had a yacht harbor, a huge swimming pool, seven bathrooms, a sauna, a massage salon, and five television sets. One TV had been specially designed in the United States, had a screen ten feet wide, and was operated by remote control—exotic technology in January 1959. "The habitation was a palace right out of *A Thousand and One Nights*," according to a Cuban who saw it. This was the same man who Philip Bennett, then a scribe at the *Boston Globe*, now the managing editor of the *Washington Post*, assures us "was aided by a complete freedom from material aspirations."

A traveling museum show titled "Che; Revolutionary and Icon" recently displayed in Manhattan's International Center of Photography and London's Victoria and Albert Museum, plays up Che as a symbol of rebellion and anti-imperialism. "Che is politics' answer to James Dean," wrote the *Washington Post's* David Segal about the exhibition, "a rebel with a very specific cause." In fact, when addressing Cuba's youth in 1962, Che denounced the very "spirit of rebellion" as "reprehensible." And as we'll learn from his former comrades in the following pages, this world-famed anti-imperialist applauded the Soviet slaughter of young, idealistic Hungarian rebels in 1956. All through the appalling massacre, Che dutifully parroted the Soviet script that the workers, peasants, and college kids battling Russian tanks in Budapest with small arms and Molotov cocktails were all "fascists." A few years later, when Cuba's countryside erupted in a similar anticommunist (really, anti–Soviet imperialism) rebellion, Che got his chance to do more than cheer the slaughter of humble rebels from the sidelines. But these he denounced as "bandits." We'll hear accounts from some of the very few who survived that communist massacre.

And what about Che the military strategist? One day before his death in Bolivia, Che Guevara—for the first time in his life—finally faced something properly described as combat. He ordered his guerrilla charges to give no quarter, to fight to their last breath and last bullet. A few hours later, with his men doing just that, a slightly wounded Che snuck away from the firefight and surrendered with a full clip in his pistol while whimpering to his captors: "Don't shoot! I'm Che, I'm worth more to you alive than dead!"

Yet on top of Hitchens's "conclusive" assertion that Che was "no hypocrite" comes Benicio Del Toro's remark that "Che was just one of those guys who walked the walk and talked the talk. There's just something cool about people like that. The more I get to know Che, the more I respect him."[1]

Del Toro's respect will surely come across clearly in his screen portrayal of his idol. The famously cagey actor based these comments (and his performance) on a screenplay based on Che's diaries, which were edited and published in Cuba, which is to say, by the propaganda ministry of the longest-reigning totalitarian dictator of modern times. Benicio Del Toro's director, Steven Soderbergh—hailed as immensely sharp and shrewd for depicting the treachery and guile of industrialists in *Erin Brockovich*, which he directed, along with the unmitigated evil of Joe McCarthy in *Good Night and*

Good Luck, which he coproduced—based his Guevara movie mostly on books edited by Fidel Castro.

Calling it "the theater of the absurd" somehow fails to describe the Che phenomenon.

The *New Yorker* writer Jon Lee Anderson wrote an 814-page biography of Che titled *Che: A Revolutionary Life.* Anderson asserts that despite his exhaustive research, "I have yet to find a single credible source pointing to a case where Che executed an innocent."[2] Yet hundreds of eyewitnesses to Che's extrajudicial murders are only a cab ride away for Anderson in New York City. Guevara himself boasted that he "manufactured evidence" and stated flat out, "I don't need proof to execute a man—I only need proof that it's necessary to execute him."[3] By which he meant the murdered man might have presented an obstacle to his Stalinization of Cuba. As Stalin himself put it: "Death solves all problems: no man, no problem." Interestingly, Che Guevara cheekily signed some of his early correspondence, "Stalin II."

"Certainly we execute," boasted Che, while addressing the U.N. General Assembly in December 1964. "And we will *continue executing* as long as it is necessary." According to *The Black Book of Communism*—not the work of embittered exiles in Miami, but the labor of French scholars, and published by Harvard University Press—the revolution's firing-squad executions had reached fourteen thousand by the beginning of the 1970s. Given Cuba's population at the time, the slaughter was the equivalent of over three million executions in the United States.

Despite this extrajudicial bloodbath, while visiting Havana in 1984, Jesse Jackson was so smitten by both his host and the lingering memory of his host's late sidekick that he couldn't contain himself. "Long Live Fidel!" bellowed Jackson to a captive crowd at the University of Havana. "Long live our Cry of Freedom!—LONG LIVE CHE!"[4]

This is the same Jesse Jackson who wrote a 224-page book against the death penalty. Even better, Che, far from reciprocating

Jackson's fond sentiments, regarded blacks as "indolent and fanciful, spending their money on frivolity and drink." Che wrote this passage in his now-famous *Motorcycle Diaries*—one of the touches that Robert Redford and Walter Salles somehow left out. Black rapper Jay-Z might keep it in mind before donning his super-snazzy Che shirt for his next MTV Unplugged session where he raps: "I'm like Che Guevara with a bling on!"[5] Mike Tyson might want to laser off his tattoo, lest he be seen as "indolent and frivolous."

What about Che the intellectual? "For Ernesto Guevara everything began with literature," writes Jon Lee Anderson. Yet Che's first official act after entering Havana (between executions) was a massive book burning. On Ernesto "Che" Guevara's direct orders, more than three thousand books were stolen from a private library and set ablaze on a busy Havana street. Around the same time, Che signed death warrants for authors and had them hunted through the streets like rabid animals by his secret police. We'll hear the whole story straight from these authors' families.

At the same time Sartre was hailing Che's towering intellect in summer 1960, *Time* magazine put him on its cover for the first time. Their feature story attributed "vast competence and high intelligence" to Guevara, who had recently been promoted to Cuba's economic minister after showing a certain acumen for numbers as Cuba's chief executioner.

Within a year of that appointment, a nation that previously had higher per capita income than Austria and Japan, a huge influx of immigrants, and the third-highest protein consumption in the hemisphere, was rationing food, closing factories, and hemorrhaging hundreds of thousands of its most productive citizens from every sector of its society.

Che responded to the unexpected economic crisis in classic manner. He opened a forced-labor camp at Guanahacabibes—Cuba's version of Siberia, but featuring broiling heat rather than cold—and filled it to suffocation by herding in Cuba's recalcitrant laborers at bayonet and machine-gunpoint.

The economic crisis fostered by Che forced the Soviets to pump the equivalent of eight Marshall Plans into Cuba. The original $9-billion Marshall Plan, applied by the United States to a war-ravaged continent of 300 million, promptly lifted its economy. All this wealth invested by the Soviets in a nation of 6.4 million—whose citizens formerly earned more than the people of Taiwan, Japan, and Spain—resulted in a standard of living that repels impoverished Haitians more than forty years later.

Che's incompetence defies not just the laws of economics, but seemingly the very laws of *physics*.

Concerning Che's military exploits, the liberal media lay it on even thicker and heavier. "One Thousand Killed in 5 Days of Fierce Street Fighting," blared a *New York Times* headline on January 4, 1959, about the final "battle" in the anti-Batista rebellion in the Cuban city of Santa Clara. "Commander Che Guevara turned the tide in this bloody battle and whipped a Batista force of 3,000 men," continued this article on the front page of the world's most respected newspaper of the time. In fact, as you'll see in the coming pages, the rebel victory at Santa Clara, where Che supposedly earned his eternal fame—like all others in which he "fought"—was accomplished by bribing Batista commanders. Total casualties on *both* sides did not exceed five. Che spent the three days of the Bay of Pigs invasion three hundred miles from the battle site braced for what he was certain was the real invasion. He'd been lured away by a rowboat full of fireworks, mirrors, and a tape recording of battle, a literal smoke-and-mirrors show concocted by the CIA for that very purpose.

Yet Che managed to earn the Cuban version of a Purple Heart in his battle against the unmanned and unarmed rowboat. A bullet had pierced Che's chin and exited above his temple, just missing his brain. The bullet came from Che's *own pistol*. "Che's military leadership was permeated by an indomitable will that permitted extraordinary feats," writes *New York Times* contributor and Che biographer Jorge Castañeda.[6]

"Extraordinary" is one way of putting it. Castañeda, also a Columbia, Harvard, and Princeton visiting professor, adds that "Che's contribution to the [Bay of Pigs] victory was crucial."

Four years later, in the Congo while planning a military campaign against crack mercenaries commanded by a professional soldier who had helped defeat Rommel in North Africa, Che confidently allied himself with "soldiers" who used chicken feathers for helmets and stood in the open waving at attacking aircraft because a *muganga* (witch doctor) had assured them that the magic water he sprinkled over them would make .50-caliber bullets bounce harmlessly off their bodies. Within six months, Che had fled Africa, narrowly saving his life and leaving behind a military disaster.

Two years later, during his Bolivian guerrilla campaign, Che made textbook mistakes for a guerrilla leader. He split his forces and allowed both units to become hopelessly lost. They bumbled around, half-starved, half-clothed, and half-shod, without any contact with each other for six months before being wiped out. Che's forces didn't even have World War II vintage walkie-talkies with which to communicate and were apparently incapable of reading compasses. They spent much of the time walking in circles, often within a mile of each other.

"Che waged a guerrilla campaign where he displayed outrageous bravery and skill," reads the *Time* encomium honoring this "Hero and Icon of the Century." The authoritative piece was written by Ariel Dorfman, who heads the Department of Latin American Studies at Duke University and previously taught at the Sorbonne. Professor Dorfman might have consulted Che Guevara's former rebel comrade, Huber Matos, now living in Miami, who recalls that while attempting to coordinate an attack on Batista's forces with him in 1958, Che admitted knowing "absolutely nothing" about military strategy. Amongst themselves communists are often quite candid. They coined the term "useful idiot," after all. But even the famously dour Nikolai Lenin might have erupted in horselaughs if he could have seen the unbridled success of Che propaganda.

Some Che biographers uncritically absorb the lies they are told by authoritative people and pass them on. Of the two most voluminous and best-selling biographies of Che, one was written by a contributor to *Newsweek* and the *New York Times* who is also a former Mexican Communist Party member and fondly recalls plastering Che's poster in his Princeton dorm room. The other, written by a columnist for *The New Yorker*, was written mostly in Cuba with Castro's full cooperation and with Aleida Guevara—a high-ranking Cuban Communist Party member—as a primary source.

Che Guevara's diaries were published by the propaganda bureau of a totalitarian regime, with the foreword written by Fidel Castro himself. Yet all Che "scholars" and the mainstream media take them at face value. Indeed, with regard to the unvarnished secrets of Che Guevara's history, his scholarly biographers treasure these Havana editions as if they were the Dead Sea Scrolls. Might there be some embellishments or omissions in these Che "diaries"—in these documents that feature so prominently in the liberal media's versions of Che's brilliance and heroism? Not according to Che "scholars." But as we'll see in the coming chapters, Che's early revolutionary colleagues, now in exile, along with the men *actually on the scene* of Che Guevara's capture, have a very different story to tell.

The book you're holding relies on testimony from people who are now free to tell the truth without fear of Castro's torture chambers and firing squads. Normally, eyewitnesses to a Hero and Icon of the Century would have to bat away the journalists, biographers, and screenwriters. Instead, for forty years, the mainstream press, scholars, and scriptwriters have shunned these invaluable sources. It appears that the journalists and scholars, no less than the screenwriters, do not want to entertain facts that conflict with the narrative they have jointly constructed with one of the century's top manipulators of the intelligentsia, Fidel Castro.

Since Castro's famous interview with Herbert Matthews of the *New York Times* in 1957, through all the fawning interviews with Dan Rather, Barbara Walters, and Andrea Mitchell, Castro always had the international media eating out of his hand like trained pigeons. The process cranked up several notches when CNN opened its Havana bureau in 1997. This was shortly after Ted Turner, during a packed speaking gig at Harvard Law School, bubbled to the crowd, "Castro is one hell of a guy! You people would like him!" (Another gushing accolade for Cuba's Maximum Leader came from the gentleman known, at the time, as "Mr. Jane Fonda." His praise was evoked by a recent hunting trip to Cuba. During Ted Turner's expedition with Castro, military helicopters drove thousands of ducks in front of their shotguns, allowing them to slaughter hundreds of hapless birds. Where was PETA on that one?) At any rate, Che lives on in part because he had Fidel Castro as a press agent.

From Castro's fervid devotion to democracy and well wishes for the United States in 1957, to his regime's glorious achievements in health care and education, to Elian's father's heartfelt yearning for the return of his son, Castro's every whopper has been respectfully transcribed and broadcast for half a century now—and by the same journalistic Torquemadas who wouldn't allow an American president to finish a sentence without erupting in cynical snorts and rude interrogations.

Much credit for the remarkable afterlife of Che Guevara goes, of course, to The Picture. To his credit, Guevara understood his role. He performed magnificently at his photo shoot in March 1960 for Alberto Korda. His "faraway eyes" and high cheekbones were perfectly highlighted. Today that's often all it takes for media stardom. Few Americans know that the famous icon photo was actually spiked by the Castro regime when it was first scheduled to run in Cuba's official paper, *Revolución*. Che's image could have overshadowed the Maximum Leader's at the time. In its place they ran a photo of Fidel sitting and chatting with two of his famous fans, Jean-Paul Sartre and Simone de Beauvoir.

Castro, better than even his chums Ted Turner and Robert Redford, always understood the power of imagery. Since his high-school days, Castro was a keen student of Nazi pageantry. The official colors of Castro's July 26 Movement's flag and armbands are black and red with a splash of white, identical to the Nazi flag and armband. Coincidence? Perhaps.

Seven years after Korda's photo shoot, when Che was safely "sleeping with the fishes" and could pose no threat to the Maximum Leader, Castro dusted off The Picture and started plastering it all over Cuba. He called the international media with a sharp whistle and said, fetch. The result is the most reproduced and idolized print of the century.

As his former comrades could have told you, "Fidel Castro only praises the dead."

Castro knows the continuing power of Che, and how to appropriate it for himself. According to UCLA professor David Kunzle, "There is no figure in 20th Century history that has produced such a body of fascinating, varied and compelling imagery as Che Guevara."[7]

Here, at long last, we encounter a truth about Che—and, as we shall learn, a truth about Fidel. Several men who were Castro's political prisoners in 1967 have revealed to me that their prison guards finally displayed that now-famous Che poster *the week before Guevara was captured and killed.* Fidel wasn't exactly surprised by the news of Che's death, having created the conditions for his death in Bolivia. He then oversaw and personally sold the media blitz for a martyred friend.

And so today The Picture adorns T-shirts, posters, watches, skis, lava lamps, skateboards, surfboards, baseball caps, beer-huggers, lighters, Rage Against the Machine CDs, and vodka bottles. Last year supermodel Gisele Bundchen took to the catwalk in skimpy underwear stamped with Che's face. Burlington put out a line of infant wear bearing Che's face. Taco Bell dressed up its Chihuahua spokesdog like Che for its "Taco Revolution" ad campaign. "We wanted a heroic leader to make it a massive taco revolution!" says Taco Bell's advertising director, Chuck Bennett. (This tribute, perhaps, is comic enough to be appropriate—as long as consumers can keep from thinking about how Che treated real dogs.) The TV shows *South Park* and *The Simpsons* have lampooned Che T-shirt wearers. Omar

Sharif and Antonio Banderas have played Che in movies. Under the pseudonym John Blackthorn, Gary Hart wrote a novel titled *I, Che Guevara*. A video game, *Guerrilla War,* plays on Che's (utterly bogus) military exploits.

Ignorance, of course, accounts for much Che idolatry. But so do mendacity and wishful thinking, all of it boosted—covertly and overtly—by reflexive anti-Americanism. This book will expose you to many eyewitness accounts of Che Guevara's cruelty, cowardice, and imbecility. The deeper investigation will be why he continues to receive so much adoration from media leftists and celebrities in the twenty-first century.

This book will succeed in some degree, however, if it merely prompts Angelina Jolie to question if her tattoos, as her website claims, are really "a reflection of her personality." If this is so, then Brad Pitt had better start watching his back.

1

New York Fetes the Godfather of Terrorism

On the evening of December 11, 1964, Che was decked out in a long trench coat, his trademark beret with the red star cocked at a jaunty angle as he strode toward the United Nations to address the General Assembly. Security was tight for the event and cops swarmed on the scene. Cuban exiles infested nearby New Jersey and many were on hand holding up placards, waving fists, and yelling "*Assassin!*" as Guevara prepared to make his grand entrance.

As Che neared the U.N. entrance, a New York cop named Robert Connolly noticed a grim-faced woman racing down Forty-third Street. He alerted his colleague Michael Marino. The two cops tensed while watching the woman pick up speed as she neared the makeshift barrier erected specifically to protect Che at the U.N. perimeter. A large knife flashed in the woman's hand.

"Watch her!" bellowed Connolly. "She's got a knife!" Connolly and Marino started sprinting toward her.

"*Arriba!*" the woman yelled, closing on Che. Only then did Che's bodyguards begin to react. She shrieked again, her little legs pumping furiously.

The cops were closing on her when she turned, yelled "*Arriba!*" a final time, and waved the huge knife. They easily dodged her knife and gang-tackled her. After a few seconds of rolling and scuffling, the inflamed woman, Gladys Perez, was subdued.

"I meant the officers no harm," Gladys panted while being led away. "The knife was meant for the assassin Guevara!"[1]

Officers Connolly and Marino were soon on their way to St. Clare's Hospital for treatment of multiple scratches and gouges inflicted by the struggle. Gladys was telling the truth. Her knife did not touch the cops. The poor officers tangled only with the buzz saw of her teeth and fingernails as she struggled to get at Che.

Unscathed, Che Guevara entered the halls of the General Assembly and started his speech. "Executions?" He paused for effect at one point. "Certainly, we execute!" he declared to the claps and cheers of that august body. "And we will *continue executing* [emphasis his] as long as it is necessary! This is a war to the DEATH against the Revolution's enemies!" The Spanish word for death is *muerte*, and Che rolled the Rs deliciously. The trilling of "*mueRRRRTE!*" resonated grandly throughout the hall.[2]

Che was merely proclaiming, of course, what the scholars of *The Black Book of Communism* would reveal—that fourteen thousand Cubans would be executed without anything smacking of due process by the end of the decade. For perspective, consider that Slobodan Milosevic went on trial for allegedly ordering eight thousand executions. The charge against Milosevic—by the same United Nations that applauded Che—was "genocide." Che let the General Assembly's ovation that greeted his "*mueRRRRRTE!*" subside and proceeded to other favored themes. "The government of the United States is not the champion of freedom," he said, "but rather the perpetuator of exploitation and oppression against the peoples of the world and against a large part of its own population!" More claps, more cheers. Yankee Imperialism was "a carnivorous animal feeding on the helpless." Another ovation.[3]

The Toast of Manhattan

Che was in New York for eight days but could barely accommodate all the Beautiful People jostling to meet him. On *Face the Nation*, Che was softballed by the *New York Times*'s Tad Szulc. "The road of liberation will go through bullets,"[4] Che said, firing rhetorical bullets through the softballs—and paying no price in reputation for this extreme display of belligerence.

Lisa Howard—Hollywood actress, Mutual Radio Network host, and ABC noontime news anchorette—hosted Che in her Manhattan penthouse. Howard had also invited Democratic senator Eugene McCarthy, a lifelong opponent of capital punishment, to fete Che. Howard, a self-appointed matchmaker between Cuba and the United States, achieved nothing but the encouragement of even more spirited denunciations of her country.

Such was Che's New York social swirl that Malcolm X had to settle for a written message, which he read in Harlem's Audubon Ballroom. "Dear Brothers and Sisters of Harlem," Malcolm read without disclosing the messenger, "I would have liked to have been with you and Brother Babu . . . Receive the warm salutations of the Cuban people and especially those of Fidel."

"This is from Che Guevara!"[5] an enraptured Malcolm X finally yelled as the room exploded in applause.

Columnist Laura Berquist conducted two reverential interviews with Che Guevara for *Look* magazine, one in November 1960, another in April 1963. *Look*'s covers and interviews featured mostly movie stars. So a Che interview must have struck *Look*'s editors as a simply *mahh-velous* idea. Berquist traveled to Havana for her interviews and in 1960 brought back the following scoop: "Che denies he's a party-line Communist." She then suggested the proper characterization for him as a "pragmatic revolutionary," to which Che smilingly agreed. "When he smiles he has a certain charm," Berquist reported. Overall she found him "fascinating . . . cool and brainy."[6]

By 1963, with Cuba officially declaring itself to be a Marxist-Leninist state, a fact it celebrated with Soviet missiles and banners of Lenin, Berquist prudently shucked the "pragmatic revolutionary" label. But she still found things to admire in Cuba—the Committees for the Defense of the Revolution, for instance. They make up a network of government spy groups set up on every city block to promptly report any "counter-revolutionary" backsliding by their neighbors to the police. Depending on the severity of the infraction, penalties range from a cut in the weekly food ration, to a stint in a prison camp, to being riddled with bullets by a firing squad. The system is novel even for communist regimes, formerly in place only in East Germany where the STASI, who helped set it up in Cuba, grandfathered it from the Nazi Gestapo. Berquist seemed charmed by them. Their role, she reported in *Look*, was "to see that children are vaccinated, and learn to read and write. And that the local butcher doles out meat fairly."[7]

The day after Che's "*mueRRRRRRTE!*" oration at the United Nations, Laura Berquist arranged a splendid and celebrity-studded evening for Cuba's mass executioner as guest of honor at the townhouse of her friend, Bobo Rockefeller. In attendance were several black activists, beat poets, and assorted literary types—in short, the very people most passionate in their support of civil rights for all people, and opposed to the death penalty. Bobo Rockefeller hosted the classic scene from *Radical Chic & Mau-Mauing the Flak Catchers* six years before Tom Wolfe wrote the hilarious essay and book.

Somehow, amidst all the media and social schmoozing, Che also found time for serious business. The details of his secret plotting were disclosed several months later when the New York Police Department uncovered a plot to blow up the Statue of Liberty, the Liberty Bell, and the Washington Monument. But for the joint work of New York's finest, the FBI, and the Royal Canadian Mounted Police, Che's terror plot would have brought the terror of September 11 to America decades earlier. The main plotters were members of the Black Liberation Army, who sneered at Malcolm X as an Uncle Tom. These American radicals were in cahoots with a Canadian separatist radical and Canadian TV anchorette named Michelle Duclos. According to the head plotter, Robert Steele Collier, who also belonged to the New York chapter of the Fair Play for Cuba Committee, the plot was hatched on his visit to Cuba in August 1964 when he met with Che Guevara. Collier, along with Duclos, met Che again on his New York U.N. visit and buttoned down the details for the explosions.

Everything seemed set. Duclos had brought in the thirty sticks of dynamite and three detonators through the Canadian border and stashed them. After the blasts, she'd provide the Black Liberation Army plotters brief refuge in her Canadian apartment until they slipped into permanent refuge in Cuba.

But the plotters had been infiltrated by Raymond Wood, a black NYPD cadet. The NYPD alerted the FBI, the Canadian Mounties, and the U.S. Border Patrol, which tailed Duclos as she crossed from Canada and watched her stash the dynamite. The FBI then staked out the locale and watched Collier drive up, look around furtively, and slink out of his car.

The agents sprang from the bushes and captured Collier just as he located the dynamite stash. Che's plot failed.[8]

Had everything gone according to plan, Che Guevara would have destroyed America's greatest monuments, killed hundreds if not thousands of visitors from around the world, and allowed the killers to slip into Cuba for safe haven. If the facts of the attack had become publicly known, President Johnson might have been forced to repudiate the Kennedy administration's noninterference agreement with the Soviet Union following the Cuban Missile Crisis. The result could easily have been catastrophic. Of course, the plot had no effect, either on American security or on Che's reputation. It fell to twenty-four-year-old Gladys Perez to wear the label "terrorist." While being booked for felonious assault, Gladys said she had

arrived from Cuba two years earlier. In Cuba, as a political prisoner, she had been tortured and raped. Asked by a court interpreter
if she regretted her actions, Gladys snapped, "No! If Guevara were
here now I'd kill him!"

The *New York Times* reported on December 14, 1964, that a
young assistant district attorney asked that the handcuffed woman
be committed for mental observation.

Consider the facts: A Cuban woman is imprisoned, tortured,
and raped by communist goons. She seeks revenge on the chief executioner of the regime that tortured her, raped her, jailed and executed thousands of her countrymen, and brought the world a hair
away from nuclear holocaust. The woman is committed for mental
observation.

Immediately after he boasted of those very executions for a
worldwide forum in the heart of their city and after he insulted his
hosts as "hyenas," fit only for "extermination," New York's media and
high society fetes Cuba's chief executioner, Ernesto "Che" Guevara.
Their honored guest had twice plotted to incinerate and entomb the
very New York now feting him. He was plotting more terrorism for
New York *during the very feting.* *Time* magazine, headquartered in
New York, then hails him as a "Hero and Icon of the Century"
alongside Mother Teresa.

Who needs "mental observation"?

Should, perhaps, a city that continues to adore a man who
wanted to destroy it be corporately committed? In 2004, the New
York Public Library was selling Che watches in its gift shop—not unlike the British Museum selling collector's items bearing the image of
Luftwaffe Chief Hermann Goering. Perhaps the library management
can be forgiven for not knowing about Che's plans for them. Less for-
givable was their benefit gala in 2005, "An Affair in Havana," which
celebrated "Literary Havana." Was the intention to celebrate Che's
book bonfire? Or was it to celebrate the sixteen librarians who today
sit in Castro's dungeons with twenty-five-year prison sentences for attempting to disseminate such subversive literature as George Orwell's

Animal Farm, Martin Luther King's "I Have a Dream" speech, and the U.N. Declaration on Human Rights? Even liberal columnist Nat Hentoff tried to make the library see reason, by calling it plainly "stupid," to no avail. And just last year Manhattan's International Center of Photography packed in the crowds for its exhibition titled "Che! Revolution and Commerce."

"Tomorrow New York is going to be here," Rudy Giuliani assured his stricken fellow citizens on 9/11. "And we're going to rebuild, and we're going to be stronger than we were before . . . I want the people of New York to be an example to the rest of the country, and the rest of the world, that terrorism can't stop us!"[9]

New York based *Time*, which places Ernesto "Che" Guevara among "The Heroes and Icons of the Century," also hailed Rudy Giuliani as its "Man of the Year" in 2001 for being 9/11's "crisis manager" and "consoler in chief," and for "teaching us how to respond to a terrorist crisis."

"We will bring the war to the imperialist enemies' very home, to his places of work and recreation," Che Guevara declared in his "Message to the Tri-Continental Conference" published in Havana in April 1967. "We must never give him a minute of peace or tranquility. This is a total war to the death. We'll attack him wherever we find him. The imperialist enemy must feel like a hunted animal wherever he moves. Thus we'll destroy him!"

And who was this imperialist enemy? "The great enemy of mankind: the United States of America!"[10]

Among the many future luminaries who attended Havana's Tri-Continental Conference was a promising young man, Abu Ammar, who would later become known as Yasir Arafat. Also in attendance was a young Ilich Ramírez Sánchez, also known as Carlos the Jackal, who became "the World's Most Wanted Terrorist." In 1967, Ramírez Sánchez was an eager recruit into Cuba's terror training camps started by Che in 1959. Through these connections, one can trace a very straight line from Che to 9/11. "I'm proud of the path of Osama bin Laden," Ramírez Sánchez told the London-based pan-Arab daily *Al-Hayat* in an interview from a French prison in 2002. "Bin Laden has followed a trail I myself blazed . . . I followed news of the September 11 attacks on the United States nonstop from the beginning. I can't describe that wonderful feeling of relief."[11]

Che wrote the first draft of the attacks of 9/11. Can anyone read him and doubt if Che were alive today, he would be anything but elated by the toppling of the World Trade Center?

Historians of the Cuban Missile Crisis have firmly established that New York's 9/11 explosions would appear like an errant cherry bomb if Che had succeeded in goading the Soviets and Americans into all-out war, which he tried to do. Only the prudence of Nikita Khrushchev stayed Che's ambitions for a red apocalypse. Nor was the Black Liberation Army plot the only terror plot Che aimed at American citizens.

On November 17, 1962, the FBI cracked another terrorist plot by Cuban agents who targeted Macy's, Gimbel's, Bloomingdale's, and Manhattan's Grand Central Terminal with a dozen incendiary devices and five hundred kilos of TNT. The holocaust was set for the following week, the day after Thanksgiving.

A little perspective: For their March 2004 Madrid subway blasts—all ten of them—that killed and maimed almost two thousand people, al Qaeda's Spanish allies used a grand total of one hundred kilos of TNT. Cuban agents planned to set off *five times* that explosive power in the three biggest department stores on earth, all packed to suffocation and pulsing with holiday cheer on the year's biggest shopping day.

Thousands of New Yorkers, including women and children—actually, given the date and targets, probably *mostly* women and children—were to be incinerated and entombed.[12]

Was this the handiwork of Che? All his biographers admit—grudgingly—that Che had a central role in establishing Cuba's security machinery, including the DGI's (Dirección General de Inteligencia) Liberation Department in charge of "guerrilla" training and foreign "liberation" plots. So it's inconceivable that Che didn't sign off on this early New York terror plot, much less that he opposed it.

The more you place Che's rhetoric and actions side by side with the adoration of him by New York–based intellectuals, the more the adoration of Che appears to be less of a fashion statement and more of a death wish.

2

Jailer of Rockers, Hipsters, and Gays

Che Guevara has given rise to a cult of almost religious hero
worship among radical intellectuals and students across
much of the Western world. With his hippie hair and wispy
revolutionary beard, Che is the perfect postmodern conduit
to the nonconformist, seditious '60s.
—*Time* MAGAZINE, MAY 1968

Christopher Hitchens recalls that "1968 actually began in 1967 with the
murder of Che. His death meant a lot to me, and countless like me,
at the time. He was a role model."[1]

In 1968, "Up Against the Wall!" echoed from Paris to Chicago,
from Milan to Mexico City. Charles De Gaulle was chased from office by student riots. "The Whole World Is Watching!" shrieked the
student protesters who turned the Democratic convention in Chicago
into an orgy of tear gas and billy clubs. "Don't trust anyone over
thirty!" was a favorite chant in places like Berkeley and Columbia
Universities, alongside "Che Lives!"

In one large Western capital in particular, some youthful protesters
were very brazen and disrespectful. They enraged and alarmed their

government, which denounced them as "hippies" and "delinquents." The government was horrified that these "antisocial elements" were "desecrating national symbols! Burning flags! Burning pictures of national heroes!"[2] These hippie groups grew long hair, dug rock and roll, and called themselves such names as "the Beats" and "the Psychedelics." They were clearly a danger to national stability and would suffer severe disciplinary measures, especially as these "delinquents" and "bums" relished trashing the images of one national hero in particular. The rigidly authoritarian national hero these young rebels targeted was known as a stern and violent disciplinarian, utterly lacking in empathy or a sense of humor. He detested rock and roll music and constantly railed against "long hair," "lazy youths," and any sign of insubordination in general. He had written that the young must always: "listen carefully—and with utmost respect—to the advice of their elders who held governmental authority." He preached constantly how students—rather than distracting themselves with idiocies like rock and roll music—must instead dedicate themselves to "study, work and military service."[3]

The reader has long since guessed that this is a description of Havana and Che.

Any shirkers of duty faced the full wrath of his notoriously brutal police. After all, in his own words, "The happiest days of [a] youth's life is when he watches his bullets reaching an enemy." And rather than indulge in frivolous pursuits during their summer vacations, students should volunteer for government service and toil there happily. Che went the Seven Dwarfs one better. For him, whistling while you work didn't suffice. He wrote that youths should not just toil for their government "happily and with great pride," but should actually "be chanting government slogans and singing government-approved songs" while in the act.[4]

And woe to those youths "who stayed up late at night and thus reported to work tardily." Youth, in particular, should learn "to think and act as a mass." Those who chose their own path were denounced as worthless lumpen and delinquents. In one famous speech, Che even vowed "to make individualism disappear from the nation! It is criminal to think of individuals!"[5]

This national hero even scorned the very "spirit of rebellion" as "reprehensible."[6]

In short, "tune in, turn on, drop out" wasn't exactly Che's thing.

It is for these reasons that longhairs and hippies burned, defaced, and ripped to pieces images of Che Guevara. Most galling to the police, to glorify Che's death, Castro had declared 1968 Cuba's "Year of the Heroic Guerrilla." With Che posters blanketing the landscape, youthful angst and rage had the perfect target. And no young people ever had more cause for angst and rage than Cuba's.

"These youths walk around with their transistor radios listening to imperialist music!" Castro raved to his usual captive audience in the Plaza de la Revolución as he announced the opening of his regime's hunting season on Cuban hippies. "They corrupt the morals of young girls—*and destroy posters of Che!* What do they think? That this is a bourgeois liberal regime? NO! There's nothing liberal in us! We are collectivists! We are communists! There will be no Prague Spring here!"[7] The famous Venceremos brigades of U.S. radicals and college students who visited Cuba to cut sugar cane and help "build Cuban socialism" started the following year. These starry-eyed leftists, with their hippie hair and hippie clothes, learned very quickly to display their Venceremos Brigade insignia prominently. A few, mistaken for homegrown Cuban hippies, had reported very disturbing encounters with Castro's police. "These young American radicals in their ritual dress," wrote French socialist Leo Sauvage at the time, "were about as safe among their Cuban 'revolutionary brothers' as they were in the streets of downtown Manhattan amidst the hardhats!"

Not that disillusionment was exactly widespread among U.S. radicals. But a few eyebrows were raised and a few troubled murmurs were overheard by the movement's high priests. Susan Sontag herself sought to lay herself as a bridge over these (slightly) troubled waters in a *Ramparts* article in the fevered spring of 1969, wherein she admitted that "the Cuban Revolution presents in part an extremely uncomfortable challenge to American radicals."

This challenge may have been "uncomfortable," but it was hardly insurmountable. Sontag went on to explain that "although their awareness of underdevelopment inevitably leads to an increasing emphasis on discipline, the Cubans are safeguarding the voluntary character of their institutions." Sontag's mass of gibberish was titled "Some Thoughts on the Right Way for Us to Love the Cuban Revolution." Sontag echoed the words used forty years earlier, when the *New York Times*'s Walter Duranty had commented on the "voluntary" character of the Ukraine's collectivization.

Charlie Bravo was a notorious "delinquent"—in other words, a Cuban college student from the sixties who finds himself in exile today. "I'd loved to have seen these Sorbonne and Berkeley and Berlin student protesters with their 'groovy' Che posters try their 'antiauthority' grandstanding in *Cuba* at the time. I'd love to have seen Che and his goons get their hands on *them*. They'd have gotten a quick lesson about the 'fascism' they were constantly complaining about—and firsthand. They would have quickly found themselves sweating and gasping from forced labor in Castro and Che's concentration camps, or jabbed in the butt by 'groovy' bayonets when they dared slow down and perhaps getting their teeth shattered by a 'groovy' machine-gun butt if they adopted the same attitude in front of Che's militia as they adopted in front of those campus cops."

Jon Lee Anderson, *New Yorker* writer and Che biographer, calls Che "the ultimate emblematic figure of what might be called the Decade of Youth. . . . That was the last period in which young people around the world rose up in revolt against the established order."[8]

Historically speaking, order has rarely been as established as under the regime cofounded by Che Guevara. According to a former Che lieutenant, Dariel Alarcon, Cuba's Ministerio del Interior (Ministry of Interior, Cuba's version of the Gestapo and KGB, indoctrinated by Che and trained by the East German STASI) runs the country lock, stock, and barrel. It constitutes Cuba's *genuine* government. Cuba's National Assembly and everything else is all smoke-and-mirror Potemkin politics.[9]

And Alarcon should know. He was a dutiful officer of the ministry for almost twenty years. If ever a fascist military-industrial complex, a secret cabal, or a hidden government of ruthless, power-mad schemers and sadists such as those Noam Chomsky and Norman Mailer constantly detect and decry in the United States actually ran a country, it's in the very country Mailer and Chomsky constantly laud: the Cuba of Castro and Che.

Che's two sons, Ernesto and Camilo, were no hippies. They attended a full five-year course at the KGB academy in Moscow. "Che played a central role in establishing Cuba's security machinery," admits his biographer, Jorge Castañeda.[10] To this day a ten-story-tall mural of Che Guevara adorns Cuba's Ministerio del Interior building. Che does live, as the face of the Cuban secret police.

Santana Loves Che's Evil Ways

Carlos Santana's grand entrance at the 2005 Oscars certainly had an impact on Cuban Americans. The famed guitarist stopped for the photographers, cast a manic smile, and swung his jacket open. TA-DA! There it was: Carlos's elegantly embroidered Che Guevara T-shirt. Half of Miami was sitting on the couch, wishing someone would say, "Tune in to this, Carlos—your T-shirt icon set up concentration camps in Cuba for anyone like you, including ordinary rock and roll fans who bought your album." A lumpen was any hapless youth who tried to listen to Yankee-Imperialist rock music in Cuba. Would Carlos Santana still be grinning if he knew that *Cuba criminalized Carlos Santana and most other rock music?*

"The stuff we had to go through!" recalls Cuban rock-and-roller Carmen Cartaya. "If you were known to have rock records, if you wore blue jeans, if you were a boy with longish hair, the police were on your tail constantly. My friend Juan Miguel Sanchez always managed to get his hands on the latest Beatles album. This wasn't easy in

Cuba, believe me, but he was a resourceful guy. Usually the only people with access to rock albums back then were the kids of the party members, the regime people, who traveled abroad. Juan Miguel wasn't one of those."

One fine day in 1965 Carmen's friend Juan Miguel vanished. "They grabbed him in one of the 'roundups,' as they called it when a group of army trucks and soldiers would surround an area known as a hangout for lumpen and round everyone up at gunpoint," recalls Carmen.

"We still had a piano in our house in 1965 and a friend had a guitar, another drums. All this was prerevolution gear, needless to say. So we'd get together and play Beatles songs; 'A Hard Day's Night' was a favorite. Then my mother would come running in. 'STOP! Are you crazy! Those so-and-sos from *El Comité* [the regime's neighborhood snitch groups] will hear it! We're in enough trouble already!' My dad was in a concentration camp at the time. My mother, as usual, was right. Listening to rock was bad enough. Listening *and* playing it was a quick way to find yourself in serious trouble with the police. Our little band didn't last long."[11]

True, Santana didn't hit it big till Woodstock in 1969, at a time when Che had already received a heavy dose of the very medicine he had dished out to hundreds of bound and gagged men and boys. This means the first inmates of his concentration camps were probably guilty of the heinous crime of listening to the Beatles, Stones, Kinks, and the like. But the regime Che cofounded kept up the practice of jailing *roqueros* well past the time Santana was hot on the rock charts.

Still, ignorance flourishes. Rage Against the Machine plaster Che's image on their shirts, guitars, and amps. "We've considered Che a fifth band member for a long time now," gushes lead guitarist Tom Morello. "Che was an amazing example."

Morello, whose music inspires so many head-banger balls, raves, and mosh pits, might be amazed to learn that upon taking over the Cuban city of Santa Clara, Che's first order of business (after summarily executing twenty-seven "war criminals," after a battle with four casualties) was to ban drinking, gambling, and dancing as "bourgeois frivolities." "I have no home, no woman, no parents, no brothers, and no friends," wrote Che. "My friends are friends only so long as they think as I do politically."[12] In short, Che, the fifth band member of Rage Against the Machine, took one of the world's most culturally vivacious countries and transformed it into a human ant farm.

"Carlos Santana smiled vacantly and gave me the peace sign," recalls a young Cuban American named Henry Gomez about a run-in with the hip guitarist in San Francisco shortly after his 2005 Oscar gig. Henry was wearing his homemade "Che's Dead—Get Over It" T-shirt when he passed the famed guitarist as he sat in a café. Santana immediately noticed the shirt and walked over.

" 'Che may be dead for you,' he said in a classic hippy-dippy drawl," says Henry. " 'But he lives in our hearts . . . Che is all about love and compassion.' "[13]

" 'Che murdered hundreds,' I said. 'It's fully documented. He urged the *opposite* of love. *Hate* as a factor of struggle. We must keep our *hatred* alive and fan it to paroxysm. *Hate* as . . . ' " But Santana wasn't listening as Henry Gomez quoted Che Guevara. "Che fought for blacks, women, and Native Americans," Carlos drawled. "Before the Cuban Revolution, women weren't allowed to enter the casinos."

Now Henry Gomez himself stared vacantly. "Where do you *begin* with this kind of space-cadet drivel?" He laughs. "In 1958 Cuba had more female college graduates per capita than the United States. And Cuban women went into any casino they desired. If not many did, it wasn't because they were barred."

But let's give Che credit. He indeed opened some Cuban establishments to women—political prisons and the execution wall.

Santana was also ignorant of Che's famous racism, of his disparaging comments on blacks and Mexicans. "Like a fool," recalls Henry, "I went on, trying to explain a few things to Carlos Santana, who was still annoyed with my T-shirt."

"You're getting hung up on facts, man," Santana slurred at one point. "We're only free when we free our hearts."

"Santana had a point," says Henry, nodding. "I was *definitely* 'hung up on facts.' So here I'm giving him facts—and he's rebutting with flower-power slogans. I should have known better. My wife was standing there highly amused by it all, not being impolite at all, simply smiling in what must have seemed to Mister Santana and his wife the typical reverential smile they get from fans. My wife was actually very hard at work stifling guffaws."[14]

"We Gotta Get Outta This Place"

When he hosted the PBS special "The 60's Experience," Eric Burdon's Che shirt shamed even Carlos Santana's, even Johnny Depp's. This was no measly T-shirt, either. It was a collared shirt, very elegant, with a huge image of the hip fellow who criminalized rock music on both front and back.

Eric was belting out the Animals' classics on the show. So naturally he sang the incomparable "We Gotta Get Out of This Place"— the exact desperate refrain of Cubans when Fidel and Che took over.

And certainly the phrase "the last thing we ever do" hits home for the families of the one in three desperate Cuban escapees who never make landfall. According to Cuban-American scholar Armando Lago, this hideous arithmetic translates into seventy-seven thousand deaths at sea over the past forty-six years—families perishing like captives of the Apaches, staked in the sun and dying slowly of sunburn and thirst, gasping and choking after their arms and legs finally give out and they gulp that last lungful of seawater. Still others are eaten alive—drawn and quartered by the serrated teeth of hammerheads and tiger sharks. Perhaps these last perished the most mercifully. Sharks don't dally at a meal.

Every year in South Florida, the INS and Coast Guard hear scores of such stories. (Were the cause of these horrors more politically correct—say, if they could somehow pin them on George Bush— we'd have no end of books, movies, and documentaries.)

A consistently hot item on Cuba's black market is used motor oil. Why? It is the poor man's shark repellent, they say. Desperate people cling to small hopes.

"I Hate the Sea" is the title of a gut-gripping underground essay by Cuban dissident Rafael Contreras. It's about some young men Rafael met on the beach near Havana. For most people, the sea soothes, attracts, infatuates. It is a symbol of liberation, travel, vacation. "Water is everywhere a protection," writes anthropologist Lionel Tiger, trying to explain the lure, "like a moat. As a species we love it." These young men Rafael met stared out to sea, cursed it, and spat into it. "It incarcerates us, worse than jail bars," they said.

So perhaps Che Guevara succeeded in fashioning his "New Man" after all. In Cuba, Che's totalitarian dream gave rise to psychic cripples beyond the imagination of even Orwell or Huxley: people who hate the sight of the sea.

Why Che's Rocking Grandson Fled Cuba

"Che exemplifies the integrity and revolutionary ideals to which we aspire," boasted Rage Against the Machine lead guitarist Tom Morello in a *Guitar World* interview. "He was an amazing example, a guy with humanitarian ideals and the will to act on them. Everywhere there was injustice, Che showed up. That's a pretty good resume."[15]

Tom Morello might benefit from a chat with a fellow heavy-metal rock guitarist named Canek Sanchez Guevara—Che's own grandson. Morello might learn a few things about the regime his "honorary fifth band member" cofounded, from which Canek Guevara was forced to flee in horror and disgust. Among the many reasons for Canek's flight was his desire to play exactly the same kind of music without being brutalized by the penal system and police put in place by his grandfather, Rage's "fifth band member." Are you listening, Tom Morello? Carlos Santana? Madonna? Eric Burdon?

"In Cuba freedom is nonexistent," Canek said in an interview with Mexico's *Proceso* magazine. "The regime demands submission and obedience . . . the regime persecutes hippies, homosexuals, free-thinkers, and poets. . . . They employ *constant* surveillance, control and repression."[16]

One day in 1991 leftist author and frequent Cuba visitor Marc Cooper was sitting on a Havana patio having coffee and chatting with the members of Cuba's *nomenklatura* hosting him. Suddenly they heard frenzied footsteps. They turned around and there came Che's grandson and a bandmate, stumbling, coughing, wheezing, and wiping their eyes. Finally catching his breath, Canek blurted that his rock band had set up to play in a nearby public square and had just started kicking out the jams when the police burst upon the scene, lobbing tear gas bombs and swinging billy clubs.

"But I'm Che's grandson!"[17] Canek protested to the cops who grabbed him.

There is a delicious irony here. Canek's grandfather had a major hand in training and indoctrinating Cuba's police force. As far as these cops were concerned, they were dutifully carrying out Canek's grandfather's revolutionary mandate. Besides his affinity for rock music, Canek further tweaked the authorities by adorning his guitar with a big decal of a U.S. dollar bill. And he wonders why his grandfather's disciples took such glee in pummeling him.

On other occasions the longhaired and punkish-looking Canek was jerked out of a movie theater line and subjected to a humiliating rectal exam by cops, presumably looking for drugs. But, all in all, Canek was immensely luckier than most Cuban "lumpen" and "delinquents." The notorious *peligrosidad predelictiva* law (rough translation: "dangerousness likely leading to crime") never got *him* shoved into a prison camp.

For what it's worth, Canek Sanchez Guevara lives in Mexico today and fancies himself an anarchist, not a conservative, Yankee stooge. He's adamant about distancing himself from those tacky and insufferable "Miami Cubans." He believes Fidel betrayed the "pure" Cuban revolution of the early sixties inaugurated by his idealistic and heroic grandfather and replaced it with an intolerant and autocratic personal dictatorship.

Canek, born in Cuba in 1974, might be excused from knowing that Cuba had never, before or since, been as vicious and Stalinist a police state as it was in the sixties. Canek's grandfather was actually *more* ideologically rigid, *more* of a Stalinist than Fidel himself— only, to his eventual misfortune, far less shrewd.

The lumpen remaining in Cuba still have Che's number. A one-time Argentine Communist Party member named Hector Navarro, also a TV reporter and law school professor, visited Cuba in 1998 to cover Pope John Paul II's visit. "A group of young Cuban musicians were playing for us tourists on the beach at Santa Maria," recalls Navarro. "So I went up to them and announced proudly that I was an Argentinean *like Che!*"

The musicians stared glumly at Navarro. So he tried again. "I even hung a picture of *Che* in my office!" he now proclaimed. More blank looks. So Navarro plowed ahead. "I'm from the town of Rosario itself—*Che's birthplace!*"

Now the musicians went from blank stares to outright frowns. "I certainly wasn't expecting this kind of thing," says Navarro. "But I continued, requesting they play a very popular song in Argentina, ti-tled 'And Your Beloved Presence, Comandante *Che Guevara!*' Now every one of them gave me a complete *cara de culo* (roughly, shitface). Only when I whipped out ten U.S. dollars and handed it to them did they start playing, but in a very desultory manner, and still with those sullen looks." Meeting after meeting with actual Cubans kept colliding with Hector Navarro's long-cherished fantasies of Cuban life. "I was in Cuba a month and a half," says Navarro. But as a fellow communist he was allowed to venture outside the tourist areas.

"This was the most important trip of my life—otherwise I might have kept believing in socialism and Che. I finally saw with my own eyes and learned that Castro's and Che's version was no dif-ferent from Stalin's and Ceausescu's."[18]

Stalinist Hippies

Almost a decade before the Summer of Love, Castro, Che, and their henchmen sported beards, long hair, and rumpled clothes. Their early popularity in the United States clearly issued from this superficial, hirsute affinity with the precursors of hippies, the Beat generation. In April 1959, Fidel Castro spoke at Harvard the same week as the similarly bearded Beat icon-poet, Alan Ginsberg. Eight years before he was grandstanding at Woodstock, Abbie Hoffman was grandstanding in Havana, observing Castro on the stump and hailing him as resembling "a mighty penis coming to life!" (Many people in Miami and Cuba, by the way, would heartily agree.)

Any photo of Che, Fidel, Raul, Camilo Cienfuegos, and company entering Havana in January 1959, after their bogus guerrilla war in the Sierra, shows how they preempted the Haight-Ashbury look by a full decade. Jean Paul Sartre acclaimed them as *Les Enfants au Pouvoir* (the children in power).[19] Raul Castro kept his blondish shoulder-length hair in a ponytail at the time. Camilo Cienfuegos's full, dark beard was identical to Jerry Garcia's a decade later. Except for his drab olive uniform, Che's *comandante* comrade, Ramiro Valdez, with his little goatee, looked like Carlos Santana circa Woodstock.

And Che himself was a ringer for Jim Morrison with a fledgling beard. Morrison always affected that "faraway look," too—that borderline scowl.

But no matter, by the mid-sixties in Castro and Che's Cuba rock and roll was associated with the United States and regarded as subversive, even if the song's performers lived in Liverpool or on Carnaby Street. "The government was always on the lookout for long hair," recalls another former Cuban delinquent and lumpen, Miguel Forcelledo. "We called rock 'midnight music,' because that was the safest time to try and listen to it. Even government snitches have to sleep, especially as these swine usually awoke very early to start their snooping. We'd form underground clubs to tap into U.S. radio stations with a

Russian-made short-wave radio someone would 'borrow' from a friend with government connections. But we were never completely safe. I was fifteen years old at the time but very lucky to get away with a brisk beating by the secret police and brief stint in jail. Many of my older friends wound up in the prison camps."

A former publicist for the Rolling Stones named David Sandison wrote a book titled *Rock & Roll People* that features reverential interviews with such musical icons as Bob Dylan, John Lennon, Paul McCartney, Mick Jagger, Keith Richards, David Bowie, Bruce Springsteen, and the Sex Pistols. He also wrote a book titled *Che Guevara*, which is even more reverential toward its subject. To Sandison it must seem perfectly congruous, one book almost an extension of the other. "A legend!" Sandison gushes on the very cover of *Che Guevara*, "a hero to radical youth to this day." In an interview Sandison prides himself on having "a great BS detector."

"All over Cuba," gushes David Sandison, "pictures of Che remind the Cuban people of their debt to this extraordinary man!"[20]

Yes indeed, Sandison. Just ask those Cuban musicians who gave *Señor* Navarro a "complete shitface" at the mere mention of Che's name, or Canek, subject of a spot rectal exam. Also ask the "Beats," the "Psychedelics," and assorted Cuban longhaired "lumpen," who stomped and shredded every Che picture they could get their hands on.

3

Bon Vivant, Mama's Boy, Poser, and Snob

Nothing could be more vicariously gratifying than Che's disdain for material comfort and everyday desires.
—DUKE UNIVERSITY PROFESSOR ARIEL DORFMAN
IN *Time* MAGAZINE

The emblematic impact of Ernesto Guevara is inconceivable without its dimension of sacrifice. Che renounces comfort for an idea.
—CHE BIOGRAPHER AND *Newsweek* WRITER JORGE CASTAÑEDA

Che was aided by . . . a complete freedom from convention or material aspirations.
—PHILIP BENNETT, *Boston Globe*

"Like so many epics," starts the opening sentence of *Time* magazine's story honoring Che Guevara as a Hero and Icon of the Century, "the story of the obscure Argentine doctor who abandoned his profession and his native land to pursue the emancipation of the poor of the earth . . ." Let's stop there.

Typically for the topic of Che, not halfway through the *very first sentence* of the *Time* story we encounter two lies. Ernesto Guevara was *not* a doctor. Though he's widely described as a medical doctor by his "scholarly" biographers (Castañeda, Anderson, Taibo, Kalfon), no record exists of Ernesto Guevara's medical degree. When Cuban-American researcher Enrique Ros asked the rector of the University of Buenos Aires and the head of its Office of Academic Affairs for copies or proof of the vaunted degree, Ros was variously told that the records had been misplaced or perhaps stolen.

And if the young Ernesto Guevara left Argentina hell-bent on "the emancipation of the earth's poor" he leaves little record of that, either. He originally headed for Venezuela, with plans to eventually come to the United States, because, in his own words in a letter to his father, those were "the best places to make money."[1]

And after the Revolution? Following a hard day at the office signing execution warrants, Che repaired to his new domicile in Tarara, fifteen miles outside Havana on the pristine beachfront, an area that today is reserved exclusively for tourists and elite Communist Party members. "The house was among the most luxurious in Cuba," writes Cuban journalist Antonio Llano Montes, of the mansion mentioned earlier with the futuristic big-screen television and remote control. "Until a few weeks prior, it had belonged to Cuba's most successful building contractor. The mansion had a yacht harbor, a huge swimming pool, seven bathrooms, a sauna, a massage salon and several television sets. . . . The mansion's garden had a veritable jungle of imported plants, a pool with waterfall, ponds filled with exotic tropical fish and several bird houses filled with parrots and other exotic birds. The habitation was something out of *A Thousand and One Nights*."[2]

Llano Montes wrote this candid description while in exile. In January 1959, he didn't go into such detail in his article, which appeared in the Cuban magazine *Carteles*. He simply wrote that "Comandante Che Guevara has fixed his residence in one of the most luxurious houses on Tarara Beach."

Two days after his article ran, while lunching at Havana's

El Carmelo restaurant, Llano Montes looked up from his plate to see three heavily armed rebel army soldiers ordering him to accompany them. Shortly the journalist found himself in Che Guevara's office in the old Spanish Fortress, La Cabana, converted into a prison, seated a few feet in front of the *comandante*'s desk, which was piled with papers.

It took half an hour, but Che finally made his grand entrance, "reeking horribly, as was his custom," recalls Llano Montes. "Without looking at me, he started grabbing papers on his desk and brusquely signing them with 'Che.' His assistant came in and Che spoke to him over his shoulder. 'I'm signing these twenty-six executions so we can take care of this tonight.'

"Then he got up and walked out. Half an hour later he walks back in and starts signing more papers. Finished signing, he picks up a book and starts reading—never once looking at me. Another half-hour goes by and he finally puts the book down. 'So you're Llano Montes,' he finally sneers, 'who says I appropriated a luxurious house.'

"I simply wrote that you had moved into a luxurious house, which is the truth," replied Llano Montes.

"I know your tactics!" Che shot back. "You press people are injecting venom into your articles to damage the revolution. You're either with us or against us. We're not going to allow all the press foolishness that Batista allowed. I can have you executed this very night. How about that!"

"You'll need proof that I've broken some law," responded Montes.

"'We don't need proof. We manufacture the proof,' Che said while stroking his shoulder-length hair, a habit of his. One of his prosecutors, a man nicknamed 'Puddle-of-Blood,' then walked in and started talking. 'Don't let the stupid jabbering of those defense lawyers delay the executions!' Che yelled at him. 'Threaten *them* with execution. Accuse *them* of being accomplices of the Batistianos.' Then Che jerked the handful of papers from Mister Puddle and started signing them.

"This type of thing went on from noon until 6:30 P.M., when

Che finally turned to his aides and said, 'Get this man out of here. I don't want him in my presence.'"[3]

The Che remembered by his innumerable victims was a man who enjoyed reducing people to powerlessness—then making them grovel for their lives. Yet in *Time*'s article, Ariel Dorfman writes of Che that "this secular saint [was?] ready to die because he could not tolerate a world where the poor of the earth, the displaced and dislocated of history, would be eternally relegated to its vast margins."Among Che's favorite guests at his Tarara estate was a Soviet GRU (Main Intelligence Directorate) officer named Angel Ciutat, who had been a close colleague of Leon Trotsky's killer, Ramon Mercader. Ciutat was actually a Spanish communist and veteran of the Spanish Civil War who fled into the arms of the Soviets after Franco battered Spain's red army. Stalin's secret police thumbed through Angel Ciutat's impressive resume as a murderer and Soviet proxy during the Spanish Civil War and promptly hired him on.

While holding court in Che's luxurious Tarara estate, Ciutat advised the admiring Guevara on the finer points of forming Cuba's secret police. After all, Ciutat had studied under the master himself—Lavrenty Beria, Stalin's police chief. And Che, as once before, in front of another Spanish communist—General Bayo, who taught him in Mexico—was all ears, a medical student, of sorts.

Angel Ciutat's guidelines for Che's firing squads were particularly adroit. These firing squads consisted of ten men and *every one* shot live ammo, bucking the norm, whereby some shot blanks to assuage their consciences. Such assuaging would contradict one of the Cuban firing squads' most vital purposes, secretly named *El Compromiso Sangriento* (the Blood Covenant).[4]

The point was to make murderers to bond with the murderous regime. The more shooters, the more murderers. The more murderers thus manufactured, the more complicit people on hand to resist any overthrow of their system. The fanatic and suicidal resistance put up by Hitler's SS troopers against the advancing Red Army saw the same theme at work. These SS troops knew they were fighting the sons and fathers of people they'd murdered in places like Babi Yar.

Under the Soviet Ciutat's orders, all cadets to Cuba's military academy were forced to serve on a firing squad. This became a prerequisite for graduation. We can imagine Che leaping in joy, slapping his forehead: "Now why didn't *I* think of that!" This policy of slaughtering Cubans—dictated by a *Soviet* officer and implemented by an *Argentine* hobo—became official in newly "nationalist" Cuba in February 1959.

Soon, "for health reasons," Che was forced to spend more and more time at his Tarara estate. But he began every day with an eager phone call to his hard-working crew in La Cabana. "How many did we execute yesterday?" he would ask.[5]

Che Carries on Family Tradition

For a communist New Man, Che had held on to a number of traditional Argentine prejudices. Anything "Yankee" was utterly loathsome. To this day polls show two-thirds of Argentines hold unfavorable opinions of the United States—the highest disapproval rate in the hemisphere. Regarding the United States, Argentina was always the France of South America—a reflexive critic.

Che had other prejudices. Many Argentines fancy themselves Europeans in a predominantly Indian and mestizo continent. The Argentine elite's snobbery toward Americans is more cultural than racial, however, and closely mimics the snobbery of the French (as well, perhaps, as that of our homegrown blue state "elites" toward red state "yokels"). Indeed, a recent poll showed that the higher a Latin American's educational level, the more pronounced his anti-Americanism.[6] In Buenos Aires, as elsewhere, a liberal arts education is especially sure to be steeped in anti-Americanism. On both sides, Che's ancestors hailed from Spanish grandees and the early viceroys of Spain's South American empire. He was also of Irish lineage.

Even here, his ancestral Lynch line was claimed as noble. Dolores Mayona Martin, a childhood friend of Che Guevara, wrote in a *New York Times* magazine article in 1968 of how the young Ernesto Guevara often boasted about descending from the original viceroy of the River Platte region, "roughly the Argentine equivalent of having had an ancestor on the *Mayflower*," she adds.[7]

Che's mother, Celia, who inherited a small fortune and a latifundium from her parents, was an early version of a feminist harridan straight from central casting. The inherited wealth, of course, made it easy. Celia was a full-blown Marxist and a noted political debater always ready to attack U.S. imperialism.[8] She always doted on her first born, little *Ernestico*.

Che's father, Ernesto, continually lost his shirt in business blunders, from trying to grow yerba mate (Argentina's version of tea), to trying to process it, to a construction business. He finally blew most of the family's inherited wealth and ended up selling the plantation to make ends meet.

There's nothing like having failed in the grubby business of business to make someone anticapitalist—and fancy himself culturally superior for it. Argentina's Guevara de la Serna y Lynch family was a perfect example of Latin America's limousine leftists—bumbling and bookish, pretentious, resentful, and haughty. The young Ernestico was *anything* but a rebel. He was a classic mama's boy, dutifully carrying on his parents' manifold petty snobberies and ideological prejudices.

Writer David Sandison mentions the Guevara children's "abiding admiration" for their parents. Most people have at least a brief period of youthful rebellion against their parents. Leave it to Che Guevara, the worldwide icon of youthful rebellion, to fail us even here.

"In camp Che always sported an annoying little smirk that drove us nuts," recalls associate instructor and Cuban Korean War vet Miguel Sanchez. "One day I simply got tired of looking at Che's little shit-eating smile and blew up. 'Twenty-five push-ups, Ernesto Guevara!'

I yelled, inches from his face, 'And *pronto!*' He grew wide-eyed, but dropped down right there and gave the twenty-five push-ups."[9]

Those who know him from posters and T-shirts thrill at Che's apparently natural look of "untamable defiance." Those who *knew* Che Guevara remember a habitual poser, an Eddie Haskell smile for Fidel, a pensive Charlie Rose–type frown when hosting Jean-Paul Sartre and Simone de Beauvoir, a Wicked Witch of the West cackle for his execution victims and their families, and a Marlon Brando smolder for Alberto Korda's camera.

At the end of his life, his Bolivian captors marveled when they opened Che's knapsack. The other guerrillas captured with him, all ragged and half-starved, carried nothing but weapons. Che carried scissors, a comb, a brush, even a little mirror. As we'll see later, Che was probably preparing for the social event of the fall '67 season— his own celebrity trial with a raucous worldwide clamor for his release. He seemed certain this would commence shortly upon his grand celebrity surrender.[10]

Cuban exile Frank Fernandez recalls a run-in between his aunt and Che Guevara in Havana in early 1959. "Che was visiting different businesses at the time, throwing his weight around, trying to cow those 'Cubiches,' as he sneered at Cubans. He barged into the office where my aunt worked and snorted that she was *una vieja burgesa* (a bourgeois old bat).

" 'Wrong,' she snapped back. 'I'm not bourgeois, I'm an *aristocrat*.' This curveball threw Che off-balance and he stood there trying to look cool.

"So my aunt she followed up with: 'And you're nothing but a brazen and insolent young punk.' "[11] She lived to tell the tale. Why? Did Che have a grudging admiration for her because the man she was speaking with considered himself an aristocrat, too?

A similar story is recounted by Cuban freedom fighter Tony Navarro, whose family owned a textile mill in Cuba.

Shortly after he became Cuba's National Bank president, Che sent his armed goons to confiscate Tony Navarro's mill, Textileras, which had always been efficient and profitable, employing hundreds and contributing much to Cuba's export sector. Navarro set up a meeting with Che to explain these things and try to make him see reason. What was the point in confiscating such an enterprise, throwing out the efficient managers, replacing them with revolutionary flunkies, and wrecking it?

An aide said, "Commander Guevara will see you now." Navarro walked into Che's office and made his best pitch as the great man pursed his lips and occasionally nodded. "Tony, have you read Kafka's *The Trial*?"

"No commander," answered a puzzled Navarro. "I've read *Metamorphosis* and *The Prison* by Kafka, but not *The Trial*."

"Read it," snapped Che. "It will explain much to you." Tony was then driven back to his home by Che's personal chauffeur.[12]

"Without having done anything wrong he was arrested one fine morning," reads the very first sentence of the book Che recommended. "A terrifying psychological trip into the life of one Joseph K., an ordinary man who wakes up one day to find himself accused of a crime he did not commit, a crime whose nature is never revealed to him," is how one reviewer sums it up. Another reviewer says, "A fictional account of an individual's arrest, trial, conviction and execution on charges that are never explained."[13]

Tony Navarro soon joined the anti-Castro underground and risked his life daily. If Che was going to kill him, well, Navarro would go down fighting. One day, after a shootout with Che's police, Navarro was arrested, but they did not get his identity right and he managed to escape and slip into the Venezuelan embassy, and on to the United States.

As with the disputatious aunt, here is another case where Che's hauteur briefly overrode his blood lust. He could have watched Tony Navarro's execution from his La Cabana office window with visitors while eating lunch, as he liked to do. Instead, in front of a cultured man like Navarro, Che felt compelled to flaunt his own highbrow tastes and erudition. Che's vanity allowed Tony Navarro to slip through his bloody paws.

It is said that Che never made one genuine Cuban friend. Even Cuban communists found Che insufferable. For all his disdain of "bourgeois" traits, old-line Cuban communists like Anibal Escalante and Carlos Rafael Rodriguez secretly complained of Guevara's own "petit bourgeois" conceits; how he preferred hobnobbing with French intellectuals rather than with Cuban Communist Party members of mixed blood. One famously portly and rumpled Cuban communist official named Francisco Brito bristled at Che's habit of bringing in immaculately tailored and coiffed Argentine and Chilean communists to staff some of Cuba's bureaucracy. Brito finally blurted out that the best thing for Che was "to get the hell out of Cuba!" because his diktats as Minister of Industries "were nothing put a pile of shit!"[14]

Che Meets Papa Hemingway

Around the time Alberto Korda snapped the famous photo of Che— now helping to sell snowboards, watches, and thong undies—he also snapped several of Che and Fidel chumming it up with Ernest Hemingway on May 15, 1960, at Havana's annual Hemingway Fishing Contest. Here, we may assume, was a mutual admiration society.

"The Cuban revolution," Hemingway wrote in 1960, is "very pure and beautiful. . . . I'm encouraged by it. . . . The Cuban people now have a decent chance for the first time."[15]

Papa Hemingway's on-again off-again friend, the novelist and author of *Manhattan Transfer*, John Dos Passos, once said that Hemingway "had one of the shrewdest heads for unmasking political pretensions I've ever run into."[16]

Alberto Diaz Gutierrez (Korda's real name) himself was a longtime Hemingway drinking chum. So his pious objections in later years against Smirnoff's plans to use Che's image on a bottle of vodka strikes many as fatuous. "I am categorically against the exploitation of

Che's image for the promotion of products such as alcohol, or for any purpose that denigrates the reputation of Che," Korda carped to the U.K. *Guardian*. "To use the image of Che Guevara to sell vodka is a slur on his name and memory."[17] (With Hemingway and Korda, vodka and slur were perhaps the right words. Apparently, though, Smirnoff considers it no slur to paste the image of a mass murderer on its product.)

But Korda did sue Smirnoff for *slurring Che* and won, on grounds of unauthorized use of the picture. After snapping his famous Che photo, Korda accepted a post as Castro's personal photographer, in which post he groveled shamelessly as a Castro court eunuch until he died of a heart attack in 2001.

In a way, John Dos Passos was right about Hemingway. Dos Passos had traveled to Spain during the Spanish Civil War along with Hemingway, but unlike him and unlike the *New York Times*'s Herbert Matthews, who also ran in his circles, Dos Passos refused to turn his head when the communists began massacring the non-Stalinist left in Madrid and Barcelona. Dos Passos finally left Spain in disillusionment and disgust—a break that had begun when he visited the Soviet Union a few years earlier. Stalin was leaving nothing to chance in Spain. He was doing advance work for what he saw as an imminent victory against Franco's forces.

As Dos Passos prepared to cross the French border out of the cauldron of murder and treachery known as Republican Spain, Hemingway's shrewdness (in professional matters at least) manifested itself. "Look, Dos," Papa warned him. "If you write negatively about the communists the reviewers will ruin you forever."[18]

Hemingway was proven right. Dos Passos's literary career crashed and burned after his return. Never mind that he wrote the truth, and as eloquently as ever.

There were hints that shortly before his suicide, Hemingway's infatuation with Castro and Che had begun to ebb. Did it happen when several thousand Cubans in his province were dragged from their homes and imprisoned or riddled with bullets by firing squads?

In *For Whom the Bell Tolls*, Hemingway seems to excuse communist massacres as "necessary murder." No, his crush on the gallant revolutionaries started ebbing when Papa found that this "pure and beautiful" revolution made it difficult for him to repair the pump on the gigantic swimming pool of his Cuban estate.

Hemingway might have thanked Cuba's minister of industries at the time, Che Guevara, for the scarcity of pool pump parts (though most Cubans were already thanking him for the scarcity of other items, such as food). Then Papa got singed by the very flames he had helped ignite. His Finca Vigia outside Havana—paid for, we may assume, from royalties earned extolling Spanish communists in *For Whom the Bell Tolls*—was finally stolen by Cuban communists, his fishing buddies.

If anyone ever fit the description of the effete bourgeois *latifundista* whom Che claimed to scorn (though the term perfectly described his own family), it was Ernest Hemingway himself. Had Papa been in a less fashionable line of business, Che would have made short work of him.

4

From Military Doofus to "Heroic Guerrilla"

Che waged a guerrilla campaign where he displayed outrageous bravery and skill.

—*Time* MAGAZINE, HAILING ITS "HEROES AND ICONS
OF THE CENTURY"

Che's most famous book is titled *Guerrilla Warfare*. His famous photo is captioned "Heroic Guerrilla." His Hollywood biopic is titled *Guerrilla*. And his most resounding failure came precisely as guerrilla warrior. There is no record of his prevailing in any bona-fide battle. There are precious few accounts that he actually *fought* in anything properly describable as a battle.

Had Ernesto Guevara de la Serna y Lynch not linked up with a Cuban exile named Nico Lopez in Guatemala in 1954, who later introduced him to Raul Castro and his brother Fidel in Mexico City, he might have continued his life as a traveling hobo, mooching off women, staying in flophouses, and scribbling unreadable poetry. Che was a revolutionary Ringo Starr, who, by pure chance, fell in with the right bunch and rode their coattails to world fame. His very name, "Che," was given him by the Cubans who hobnobbed with him in Mexico. Argentines use the term "Che" much as Cubans use "chico," or Michael Moore fans use "dude." The term has an Italian rather than a Spanish pedigree. The Cubans noticed Ernesto Guevara using it, so it stuck. Fidel Castro recruited his new friend to serve as the rebel army's doctor (on the strength of his bogus credentials) before their "invasion" of Cuba. On the harrowing boat ride through turbulent seas from the Yucatan to Cuba's Oriente province in a decrepit old yacht, the *Granma,* a rebel found Che lying comatose in the boat's cabin. He rushed to the commander. "Fidel, looks like Che's dead!"

"Well, if he's dead, then throw him overboard," replied Castro.[1] Guevara, suffering the combined effects of seasickness and an asthma attack, stayed on board.

Baptism of Fire

Guevara's condition did not immediately improve upon landfall. At one point, he declared: "Doctor! I think I'm dying!"[2] That was "doctor" himself, Ernesto Che Guevara, gasping to fellow rebel (and bona-fide physician) Faustino Perez during their Cuban baptism of fire. The Castro rebels had landed in Cuba three days earlier on the *Granma* from Mexico. The Cuban army, alerted by a peasant who didn't seem to recognize his self-appointed liberators, had ambushed them near a cane field in a place named Alegria del Pio.

In Che's Havana-published diaries (primary source for most of his biographers and media stories), he uses slightly different terminology regarding the incident. Much like John Wayne in *Sands of Iwo Jima,* Che recalls saying, "I'm hit!" But far be it from Che Guevara to stop there, so his official diary gushes forth: "Faustino, still firing away, looked at me . . . but I could read in his eyes that he considered me as good as dead. . . . Immediately, I began to think about the best way to die, since all seemed lost. I recalled an old Jack London story where the hero, aware that he is bound to freeze to death in the wastes of Alaska, leans calmly against a tree and prepares to die in a dignified manner. That was the only thing that came to my mind at that moment."

In fact Faustino Perez later recounted that he was nearly wounded himself—not by the whizzing bullets, but by a hernia while trying to stifle his laughter at the look on Che's face, especially after seeing the nature of Che's wound. "It's a scratch!" Perez blurted. "Keep walking."[3] A bullet had barely grazed the back of Che's neck.

And what about Fidel? Upon hearing the first shots fired in anger against his glorious rebellion, this hands-on *comandante*-in-chief vanished, leaving his men to scramble and scrounge for themselves. The future Maximum Leader's headlong flight from the skirmish site, through rows of sugarcane, leaping over brambles, dodging trees, was so long, and his speed so impressive, that one wonders if he really had missed his true calling, playing major league baseball, as urban legend has it.

None of his men, including Che, could find Castro for the rest of the day. But in the middle of the night, after miles of walking, Faustino Perez heard a tentative voice: "Mr. Perez? . . . Mr. Perez?" And out came Fidel Castro from a cane field, accompanied by his bodyguard, Universo Sanchez.[4] "Later I learned that Fidel had tried vainly to get everybody together into the adjoining cane field," is how the ever-faithful Che covers for Fidel in his diaries. Considering the length and breadth of Cuban cane fields in that area, "adjoining" is technically correct for a place three miles away.

A few weeks after this skirmish, when the only thing Fidel Castro commanded was a raggedy band of a dozen "rebels" in Cuba's Sierra Maestra mountains, he was approached by some of his rebel group's many wealthy urban backers. "What can we do?" they asked. "How can we help the glorious rebellion against the upstart mulatto scoundrel Batista? We can write you some checks. We can buy you some arms. We can recruit more men. Tell us, Fidel, what can we do to help?"

"For now," Castro answered, "get me a *New York Times* reporter up here."

The rest is history. Castro's July 26 Movement's efficient and well-heeled communications network fell promptly to the task. Lines hummed from Santiago to Havana to New York. Within weeks, the *New York Times*'s ranking Latin American expert, Herbert Matthews, was escorted to Castro's rebel camp with his notepad, tape recorder, and cameras. Castro was being hailed as the Robin Hood of Latin America on the front pages of the world's most prestigious papers. The following month CBS sent in a camera crew. Within two years Castro was dictator of Cuba, executing hundreds of political prisoners per week and jailing thousands more—all the while being hailed as "the George Washington of Cuba" by everyone from Jack Paar, to Walter Lippmann, to Ed Sullivan, to Harry Truman.

While Castro and Che failed to launch a successful military invasion, they invaded nonetheless, riding rivers of ink.

Shooting Back at Che

On their march from the Sierra mountains of eastern Cuba to Las Villas province in central Cuba during the fall of 1958, Che's "column" somehow ran into a twenty-member band of Cuba's Rural Guard, who started shooting. Che and his band scattered hysterically, bewildered and shocked by hearing hostile gunfire. In this mad melee, they fled from a band of country boys whom they outnumbered four to one. In their fright, the gallant *guerrilleros* abandoned two stolen trucks crammed with arms and documents.

"We found Guevara's own diary and notebooks in one of the trucks," recalls Cuban air force lieutenant Carlos Lazo, who had made a recon flight over the area and notified the Rural Guard of the Che column.[5] The sight of Lieutenant Lazo's plane overhead had greatly exacerbated Che's column's panic attack and spurred on their frantic flight. The "Heroic Guerrilla's" voluminous writings, and those of his biographers, somehow overlook this exhilarating military engagement.

Oddly, the notebook and diaries found by Lazo differ dramatically from the "Che Diaries," the "Secret Papers of a Revolutionary," and the "Reminiscences of the Cuban Revolutionary War" later published by Castro's government under Che Guevara's byline, with a foreword by Fidel Castro himself. It is at this juncture that we see how mainstream historical research was poisoned, and the myth of Che the heroic guerrilla was created. On one hand, historians had access to a mass of confidential memos snatched from a frantically fleeing Che. On the other hand, a Stalinist regime published—with a deafening fanfare of trumpets—Che's "official" diaries and reminiscences. And which set of writings became the source material for all those hard-nosed *New York Times* reporters, all those diligent Che biographers and erudite Ivy league scholars? The propaganda, of course.

"Those confidential notebooks and diaries we found in Che's truck confirmed everything we were already saying about Che," says Lazo. "First off, Guevara complained that his column was getting absolutely no help from the country people, whom he claimed were all *latifundistas* (large landholders). The first part was true, the country folk mostly shunned them. The second part was patently untrue, these weren't huge landholders. They were simply anticommunist. That was enough for Che to mark them for reprisal. I saw where several boys, one of them seventeen, another eighteen, had been marked for execution in his diary. These were not 'war criminals' in any sense of the word. They were simply country boys who had refused to cooperate with him. I guess these had really annoyed him somehow. Shortly after the rebel victory these were rounded up and executed as 'war criminals.' "

The *New York Times*, *Look*, and CBS weren't around for these murders. Even those labeled "war criminals" by the rebels were often simply Cuban military men who had shot back. If they'd actually taken their oath and duty seriously, if they'd actually pursued Che's rebels, fought them, and inflicted casualties—well, then Che's henchmen went after them with particular zeal. Lieutenant Orlando Enrizo was one such. "They called us Batista war criminals," he recalls from

Miami today. "First off, I had nothing to do with Batista, didn't even like the guy. He didn't sign my checks. Me and most of my military comrades considered ourselves members of Cuba's Constitutional Army.

"The Castro rebels whom we knew to be communist-led—though many were not communists themselves, simply dupes—start ambushing us, start killing our men in their barracks, destroying roads and bridges, terrorizing the countryside, and we're supposed to greet them with kisses? Not me," says Enrizo. "I fought them. I met an ex-rebel in exile later who told me point-blank that Che's people would murder *campesinos* for not cooperating, or for being suspected informers, or whatever. Then they'd promptly blame it on us."

And sure enough, the media, both in the United States and in Cuba at the time, took the rebels' word as gospel that the men of the Cuban army were the murderers. Castro and his network always had the media's ear.

"Well, I'll admit it," says Enrizo. "I fought the rebels hard. I shot during combat when people were shooting at us. I pursued them. I'm damn proud of my record. Let Che's biographers and anyone else call me a war criminal. I murdered no one. How many of the rebels—much less Che—can claim that?"

Che never forgot Lieutenant Enrizo's assault on his "column." "I knew the dragnet was out for us after the rebel victory and escaped to Miami," Enrizo says. Like most Cuban exiles of the time, Enrizo expected his exile to be short. One day shortly after he arrived in Miami, Lieutenant Enrizo met two men in a diner he had known in Cuba as Castro rebels. "Just the man we've been looking for!" they said to Enrizo as they surrounded him. Che Guevara himself had sent these men to Miami on a special mission to kidnap Orlando Enrizo and haul him back to Cuba for a spectacular show trial and public firing-squad execution, much like the famous trial held in February 1959 for Cuban army commander Jesus Sosa Blanco for which the international press was invited to attend. The kidnappers had been jubilant with the assignment and expressed their excitement to Che himself.

"They were excited with the assignment all right," says Enrizo, "because it allowed them to finally scoot out of Cuba, something they'd been planning for a while, but couldn't find a way out. Those guys still live here in Miami. We're friends."[6]

Enrizo's fellow fighter, Lieutenant Lazo, uncovered much of interest in Che's personal papers. "Every last one of the contacts Guevara had listed in his notebooks was a well-known Cuban Communist Party member." Cuba's Communist Party was rigidly Stalinist and slavishly followed Moscow's orders. But to this day, assert that Castro's rebels had communist support or were communists themselves, and you will find yourself labeled a crackpot by mainstream academia.

All serious scholars will tell you that only "Yankee bullying" pushed a reluctant Castro and Che into the arms of the Soviet Union. This wall of resistance to the truth has proven more durable than the concrete and steel of the Berlin Wall. It has been impervious to a half-century of contrary evidence, including declassified Soviet documents that list Raul Castro as a reliable KGB contact since 1953. This myth persists in the face of innumerable telling details, like the fact that when Che Guevara was arrested in Mexico City in 1956, he was actually carrying the card of the local KGB agent, Nikolai Leonov, in his wallet.

In short, Lazo's documents are the Cuban version of the Venona papers. Declassified in 1995, the Venona project was a U.S. intelligence project that broke Soviet codes and revealed Soviet spies in the U.S. It makes no difference to academia, the major media, or other apologists. "War with the U.S. is my true destiny," Castro had written to a confidant in early 1958.

The Batista government made all the information found in Che's private papers known to the U.S. government. It did no good. The U.S. government held tough on its arms embargo against Batista, while the U.S. media lionized Castro.

The Battle of Santa Clara

Che's most famous military exploit as a Cuban *comandante* was "The Battle of Santa Clara," the December 1958 confrontation that caused Batista to lose hope and flee Cuba. "One Thousand Killed in 5 days of Fierce Street Fighting," blared a *New York Times* headline in a January 4, 1959, article about the battle. "Commander Che Guevara appealed to Batista troops for a truce to clear the streets of casualties," continued the article. "Guevara turned the tide in this bloody battle and whipped a Batista force of 3,000 men." "Santa Clara became a bloody battleground," writes Jon Lee Anderson. "Pitched battles were fought in the streets. Tanks fired shells, airplanes bombed and rocketed . . . both civilian and guerrilla casualties began to pile up in hospitals."

Exiles who were at Santa Clara tell a very different story. "I was there," recalls Manuel Cereijo. "I lived in Santa Clara. Sure there was a little shooting, but people were actually going outside to see the show. Best I could gather, a grand total of two civilians and two or three rebels died."

In fact, the Battle of Santa Clara—despite the reporting of ur–Jayson Blairs—was a puerile skirmish. The *New York Times* was still very much in Castro's thrall and reported on that battle accordingly, though no reporters were actually on hand. So who were Anderson's other impeccable sources? Che's widow and the Castro regime, thirty years after the fact. Che Guevara's *own diary* mentions that his column suffered *exactly one casualty* (a soldier known as *El Vaquerito*) in this ferocious "battle." Other accounts put the grand total of rebel losses at from three to five men. Most of Batista's soldiers saw no reason to fight for a crooked, unpopular regime that was clearly doomed, so they didn't fire a shot, even those on the famous "armored train" that Guevara supposedly attacked and captured.

"Che targeted all enemy positions but concentrated on the armored train," writes the ever-starstruck Anderson, who then resorts to quoting Che's own Havana-published diaries. "The men were forced out of the train by our Molotov cocktails . . . the train became a veritable oven for the soldiers,"[7] he claims.

Actually the men were "forced out of the train" by a bribe from Che to their commander before a shot was fired, much less any "Molotov cocktails" thrown.

Today that armored train features as a major tourist attraction in Santa Clara. The train, loaded with 373 soldiers and $4 million worth of munitions, had been sent from Havana to Santa Clara in late December by Batista's high command as a last-ditch attempt to halt the rebels. Che's rebels in Santa Clara bulldozed the tracks and the train derailed just outside of town.

Then a few rebels shot at the train and a few soldiers fired back. No one was hurt. Soon some rebels approached brandishing a truce flag and one of the train's officers, Enrique Gomez, walked out to meet them. Gomez was brought to meet *Comandante* Guevara.

"What's going on here!" Che shouted. "This isn't what we agreed on!"

Gomez was puzzled. "What agreement?" he asked. Turned out, unbeknownst to the troops inside, the train and all its armaments had been *sold*, fair and square, to Guevara by its commander, Colonel Florentino Rossell, who had already hightailed it to Miami. The price was either $350,000 or $1 million, depending on the source.[8]

"The whole thing was staged for the cameras," says Manuel Cereijo. "The train had already been sold to Che without a shot fired from either side. Then Che ordered the train to back up a bit so they could bulldoze the tracks, then have the train come forward so they could stage the spectacular 'derailment,' for the cameras."[9]

Seems that Che was finally learning from Fidel how to wage a "guerrilla war." Che had every reason to be upset. Actual *shots* fired against his troops? Here's another eyewitness account regarding Che's famous "invasion" of Las Villas province shortly before the famous "battle" of Santa Clara.

"Guevara's column shuffled right into the U.S. agricultural experimental station in Camaguey. Guevara asked manager Joe McGuire to have a man take a package to Batista's military commander in the city. The package contained one hundred thousand dollars with a note. Guevara's men moved through the province almost within sight of uninterested Batista troops."[10]

Francisco Rodriguez Tamayo was a rebel captain who had been in on many of these transactions, defecting mere months after the rebel victory. In an *El Diario de Nueva York* article on June 25, 1959, he claimed that Castro still had $4.5 million left in that "fund" at the time of the revolutionary victory. "I don't know what might have happened to that money," Rodriguez Tamayo adds.

"Castro kept the money in jute sacks at his camp," recalls former rebel Jose Benitez. "I saw bags stuffed with pesos."[11]

In January 1959, Che's men arrested a Batista army colonel named Duenas at his office in Camaguey, Cuba. "What's going on here!" the indignant colonel protested. "You people have to show me respect! I'm the one who let you through this province without a shot! Just ask Fidel! He'll tell you!"[12]

Yet immediately after the Santa Clara bribe and skirmish, Che ordered twenty-seven Batista soldiers executed as "war criminals." Gratitude was never his strong suit. Dr. Serafin Ruiz was a Castro operative in Santa Clara at the time, but apparently an essentially decent one. "But, *comandante*," he responded to Che's order, "our *Revolución* promises not to execute without trials, without proof. How can we just . . . ?"

"Look, Serafin," Che snorted back, "if your bourgeois prejudices won't allow you to carry out my orders, fine. Go ahead and try them tomorrow morning—but execute them *now!*"[13] Che might have known Lewis Carroll as well as his Kafka, perhaps recalling the Queen of Hearts's famous line to Alice in Wonderland: "Sentence first—verdict afterwards!"

"Surrounded by death, it is a normal human reaction to reach out for life and even Che was not immune to this instinct,"[14] Che hagiographer and *New Yorker* writer Anderson states, referring to

Che's actions during the apparently Stalingradesque battle of Santa Clara.

In fact, the only death Che was "surrounded by" was the flurry of executions without trial he ordered against his future enemies. "Damn, but Che has drowned this city in blood!" exclaimed his rebel comrade Camilo Cienfuegos upon passing through Santa Clara. "Seems that on every street corner there's the body of an execution victim!"[15]

And that reaching out for life by Che was the ditching of his squat and homely Peruvian wife, Hilda Gadea, for an illicit affair with his new flame, the trim blonde Cuban Aleida March. Officials in Cuba's U.S. embassy at the time became a little skeptical about all the battlefield bloodshed and heroics reported by the *New York Times,* CBS, *Look*, and *Boys' Life* (honest, even they braved the perils of this war of bribery for a Castro interview). U.S. officials ran down every reliable lead and eyewitness account of what the *New York Times* kept reporting as bloody civil war with thousands dead in single battles. They found that in the entire Cuban countryside, in those two years of "ferocious" battles between rebel forces and Batista troops, the total casualties on *both* sides actually ran to 182.[16]

Che Guevara's own diary puts the grand total of his forces' losses during the *entire two-year-long* "civil war" in Cuba at twenty, about equal to the average number dead during Rio de Janeiro's carnival every year. In brief, Batista's army barely fought.

Stalinist Hit Man

During the Spanish Civil War Stalinists attempted to ensure their future rule by butchering their leftist allies. This butchery commenced well before they foresaw any victory over the common rightist foe, Franco. One year into that war, Spanish Stalinists were already piling up the bodies of anarchists, Trotskyites, and socialists in mass graves, each with a bullet hole in the nape of the neck. This leftist rabble had been useful as cannon fodder against Franco for a time. But by 1937 the time had come to get the house in order.

One leftist who narrowly escaped was George Orwell, who had volunteered for the anti-Franco anarchist militia and been wounded in battle. Unlike the rest of the literati (the always blustering Ernest Hemingway comes to mind here), Orwell actually enlisted in the Spanish Republican forces and fought—long, hard, and bravely. His *Homage to Catalonia* tells the whole story. Orwell scooted out of Spain in disguise and just in time—with Stalinist death squads hot on his tail.

There's ample evidence that Ernesto "Che" Guevara was a very willing tool in similar Stalinist butchery against Cuban anticommunists and noncommunists during the anti-Batista rebellion. "For some reason," recalls anti-Batista rebel Larry Daley, "it was always the known anticommunists who kept disappearing from our ranks. Che's march from the Sierra to Las Villas and Santa Clara involved very little fighting by his column. His path had been cleared by another column led by rebel commander Jaime Vega, who was known as a noncommunist. Vega's forces kept running into ambushes by the Cuban army and air force and took fairly heavy casualties (relatively speaking). We suspect they were being ripped off by Castro and Che confidants."

From Havana to Santiago, the Castroites had a history of this type of treachery. Some of the known anticommunists among the rebels were executed by the rebels outright, but others, like Frank Pais and Rene Latour, kept running blindly into Batista's army or police and were ambushed, or left to die in skirmishes where most communists survived. One entire boatload of eighty anti-Batista rebels who landed in Oriente province in a yacht known as the *Corinthia* from Florida was promptly defeated and captured by a Batista force. Heaven knows, such lethal efficiency was not characteristic of the bulk of Batista's army. The *Corinthia* crew were known to be noncommunist, and had no affiliation with Castro whatsoever, but were probably infiltrated by his agents. Another tipoff? Many anti-Batista people of the time strongly suspect it.

A bit earlier, in the Sierra, a brave and well-known anticommunist named Armando Cañizarez had a famous run-in with Guevara at his camp. They didn't see eye to eye on the recent Soviet invasion of Hungary. "Che was all for it," recalls Armando's brother Julio, who was also a rebel and witnessed the encounter. " 'The Soviets had every right—even a duty—to invade Hungary,' Che said outright. The Hungarian rebels were 'fascists! CIA agents!'—the whole bit. It sounded like he was reading straight out of *Pravda* or Tass. We gaped.

"Sure, to hear of Che Guevara reading straight from communist propaganda sheets may not sound odd *now*," says Julio. "But remember, in 1957 Castro and all the rebel leaders claimed to be anticommunist, prodemocracy, etcetera. And many of us rank and file were indeed anticommunist.

"So Che's attitude caught us off-guard. Armando kept getting hotter and hotter as he argued with Guevara. I could see it in his face. He couldn't believe this Argentine guy—remember, this was early, Che wasn't a famous *comandante* yet—was defending that naked aggression and terrible slaughter of Hungarians who were only fighting for their freedom and national independence, which we thought we were doing at the time ourselves. Armando stepped back and I could see he was balling his fist. He was preparing to bash Guevara—to punch his lights out!

"So I moved in and asked Armando to come over by me. But he was so worked up I had to grab him by the arm and drag him over. A little while later, after we'd cooled off a bit, another rebel soldier came up and whispered to us that we'd better get the hell outta there—and fast. We did get away from Guevara, but continued in the anti-Batista fight."[17]

After the victory, the Cañizarez brothers watched in fury as Che and Castro implemented their covert plan to communize Cuba. They both came to the United States and promptly returned to Cuba with carbines in hand at the Bay of Pigs, where Armando gave his life for Cuban freedom after expending his last bullet. To this day, his family doesn't know where Armando Cañizarez is buried.

"We have to create *one* unified command, with one *comandante-in-chief.*" Che laid down this Stalinist ground rule to his astonished Bolivian guerrillas shortly after he snuck into that country to start his guerrilla war. "That's how we did it in Cuba. The guerrilla chief has to take all measures that will assure his future control of power, *totally.* We have to start early in destroying any and all other revolutionary groups that presume to exist outside of our control. Now, we may use other groups to help eliminate the primary enemy. But that doesn't mean we'll share any power with them after the victory. The Cuban experience is valid for the entire continent."[18]

Castro's Press Hut

At one point, when it seemed there were more newsmen in Cuba's mountains than guerrillas or soldiers, it got so bad that a shack in Castro's "guerrilla camp" in the Sierra Maestra actually had a sign, "Press Hut," to accommodate the parade of American newspeople lugging their cameras, lighting equipment, sound equipment, makeup, and lunch baskets.[19]

In March 1957, CBS had sent two reporters, Robert Taber and Wendell Hoffman, into the Sierra with their microphones and cameras to interview Castro and his rebel "fighters." The CBS men emerged with "The Story of Cuba's Jungle Fighters," a breathtaking news-drama that ran on prime-time U.S. TV.

For the record: Botanically speaking, Cuba has no "jungle," the "fighters" numbered about two dozen at the time (though both the *New York Times* and CBS mentioned "hundreds"), and the "fighting" itself up to that time had consisted of a few ambushes and murders of Batista soldiers, usually while they were asleep in their rural barracks.

CBS correspondent Robert Taber's services to Castro had just begun, however. A few years later he was a founding father of the Fair Play for Cuba Committee, an outfit whose fifteen minutes of fame came in November 1963 when member Lee Harvey Oswald *really* racked up some headlines. Dan Rather soon picked up the torch from the "unbiased" Robert Taber.[20]

The U.S. embassy's public affairs officer in Havana, Richard Cushing, even served as an unofficial tour guide for the throngs of American newspeople flocking into the Sierra to interview the Cuban rebels. And one rebel who hadn't seen Castro since their days in joint Mexican exile met up with him in his mountain camp. "*Pero Chico!*" he blurted. "You're getting so fat! How much weight you've put on!"

Didn't he realize? Castro's gut-busting "guerrilla war" was a moveable feast.

Typically, Che Guevara doesn't even merit credit for the perfectly sensible scheme of bribing Batista's army, then portraying little skirmishes to the international press as Caribbean Stalingrads. What about the source of these funds? They came, as we saw, from Fidel's snookering of Batista's wealthy political opponents. How had he convinced these hard-nosed businessmen to fund his July 26 Movement? By speaking the language of democracy and prosperity.

In late 1957, Castro signed an agreement called the Miami Pact with several anti-Batista Cuban politicians and ex-ministers in exile at the time. Che Guevara, never one to grasp the subtleties of Castro's schemes, went ballistic over the Miami Pact, denouncing it as a shameful deal with "bourgeois" elements. "I refuse to lend my historic name to that crime!" he wrote. "We rebels have proffered our asses in the most despicable act of buggery that Cuban history is likely to recall!"[21] Che underestimated the craftiness of Castro, mistaking the bugger*ers* for the bugger*ees*.

That a "guerrilla war" with "peasant and worker backing" overthrew Batista is among the century's most widespread and persistent academic fables. But no Castroites who participated actually believed it—except, of course, Guevara. The Associated Press dispatches about Castro and Che's "war" were actually concocted and written by Castro's own agent in New York, Mario Llerena, who admits as much in his book, *The Unsuspected Revolution*. Llerena was also the contact with Herbert Matthews. (*National Review's* famous cartoon in 1960 showing a beaming Castro saying, "I got my job through the *New York Times!*" nailed it.)

To give them credit, most of Castro's *comandantes* knew their Batista war had been an elaborate ruse. After the glorious victory, they were content to run down and execute the few Batista men motivated enough to shoot back (most of these were of humble background), settle into the mansions stolen from *Batistianos*, and enjoy the rest of their booty.

British historian Hugh Thomas, though a Labor member who sympathized with Castro's revolution in his younger years, studied mountains of records (outside Castro's Cuba) and simply could not evade the truth. His massive and authoritative historical volume *Cuba, or The Pursuit of Freedom* sums it up very succinctly: "In all essentials, Castro's battle for Cuba was a public relations campaign, fought in New York and Washington."

"The Guerrilla war in Cuba was notable for the marked lack of military skills or offensive spirit in the soldiers of either side," writes military historian Arthur Campbell, in his authoritative *Guerillas: A History and Analysis*. "The Fidelistas were completely lacking in the basic military arts or in any experience of fighting as a co-coordinated force. Their tactics . . . were confined to road ambushes which were seldom carried to close quarters, to patrols whose sole object was to fire at some isolated target far removed from the main communication arteries. . . . The *Batistianos* suffered from a near-paralysis of the will to fight . . . Fidel Castro was opposed by a weak and inefficient regime which had virtually worked its way out of power before the guerrilla war even started . . . this short campaign was noted . . . for its low number of casualties."

As we shall see, Che Guevara possessed an immense capacity for self-deception regarding his "guerrilla war," helping to set the stage for his doom in Bolivia. In Cuba few fought against him. In the Congo few fought with him. In Bolivia, Che finally started getting a taste of both. In short order, he would be betrayed by the very peasants he was out to "liberate."

Che as Guerrilla Professor

Left-wing scholars also excuse Che's radicalism as a response to the April 1961 Bay of Pigs attack against an innocent nationalist revolution that wished only to be left alone. They ignore the fact that every single invader, including the commanders, was a Cuban. If anything, the documentary evidence shows that Castro and Che dispatched five of their own versions of the Bay of Pigs invasions before the United States had even started contingency planning for theirs.

Shortly after entering Havana, Che had formed "the Liberation Department" in Cuba's State Security Department and was already advising, equipping, and dispatching guerrilla forces to attempt to duplicate the Cuban rebellion (as he saw it) in the Dominican Republic, Haiti, Panama, and Nicaragua. Every one of those guerrilla forces, Cuban-communist led and staffed, was wiped out in short order, usually to the last man. Rafael Trujillo in the Dominican Republic and Luis Somoza in Nicaragua weren't about to follow Batista's example in Cuba of pussyfooting around against guerrillas. A few years later Che equipped, advised, and sent more guerrillas to Argentina and Guatemala. Again, they were stomped out almost to a man. These guerrilla expeditions cost the lives of two of Che's fatally credulous friends: the Guatemalan Julio Caceres and the Argentine Jorge Massetti. The story of the latter is worth retelling. Shortly after Che became the jailer and executioner of La Cabana, he flew in his Argentine flunkie friends. He ensconced them in stolen Cuban mansions and had them chauffeured around Havana in stolen Cuban cars. Che's comrades were quite impressed with the local boy who had made good. Among these Argentines was an unemployed journalist, the ill-fated Jorge Massetti, whom Che had brought to Cuba to start a press agency, an unemployed lawyer named Ricardo Rojo, who later authored the reverential tome *My Friend Che,* and an unemployed caricaturist and ceramic artist named Ciro Bustos, who became a globe-trotting and self-professed intelligence ace.

One day in 1962, while meditating in his Havana office, Che had divined that "objective conditions for a revolution"[22] had suddenly sprouted in his native Argentina and hatched a plan. He decided that his hardy and intrepid Argentine friends could be the revolutionary vanguard to hack their way into the northern Argentine jungle, set up a guerrilla *foco* and lead the masses to storm Buenos Aires's Presidential Palace as boldly as Paris's *vainqueurs* had stormed the Bastille.

Soon Che's friends had graduated from Che's Cuban academy of guerrilla war and proclaimed themselves "the People's Guerrilla Army." Weeks later, with the help of Cuban officers, they slipped through Bolivia and into northern Argentina, where they had set up a clever "underground" of rugged revolutionary sleuths and gunslingers consisting mainly of professors and administrators from Cordoba University's Faculty of Philosophy and Letters. A few philosophy students and bored bank tellers also rallied to the cause, hobbling into the guerrilla *foco* with severely blistered feet and plucking fleas from their legs—but boosting the ranks of "the People's Guerrilla Army" to almost two dozen.

Soon all *guerrilleros* were issuing fire-breathing "War Communiques" from their bug- and snake-infested camp, poised to overthrow the democratically elected Argentine government.

The only Argentine "people" they ever recruited were a few more students and professional misfits like themselves. Within a month they were starving, aching from more blisters and sprained ankles, and scratching maniacally at mosquito and tick bites, all the while bickering and betraying each other. Within two months, and before a shot had been fired in anger against any Argentine force, three "guerrilla" slackers were executed by firing squad on Massetti's orders. Che had taught Massetti well.

Local *campesinos* finally got tired of all the pasty-faced intellectuals skulking around. Buenos Aires dispatched a couple of patrols and wiped them out in a few days.

Che never got a chance to make his grand guerrilla entrance into his homeland, and the ever-acute Bustos had slipped away before things got really hot. (We'll encounter him later in Bolivia.)

An escapee from one of Che's "guerrilla schools," Juan de Dios Marin, tells a blood-curdling story.

Juan was a Venezuelan recruit into one such camp that sprang up on the vast property of Che's stolen luxurious seaside estate, Tarara, fifteen miles east of Havana, which Che had "requisitioned" for health reasons. "I am ill," Che wrote in the Cuban newspaper *Revolución*. "The doctors recommended a house in a place removed from daily visits." Apparently, Che's doctors also prescribed a yacht harbor, as well as that huge swimming pool with the waterfall, and, of course, the futuristic television.

"This guerrilla school had fifteen hundred recruits," recalls Marin. "We trained sixteen hours a day, seven days a week. The training lasts four months and six thousand communist guerrillas were turned out every year. The program was run by Spanish Civil War veteran Alberto Bayo. Our instructors were mainly Russians and Czechs. . . . The trainers and guides watched us constantly. Two boys who tried to sneak out one night were hauled in front of a firing squad and shot. The primary training manual is titled *150 Principles Every Guerrilla Should Know* by Alberto Bayo." Che did not instruct, and the Russians knew better than to use *his* manual.

Juan de Dios Marin finally became disillusioned and tried to escape. He was caught, savagely beaten, and finally lined up in front of a firing squad. "The wall was splattered with dried blood, and without a blindfold I found myself staring at the muzzles of six rifle barrels," he recalls. "The shots went off and I thought I'd passed out. In a few seconds I realized they had shot blanks."[23]

This was a favorite interrogation technique for the Che-trained police, a sort of good-cop/bad-cop ploy that often bore fruit when the rattled prisoner suddenly realized he was alive.

The only open skeptic of these revolutionary cadres was Castro. "These foreigners are nothing but troublemakers," he told a Cuban rebel named Lazaro Ascencio right after the revolutionary triumph. "Know what I'm going to do with Che Guevara? I'm going to send him to Santo Domingo and see if Trujillo kills him."[24]

How serious was Castro here? We can only guess. Castro's immediate solution to occupying Che was to assign him as commander of La Cabana, an assignment shrewdly matched to Che's aptitude and abilities.

Che and "Imperialism's First Defeat" (the Bay of Pigs)

Castro and his court scribes declare the Bay of Pigs invasion "Imperialism's First Defeat." This should have been Che's crowning moment, the highlight of his career, such as it was. Instead, most of the fourteen hundred freedom fighters trapped on that bloody beach saw more combat in three days than the "Heroic Guerrilla" saw his entire life—probably twice as much.

The invasion plan included a CIA squad dispatching three rowboats off the coast of Pinar del Rio in western Cuba, 350 miles from the true invasion site. They were loaded with time-release Roman candles, bottle rockets, mirrors, and a tape recording of battle. This area of Cuba was closest to the United States, making it a logical choice for any amphibious landing. So the ruse made sense, just as in World War II when Hitler was tricked into believing that the main Allied landing was coming at Calais, even as the invasion stormed Normandy.

Castro, as well as Che, decided that the action three hundred miles away at the Bay of Pigs was a transparent ruse. The *real* invasion was coming in the western Pinar del Rio right on the Yankees' doorstep and—as luck would have it—Che Guevara's area of command!

Che stormed over with several thousand troops, dug in, locked, loaded, and waited for the "Yankee-mercenary" attack. They braced themselves as the sparklers, smoke bombs, and mirrors put on a show just offshore.

It was later revealed that during the smoke-and-mirror show Che had managed to almost lobotomize himself with a misfire. The bullet pierced Che's chin and exited above his temple, just missing his brain. The scar is visible in all post–April-1961 pictures of the gallant Che. Che hagiographers Jon Lee Anderson, Jorge Castañeda, and Paco Taibo all admit that Che's *own* pistol went off just under his face.

That Che missed a direct role in the defeat of imperialism troubles his hagiographers almost as much as it troubled Che himself. Ivy League luminary, Mexican politician, and *Newsweek* writer Jorge Castañeda explained that "Che's contribution to the victory was crucial" in his *Compañero: The Life and Death of Che Guevara.* "Cuba's 200,000 militiamen played a central role in the victory. They allowed Castro to deploy lightly armed, mobile forces to all possible landing points, forming a huge early-warning network. The militia's training was entrusted to the Department of Instruction of the Rebel Armed Forces, *headed by Che* since 1960. His contribution to the victory was thus crucial. Without the militias, Castro's military strategy would not have been viable; without Che the militias would not have been reliable."[25]

This is a lie of a sort to make Alan Dershowitz and the late Johnnie Cochran eat their hearts out.

In fact, all who were on that beachhead and are now free to speak could set Castañeda straight about that Che-trained militia's military prowess. A couple of strafing runs by a couple of Skyhawk jets from the U.S. carrier *Essex* lying just offshore would have sent Castro's Che-trained forces scrambling even more frantically than they had done at first anyway, when they thought they actually faced a fully backed invasion. Indeed, *any* show of force at all from the invaders' "allies"—a few salvoes from the destroyers cruising just offshore, *anything*—would probably have done the trick.

"When we first hit the beach and started shooting, the *milicianos* surrendered in droves," recalls Bay of Pigs survivor Nilo Messer. "One entire battalion of *milicianos* surrendered en masse. So a couple of our guys are sitting there guarding a few hundred *milicianos*! But finally the Castro troops caught on. They saw we'd been abandoned, saw nothing else was coming, and realized how badly they outnumbered us."

Denied air cover and naval fire by Camelot's best and brightest, Brigada 2506 took more casualties (proportionately) its first day ashore at the Bay of Pigs than the U.S. forces who hit Normandy took on June 6, 1944. But they sucked it up and ripped into Castro and Che's forces with a ferocity that amazed their U.S. trainers, men who'd earned their spurs in such fights as the Battle of the Bulge and Iwo Jima.

The Castro-Che communist forces outnumbered these men almost fifty to one, and almost lost the battle, suffering casualties of twenty to one from the abandoned invaders. There was no navel-gazing about "why they hate us" by these mostly civilian volunteers. They didn't need a Frank Capra to explain in brilliant documentaries "Why We Fight." They'd seen communism point-blank: stealing, lying, jailing, poisoning minds, murdering. They'd seen the midnight raids, the drumbeat trials. They'd heard the chilling *"Fuego!"* as Che's firing squads murdered thousands of their brave countrymen. More important, they heard the *"Viva Cuba Libre!"* and the *"Viva Cristo Rey!"* from the bound and blindfolded patriots, right before the bullets ripped them apart.

"They fought like Tigers," wrote their U.S. comrade in arms and trainer Grayston Lynch, who himself had landed on Omaha Beach, helped throw back Hitler's panzers at the Battle of the Bulge six months later, and fought off human wave attacks by Chi-Coms on Korea's Heartbreak Ridge six years after that.[26] "They fought hard and well and inflicted terrible casualties on their opponents," writes another of the Cubans' trainers, U.S. Marine Corps colonel Jack Hawkins, who might also be considered judicious in these matters.

Hawkins is a multidecorated veteran of Bataan, Iwo Jima, and Inchon. "They were *not* defeated," continues Hawkins about Brigada 2506. "They simply ran out of ammunition and had no choice but to surrender. And that was not their fault. They fought magnificently. They were abandoned on the beach without the supplies, protection, and support that had been promised by their sponsor, the government of the United States."[27]

"For the first time in my life I was ashamed of my country," admits Grayston Lynch about the Bay of Pigs. "Tears filled my eyes."[28]

An abandoned invader named Manuel Perez-Garcia, who parachuted into that inferno of Soviet firepower known as the Bay of Pigs, epitomizes the depth of this betrayal. Shortly after Pearl Harbor, he had volunteered for the U.S. Army and made paratrooper with the famed Eighty-second Airborne Division. "The Philippine theater of operations is the locus of victory or defeat," said General Douglas MacArthur. And it was exactly into that locus that Cuban-born Manuel Perez-Garcia parachuted after battling through New Guinea.

At war's end the Eighty-second presented a special trophy to the U.S. soldier who had racked up the most enemy kills in the Pacific theater. Today that trophy sits prominently in Miami's Bay of Pigs Museum, donated by the man who won it, Bay of Pigs veteran and Cuban-born Manuel Perez-Garcia. The trophy sits alongside the three Purple Hearts, three Bronze Stars, and three Silver Stars Perez-Garcia earned in the Pacific.

When Japan's ferocious General Tomoyuki Yamashita, the infamous "Tiger of Malaya," finally emerged from his headquarters to surrender his pistol, samurai sword, and battle flag to the first U.S. soldier he saw, he found himself facing Manuel Perez-Garcia. "Manuel was always out front," recalls his brother-in-arms José M. Juara Silverio, a fellow paratrooper at the Bay of Pigs.[29]

"The tip of the spear," military historian John Keegan calls the place Perez-Garcia always scrambled to occupy. In fact, Perez-Garcia ranks right behind Audie Murphy in the enemy kills by a U.S. soldier in World War II, with eighty-three Japanese soldiers killed in combat. (General Yamashita's battle flag and sword, by the way, are also on display at the Bay of Pigs Museum.)

When Kim Il Sung blitzkrieged South Korea in June 1950, Manuel Perez-Garcia rallied to the U.S. colors again, volunteering for the U.S. Army at age forty-one. It took a gracious letter from President Harry Truman himself to explain that by U.S. law he was slightly overaged but that, "You, sir, have served well above and beyond your duty to the nation. . . . You've written a brilliant page in service to this country."

Perez-Garcia's son, Jorge, however, was the right age. He joined the U.S. Army, made sergeant, and died from a hail of bullets while leading his men in Korea on May 4, 1952. To fight America's enemies, Perez-Garcia and his son were shipped thousands of miles to distant continents. When he tried fighting a tyrant every bit as rabid and murderous as Tojo or Kim Il Sung, but only ninety miles away, he was abandoned.

Here's a summary of the battle of the Bay of Pigs, and the Che-indoctrinated militia's performance: forty-one thousand Castro troops and militia with limitless Soviet arms, including tanks, planes, and batteries of heavy artillery, met fourteen hundred mostly civilian exile freedom fighters, most with less than a month's training. These men carried only light arms and one day's ammo. The Che-trained militia was immediately halted, before fleeing hysterically.

They were ordered back, probed hesitantly, got mauled again, and retreated in headlong flight. They marched back *again*, many at gunpoint, and rolled in battery after battery of Soviet 122mm howitzers. They rained two thousand rounds of heavy artillery fire into lightly armed men they outnumbered twenty to one. ("Rommel's crack Afrika Korps broke and ran under a similar bombardment," writes Bay of Pigs historian Haynes Johnson.) Then Castro's unopposed air force strafed the invaders repeatedly and at will.

The invaders stood their ground, and the militia was forced to probe yet again, but with heavy reinforcements (twenty-to-one odds weren't enough). Then they rained *another* Soviet artillery storm on the utterly abandoned and hopelessly outnumbered invaders.

Finally they moved in and overwhelmed the freedom fighters— after three days of effort, and only when the invaders, who hadn't eaten or slept in three days, were *completely out of ammo with no more coming.* When the smoke cleared and all their ammo had been expended, when a hundred of them lay dead and hundreds more wounded, after their very mortar and machine-gun barrels had melted from their furious rates of fire, after three days of relentless battle, barely fourteen hundred of them had squared off against fifty-one thousand troops trained by Che's Department of Instruction of the Rebel Armed Forces, as well as Castro's entire air force and squadrons of Stalin tanks. In the process, Castro's forces took *3,100 casualties*. The invaders took *114 casualties*.[30] They did it while being denied the air support and cover they expected from the Kennedy administration.

Nilo Messer, Jose Castaño, and Manuel Perez-Garcia, along with their thousand-plus surviving Band of Brothers from Brigada 2506, have never seen fit to write an instructional book an amphibious warfare. Manuel Perez-Garcia, in particular, might be expected to know a thing or two regarding combat. The few long-fighting Escambray rebels who managed to survive the Castroite massacres have also refrained from expounding in print on their experiences.

Leave it to Che Guevara (characterized as "modest" by his biographers), after a few skirmishes that the Cripps or Bloods would shrug off as a slow week, to deliver to the world his book *Guerrilla Warfare*, his opening chapter titled "Guerrilla Warfare: A Method." "You really have to laugh at that book," says retired CIA officer Mario Riveron (himself a Bay of Pigs survivor), whose job was to study, track, and finally capture Che in Bolivia. "Guevara's name is certainly on the cover of that book. But no one who actually fought against him believes those were *his* ideas. The man was a complete failure as a guerrilla. He constantly got lost. He didn't have reliable maps. He split his forces in two and they *both* got lost, without any contact with each other for several months, though they were often bumbling around a mere mile from each other. He abandoned campsites and carelessly left documents and pictures and supplies where we could easily find them. He knew nothing about the use of aerial reconnaissance or helicopters against guerrillas, which strengthens the suspicion that he lifted his stuff straight from Mao. Best of all, he was unable to recruit *one single peasant* into his guerrilla ranks. And here were the people he was there to 'liberate.' "[31]

Many who fought *alongside* Che Guevara were also astounded by his thundering military ineptitude. "When I got to the Sierra," recalls former rebel *comandante* Huber Matos in an interview with Pedro Corzo for the documentary *Anatomia de un Mito*, "Che had already been fighting for over a year. He commanded a column. I was assigned to form a defense line—a line of fortifications in an area under his command. So I consulted him, asked him about it, asked him to help me with the plan.

" 'Look Huber,' he replied straight to my face, 'I don't know anything about that sort of thing.' 'But *you're* the commander here?' I answered. 'I mean, we have to coordinate this thing, have to come up with some kind of tactical plan. I'm assigned to this so I'd like to know how many men to use, and where to place them. I want to make sure that my defense line is coordinated with your own defense plan for the area.' 'But I don't have *any* plan,' Che answered. Several times after that he confessed to me that he knew nothing about tactical military matters."[32]

Che did show up at the Bay of Pigs battle site—on the day the shooting ended. He walked into a building strewn with captured and wounded freedom fighters and looked around with his wry Argentine smile. "We're going to execute every one of you," he barked. Then he turned on his heels and walked out.[33] (As usual, Castro had a plan for these prisoners that was much shrewder. By returning them, Castro's regime reaped a propaganda windfall, as well as a $62-million ransom payment from JFK.) Jon Lee Anderson describes the scene of Che's arrival with ghoulish humor: "Upon recognizing Che, one of the POWs was so terrified he urinated in and soiled his trousers."[34] One of Anderson's primary sources for his book was the Castro government, so the story should be suspect. No *Brigadista* I've interviewed recalled it. Assume, however, for the sake of argument, that this incident of the "terrified" captive actually happened. What this captive feared was Che's well-known treatment of *defenseless* men. Anderson has a remarkable sense of humor, indeed.

Along with his fellow prisoners from Brigada 2506, Manuel Perez-Garcia lived for almost two years under a daily death sentence in Castro's dungeons. Escaping it would be a simple matter of signing the little confession eagerly presented almost daily by his communist captors. The little piece of paper denounced the United States, the very nation that had left them to die.

Neither Manuel, Jose, Nilo, nor any of their brothers in arms signed that document. Many spat on it, figuring they were signing their own death warrants in the act. After all, Castro and Che's firing squads were murdering hundreds of Cubans a week for trivial offenses. These men were avowed enemies of the regime.

"We will die with dignity!" snapped Brigada 2506 second-in-command Erneido Oliva to the furious communists day after day. An attitude like Brigada 2506's not only enrages but baffles the likes of Castro—and Che, as we will see from his behavior in Bolivia.

The comrades of Manuel Perez-Garcia recall he was particularly defiant and scornful toward his strutting Castroite captors, who after the shooting stopped, lorded over captive men with new-found bravery. Having observed these Che-trained men in battle—and considering his own experience in battle—Perez-Garcia must have found a few snorts and wisecracks irresistible. General Yamashita himself, after conquering half of Britain's Asian empire with a fraction of the empire's Asian forces, never put on such airs as Fidel and Che as they toyed with these prisoners.

Fellow prisoner Jose Castaño recalls one morning in Havana's El Principe prison when Manuel Perez-Garcia made a particularly snide comment to one of his captors. "That commie guard was probably around twenty-five years old, and held a loaded Czech machine gun," Jose says. "He was *still* afraid of the fifty-one-year-old, half-starved prisoner, Manuel! So he called over a couple of his buddies and they were moving in on Manuel—who quickly jerked off his belt and wrapped one end around his fist. He sneered at them, 'Come on!' and started snapping the buckle end of the belt like a bullwhip. "Suddenly an officer rushes up and whispers something into the guards' ears. This defused the scene immediately," Jose recalls. "Manuel's history was well known even by the Castroites."[35]

In private, Castro was *fuming* at his own militia's performance. A week after the battle, Castro visited some of the freedom fighters in their Havana prison cells. One had been an old acquaintance from college. "*Hombre,* if I had twenty thousand men like you guys, I'd have all of Latin America in my hands right now," Castro told his old friend.[36]

Che Thanks the Best and Brightest

Four months after the Bay of Pigs invasion the Organization of American States held a conference in Punta del Este, Uruguay. At this event, JFK's special counsel and speechwriter Richard Goodwin represented the United States and had a long and amiable chat with the Cuban representative, Ernesto "Che" Guevara.

"Behind the beard his features are quite soft, almost feminine," Goodwin wrote in a memo to JFK, declassified in 1999. Guevara "has a good sense of humor, and there was considerable joking back and forth during the meeting . . . his conversation was free of propaganda and bombast. He spoke calmly, in a straightforward manner, and with the appearance of detachment and objectivity . . . he went on to say that he wanted to thank us very much for the [Bay of Pigs] invasion—that it had been a great political victory for them—enabled them to consolidate. At the close he said that he would tell no one of the substance of this conversation except Fidel. I said I would not publicize it either.

"After the conversation was terminated I left to record notes on what had been said. [Che] stayed at the party, and talked with the Brazilian and Argentine representatives. The Argentine fellow—Larretta—called me the next morning to say that Guevara had thought the conversation quite profitable, and he told him that it was much easier to talk to someone of the 'newer generation.' "[37]

In this recently declassified document, Goodwin revealed no discomfiture or skepticism regarding any of Che's statements. Nor did he offer the mildest rebuttal to Guevara. Apparently they were occupied with all that "considerable joking back and forth." Che indeed had ample reason to be grateful to the Best and Brightest of the Kennedy administration. As Castro often remarked during 1960, "We'd better hope Kennedy wins the election. If Nixon wins our revolution won't last."[38] Goodwin, a Harvard Law School graduate, typified the indulgent attitude of many of the young, new left in America toward Castro. "I believe this conversation [with Guevara]—coupled with other evidence which has been accumulating—indicates that the Soviet Union is not prepared to undertake the large effort necessary to get [Cuba] on their feet," wrote Goodwin, "and that Cuba desires an understanding with the U.S. They would have free elections—but only after a period of institutionalizing the revolution had been completed. . . . They could agree not to make any political alliance in the East. Che said they did not intend to construct an Iron Curtain around Cuba . . . [the U.S.] should seek some way of continuing the belowground dialogue which Che has begun. We can thus make it clear that we want to help Cuba and would help Cuba if it would sever communist ties and begin democratization."[39]

Of course, Goodwin was outsmarted. At the time of that meeting, Che Guevara himself was the Cuban regime's chief champion of a Soviet alliance—"the scion of the Soviet Union," his biographer Jorge Castañeda labeled Guevara. Che was the "vital link" with the Soviets, was how Anderson put it. The Soviet ambassador to Cuba at the time, Alexander Alexiev, reports that while planning the secret placement of nuclear missiles in Cuba, Che was consistently the most gung-ho—"the most active" is how Alexiev describes the eager Guevara during the meetings.

The Cuban Missile Crisis

During the October 14, 1962, broadcast of a Sunday chat show, *Issues and Answers,* a disdainful McGeorge Bundy, JFK's national security advisor, told a national audience there were no Soviet missiles in Cuba. "Refugee rumors," he called the eyewitness reports from Cuban exiles about those missiles—reports they'd been giving the State Department and CIA for months by then, after risking their lives to obtain them.

"Nothing in Cuba presents a threat to the United States," continued Bundy, barely masking his scorn. "There's no likelihood that the Soviets or Cubans would try and install an offensive capability in Cuba."[40] After all, at Punta del Este, Che Guevara had confided that valuable piece of information to Bundy's colleague Richard Goodwin. And between those insufferable Cuban refugees and the "straightforward" Che Guevara, the Best and Brightest had chosen to trust the latter.

President Kennedy himself sounded off the following day. "There's fifty-odd thousand Cuban refugees in this country," he sneered, "all living for the day when we go to war with Cuba. They're the ones putting out this kind of stuff."[41]

Exactly two days later JFK had photos taken by a U-2 spy plane of those "refugee rumors." He saw nuclear-armed missiles pointing at American cities. The response of Kennedy and his team to the Cuban Missile Crisis has been the stuff of legend, told and retold in movies as a victory of shrewd dealing and brinksmanship. In fact, the solution from the best and the brightest was to team up with the Soviets and grant the Cuban communist regime its mutually assured protection.

"Many concessions were made by the Americans about which not a word has been said," said Castro himself. "Perhaps one day they'll be made public."[42]

"We can't say anything public about this agreement," said Robert F. Kennedy to Soviet ambassador Anatoly Dobrynin when closing the deal that ended the so-called crisis. "It would be too much of a political embarrassment for us."[43] For its part in the Kennedy-Khrushchev deal, the administration secretly agreed not to oppose Castro's government in Cuba.

On October 28, 1962, when news that part of the "resolution" of the Cuban Missile Crisis meant removing the missiles from Cuba, thousands of Cuban troops suddenly surrounded the missile sites. A rattled Soviet foreign minister, Anastas Mikoyan, rushed to Havana and met with Castro. The KGB itself feared the Cuban commandos might attack, take control of the missiles, and start World War III.

Mikoyan somehow defused the situation during his meeting with Castro, no doubt explaining that his regime had come out of the deal smelling like a rose. "Mutually Assured Protection," you might call it, with Castro and Che protected by both the Soviets *and* the United States. True to its word, the United States immediately started rounding up the Cuban exiles who had been launching commando raids against Castro from South Florida.

The Kennedy administration launched into this effort with gusto, giving the U.S. Coast Guard six new planes and twelve new boats and boosting their manpower by 20 percent. JFK called British prime minister Harold Macmillan and informed him that some of those crazy Cubans had moved their operations from South Florida to the Bahamas. Her Majesty's Navy was only too happy to help. Thus, the very Cuban exiles being trained and armed to launch raids on Cuba by the CIA only the week before were now being arrested by U.S. and British forces.[44]

What about Goodwin's belief that Che lacked "propaganda or bombast"? A month later—thinking he was speaking off the record to the *London Daily Worker*—Che Guevara explained: "If the missiles had remained *we would have used them against the very heart of the*

United States, including New York. We must never establish peaceful coexistence. We must walk the path of victory even if it costs millions of atomic victims!"[45]

Che Guevara himself, of course, did not want to be one of the victims of a nuclear exchange he was only too ready to start. He and Fidel had priority reservations in the Soviet bomb shelter outside Havana. The Soviet ambassador of the day, Alexander Alexiev, reports that Castro and Che had made sure of that.[46]

As early as 1955, Ernesto Guevara had written to his doting mother that a struggle against the United States was his "true destiny." "We must learn the lesson of absolute abhorrence of imperialism. Against that class of hyena there is no other medium than extermination!"[47] In October 1962, Guevara had gotten tantalizingly close to that medium.

Richard Nixon summed up the Cuban Missile Crisis "resolution" best. "First we goofed an invasion—now we give the Soviets squatters' rights in our backyard."[48]

Safeguarded by U.S. policy and lavished with Soviet arms, the Cuban communists' revolution had a secure base to hatch and breed guerrilla wars in pursuit of the dream of "continental liberation" with the Andes as the "Sierra of the continent." All the odds were with them. With a halfway-competent guerrilla leader as head of the DGI's "Liberation Department," they might have pulled it off. Instead they had Ernesto "Che" Guevara.

5

Fidel's Favorite Executioner

[Che presented a] Christlike image . . . with his mortuary gaze it is as if Guevara looks upon his killers and forgives them.
—*Newsweek* WRITER AND CHE BIOGRAPHER JORGE CASTAÑEDA

[Che's image] derives from a visual language . . . it also references a classical Christ-like demeanor.
—TRISHA ZIFF, GUGGENHEIM MUSEUM CURATOR

It was out of love, like a perfect knight, that Che had set out. In a sense he was like an early saint.
—*The Nation* COLUMNIST I. F. STONE AFTER MEETING GUEVARA

Che's prescription for the ideal revolutionary as an "effective, violent *cold* killing machine" implies a certain detachment or nonchalance toward murder. In fact, Che gave ample evidence of taking to the task with relish. Except in battle, Che was always quite a *warm* killing machine.

"Crazy with fury I will stain my rifle red while slaughtering any enemy that falls in my hands! My nostrils dilate while savoring the acrid odor of gunpowder and blood. With the deaths of my enemies

I prepare my being for the sacred fight and join the triumphant proletariat with a bestial howl!" This is a passage from Che's famous *Motorcycle Diaries* that Robert Redford somehow managed to omit from his touching film. The "acrid odor of gunpowder and blood" rarely reached Guevara's nostril from actual combat. It always came from the close-range murder of bound, gagged, and blindfolded men and boys.

Thirsting for Blood

In late January 1957, a few weeks after his dauntless Baptism of Fire when "all seemed lost," and Che stoically braced for a "dignified death" (from a wound that didn't require one stitch), he sent a letter to his discarded wife, Hilda Gadea. "Dear *vieja,* I'm here in Cuba's hills, alive and *thirsting for blood.*"[1] His thirst would soon be slaked.

In that very month of January 1957, Fidel Castro ordered the execution of a peasant guerrilla named Eutimio Guerra, accused of being an informer for Batista's forces. Castro assigned the killing to his own bodyguard, Universo Sanchez. To everyone's surprise, Che Guevara—a lowly rebel soldier/medic at the time, not a *comandante* yet—volunteered to accompany Sanchez and another soldier to the execution site. The Cuban rebels were glum as they walked slowly down the trail in a torrential thunderstorm. Finally the little group stopped in a clearing.

Sanchez was hesitant, looking around, perhaps looking for an excuse to postpone or call off the execution. Dozens would follow, but this was the first execution of a Castro rebel. Without warning, Che stepped forward and fired his pistol into Guerra's temple. "He went into convulsions for a while and was finally still. Now his belongings were mine," Che wrote in his diaries.

Che's father in Buenos Aires received a letter from his prodigal son. "I'd like to confess, Papa, at that moment I discovered that I really like killing."[2]

This can-do attitude caught Castro's eye. More executions of assorted "deserters," "informers," and "war criminals" quickly followed, all with Che's enthusiastic participation. One was of a captured Batista soldier, a seventeen-year-old boy totally green to the guerrilla "war"—hence his easy capture. First Che interrogated him.

"I haven't killed anyone, *comandante!*" the terrified boy answered Che. "I just got out here! I'm an only son, my mother's a widow, and I joined the army for the salary, to send it to her every month . . . don't kill me! Don't kill me!—*why?*"[3]

Che barked the orders and the boy was trussed up, shoved in front of a recently dug pit, and murdered. This was the same man Ariel Dorfman wrote of in *Time* as the "generous Che who tended wounded enemy soldiers."

Castro thought executing Batista soldiers was incredibly stupid, compared to the propaganda value of releasing them. But he recognized Che's value as an ardent executioner. Castro was already thinking ahead to his stealth takeover of Cuba, planning his version of Stalin's Katyn massacre, and with the same rationale: to decapitate—literally and figuratively—any future counter-revolutionaries, future *contras*. So by summer 1957, Che had been promoted to full-fledged major or *comandante,* the rebel army's highest rank. His fame was spreading.

But not all were favorably impressed. In mid-1958, a rebel soldier, Reynaldo Morfa, was wounded and made his way to Dr. Hector Meruelo in the nearby town of Cienfuegos. The good doctor patched him up and a few weeks later informed him that he was well enough to return to Che's column.

"No, doctor," Reynaldo responded. "Please be discreet with this because it could cost me my life, but I've learned that Che is nothing but a murderer. I'm a revolutionary but I'm also a Christian. I'll go and join Camilo's column—but never Che's."[4]

Agustin Soberon was the first Cuban reporter to visit Che's Sierra Maestra camp to interview him. "I was a reporter for the Cuban magazine *Bohemia* and visited Che in March 1958 at his camp in La Plata," he recalls. "It was impossible to break the ice with Guevara,

I've never met anyone with such a despotic and arrogant nature. First I asked him about his wife, Hilda, whom he left in Mexico to come on the *Granma* with Fidel. 'I don't know anything about her since I left—and I don't care anything about her,' he snapped. Okay, so I then ask him about his profession of medical doctor. 'I'm not interested in medicine at all,' he snaps. 'I dislike it.'" Soberon continues: "That night I slept in a hut at the camp. A young rebel sleeping next to me was having what looked to me like a terrible nightmare. He was rolling back and forth, murmuring, 'Execute him—execute him—execute him.' So the next morning I asked him about it. I'll never forget this, the young rebel's name was Humberto Rodriguez and he explained how he'd been put in charge of firing squads. What he'd been saying during the nightmare were Che's constant commands, still ringing in his ears. Apparently they troubled him. A little while later, Che himself comes over and announces they're tying a victim to the stake. Would I like to come over and watch the firing squad at work? I didn't. I'd seen enough and heard enough. I left."[5]

All these victims were *campesinos*, peasants, of whom Che himself wrote that their "cooperation comes after our planned terror."[6]

Ten months after Soberon's visit to his Sierra campsite, Che entered Havana and moved promptly into that infamous old Spanish fortress, La Cabana. "The shouts of *Viva Cuba Libre!* and *Viva Cristo Rey!* followed by the firing-squad blasts made the walls of that Fortress tremble," recalls Armando Valladares, who served twenty-two years in Castro's Cuban prisons.

During these bloody months, *Time* magazine featured Cuban revolutionary *comandante* Ernesto "Che" Guevara on its cover and crowned him the "Brains of the Cuban Revolution." (Fidel Castro was "the heart" and Raul Castro "the fist.") "Wearing a smile of melancholy sweetness that many women find devastating," *Time* gushed, "Che guides Cuba with icy calculation, vast competence, high intelligence and a perceptive sense of humor."

The tone of the *Time* article was in perfect league with other major media—and utterly wrong. Guevara was no more the brains of the Cuban revolution than Feliks Dzerzhinski had been the brains of the Bolshevik revolution, or Himmler the brains of the National Socialist revolution, or Beria the brains behind Stalinism. Che performed the same role for Fidel Castro that Dzerzhinski performed for Lenin, Himmler for Hitler, and Beria for Stalin. He was the snarling enforcer, the regime's chief executioner.

Under Che, La Cabana fortress had been converted into a Caribbean Lubyanka. His approach was thoroughly Chekist. "Always interrogate your prisoners at night," Che commanded his goons, "a man is easier to cow at night, his mental resistance is always lower."[7]

Exact numbers may never be known, but the orders of magnitude of these murders are not in doubt. José Vilasuso, a Cuban prosecutor who quickly defected in horror and disgust, estimates that Che signed 400 death warrants during the first three months of his command in La Cabana. A Basque priest named Iòaki de Aspiazu, often on hand to perform confessions and last rites, says Che personally ordered 700 executions by firing squad during that period. Cuban journalist Luis Ortega, who knew Che as early as 1956, writes in his book *Yo Soy El Che!* that Guevara sent 1,892 men to the firing squad.

In his book *Che Guevara: A Biography*, Daniel James writes that Che himself admitted to ordering "several thousand" executions during the first year of the Castro regime. Felix Rodriguez, the Cuban-American CIA operative who helped track down Che in Bolivia and was the last person to question him, says that Che during his final talk admitted to "a couple thousand" executions. But he shrugged them off as all being of "imperialist spies and CIA agents."

Che's bloodbath in the first months of 1959 was not conducted for either vengeance or justice. Like Stalin's massacre of the Polish officer corps in the Katyn forest, like Stalin's Great Terror against his own officer corps a few years earlier, Che's firing-squad marathons were a perfectly rational and cold-blooded exercise.

Five years earlier, while a communist hobo in Guatemala, Che had seen the Guatemalan officer corps, with CIA assistance, rise against the regime of Jacobo Arbenz, sending him and his communist minions into exile. (For those leftist scholars who still claim that Jacobo Arbenz was an innocent "nationalist" victimized by the fiendish United Fruit Company and its CIA proxies, please note: Arbenz sought exile, not in France, or Spain, or even Mexico, the traditional havens for deposed Latin American politicians, but in Czechoslovakia, within the Soviet bloc. The coup went into motion, not when Arbenz started nationalizing United Fruit property, but when a cargo of Soviet-bloc weapons arrived.) "Arbenz didn't execute enough people," was how Ernesto Guevara explained the Guatemalan coup's success.[8]

Fidel and Che didn't want a repetition of the Guatemalan coup in Cuba. Their massacres cowed and terrorized. Public show trials underscored the message. And the executions, right down to the final shattering of the skull with the coup de grace from a massive .45 slug fired at five paces, were often public, too. Visitors to La Cabana, even prisoners' families, all walked in front of the blood-spattered *paredon*. This was no coincidence.

"It was a wall painted in blood," recalls Margot Menendez, who entered to try to convince Guevara that her brother was innocent. "You couldn't miss that horrible wall. It seemed to announce that we were entering hell."

"Your brother wore the wrong uniform," Che smirked at the sobbing Margot Menendez. That very night Che's firing squad murdered the boy. Another jailed at La Cabana by Che in the early months of the revolution was a Cuban gentleman named Pierre San Martin. "Sixteen of us would stand while the other sixteen tried to sleep on the cold filthy floor," San Martin recalled in 1997. "We took shifts that way. Dozens were led from the cells to the firing squad daily. The volleys kept us awake. We felt that any one of those minutes would be our last.

"One morning the horrible sound of that rusty steel door swinging open startled us awake and Che's guards shoved a new prisoner into our cell. He was a boy, maybe fourteen years old. His face was bruised and smeared with blood. 'What did you do?' we asked, horrified. 'I tried to defend my papa,' gasped the bloodied boy. 'But they sent him to the firing squad.'"

Soon Che's guards returned. The rusty steel door opened and they yanked the boy out of the cell. "We all rushed to the cell's window that faced the execution pit," recalls San Martin. "We simply couldn't believe they'd murder him.

"Then we spotted him, strutting around the blood-drenched execution yard with his hands on his waist and barking orders—Che Guevara himself. 'Kneel down!' Che barked at the boy.

" 'Assassins!' we screamed from our window.

" 'I said: KNEEL DOWN!' Che barked again.

"The boy stared Che resolutely in the face. 'If you're going to kill me,' he yelled, 'you'll have to do it while I'm standing! Men die standing!' "

"Murderers!" the men yelled desperately from their cells. "Then we saw Che unholstering his pistol. He put the barrel to the back of the boy's neck and blasted. The shot almost decapitated the young boy.

"We erupted, 'Murderers!—Assassins!' Che finally looked up at us, pointed his pistol, and emptied his clip in our direction. Several of us were wounded by his shots."[9]

"The blond boy could not have been much over fifteen," recalls NBC correspondent Edward Scott about another execution he witnessed at La Cabana in February 1959. "As they wrestled him to the stake the boy spoke eloquently to the firing squad, telling them repeatedly that he was innocent." This seemed to rattle the firing-squad members, and at Herman Marks's order of "*Fuego!*" only one bullet struck the bound boy. A furious Marks walked up and demolished the boy's skull with two blasts from his .45. Then he summoned his bodyguards and ordered the entire firing squad arrested. Apparently they'd fallen down on the job.[10] Who was Herman Marks? He was an American, an ex-convict, Marine deserter, and mental case with the U.S. law close on his heels in 1957. At age 30, Marks was convicted of raping a teenage girl and sent to the state prison in Waupun, Wisconsin for 3½ years.[11] He was also one of the very few people to whom Che was close.

Marks escaped to Cuba, joined Che's rebels in the Sierra Maestra, became a gung-ho "revolutionary," and was quickly promoted to "captain" (apparently theft and rape constituted no "crime against revolutionary morals"). As early as the Sierra skirmishes, Marks's specialty had been jumping into the freshly dug pit and shattering the skulls of Che's firing-squad victims with the coup de grace blast from his .45 pistol. Later, during the Che-ordered firing-squad marathons in La Cabana, Marks really started earning his keep. He named La Cabana his personal "hunting lodge," and his .45 barely had time to cool between assignments.

Che's Room with a View

In La Cabana, Marks would bring his pet dog to work with him. "A huge dog," recalls Roberto Martin-Perez, who suffered twenty-eight years in Castro's Gulag (over three times as long as Alexander Solzhenitzyn and Natan Sharansky spent in the Soviet Gulag) and is today married to Miami radio star Ninoska Perez. "The dog looked like a German shepherd–hound cross of some kind. He followed Marks everywhere."

Whatever his pedigree, the dog's specialty was happily bounding up after the firing-squad volley and lapping up the blood that oozed from the shattered heads and bodies of the murdered. We can assume that Che was watching and gloating from his window. After all, one of Che's first acts upon entering La Cabana was to order a section of wall torn out from his office so he could watch his beloved firing squads at work.

Another of Marks's amusements was walking down the dark, dank halls of the prison fortress, laughing crazily and rattling the bars of the cells. After he got the attention of the condemned men and boys, he'd ask them behind which ear they wanted the coup de grace from his .45 pistol. A real cut-up, this Herman Marks. "Marks was like a butcher killing cattle in an abattoir," finally wrote (of all people!) Herbert Matthews of the *New York Times*.

"We'd hear the clump of the bootsteps coming down the hall and wondered who was next," remembers one prisoner, Roberto Martin-Perez. "Sometimes it was Marks who would stop in front of a cell and point. Then he'd walk to the next one and point. He might pass two more, then stop again. Men were dragged out of the cell and a bit later we'd hear the volley. It was hard to sleep under such conditions. You never knew when your turn was coming. Somehow I made it, but I lost many friends. During one week in 1962, we counted four hundred firing-squad blasts."

Technically, Che Guevara was no longer in command of La Cabana after September 1959. But it was still *his* system of justice, with firing squads piling up corpses throughout Cuba. Guevara established it, on Castro's orders, cranked it into high gear, and always claimed it proudly, as we saw in his famous U.N. speech. "Executions? Certainly, *we* execute!"

"There was something seriously wrong with Guevara," says Roberto Martin-Perez. "Castro killed and ordered killing—*for sure* he killed. But he killed, it seemed to us, motivated by his power lust, to maintain his hold on power, to eliminate rivals and enemies— along with *potential* rivals and *potential* enemies. For Castro it was a utilitarian slaughter, that's all. Guevara, on the other hand, seemed to *relish* it. He appeared to revel in the bloodletting for its own sake. You could somehow see it in his face as he watched the men dragged out of their cells."

As it happened, *Señor* Roberto Martin-Perez was childhood friends with Aleida March, Che Guevara's widow. The Castroites certainly had utilitarian reasons to jail Roberto Martin-Perez. "More than hating Castro, Che, and their toadies, I despised them," he admits. "Knowing how they'd taken power, I felt contempt. All that guerrilla war stuff was utterly bogus. It was a huge con job. They had a few shootouts, a few skirmishes, that's all. There's nothing wrong with taking power without much bloodshed. But then to start strutting around like they were battle-hardened heroes and 'mighty guerrilla warriors,' etcetera. It was almost laughable. As a kid, I'd known one of their bunch, Efigenio Ameijeiras, who after their victory was suddenly promoted to 'head of the revolutionary national police,' where he immediately started jailing and torturing people.

"Ameijeiras had been a purse snatcher and a hubcap thief a few months before. He even tried to sell *me* some stolen hubcaps and stolen watches—good grief! So then I have to see this bunch acclaimed as 'heroes' and 'idealists,' etcetera by the *New York Times*? Had I gotten out? In ten seconds I'd have grabbed a gun and gone against them again," says Martin-Perez.[12]

He was incapable of masking his scorn, and in prison he suffered horribly for it. Even at age nineteen, Martin-Perez was known among his captors and prison guards as "*El Cojuno*" (the ballsy one). "One day I'd gotten particularly smart-mouthed, I guess," he remembers. "So they dragged me down to the torture cell and hung me by my wrists, behind my back, with my feet exactly an inch from the floor. I could touch it with my tippy-toes every now and then. They had the elevation exactly right. After all, Che himself had called in the KGB to train the Cuban police. They hung me there for seventeen days—exactly seventeen. I still remember it well."

Roberto Martin-Perez was moved from La Cabana to another prison, where his reputation had preceded him. "Hah! So you're *El Cojuno*?" sneered the new prison chief upon calling him out. Then he took out his pistol and aimed carefully. "He hit me in the leg," recalls Martin-Perez, "and I fell grimacing. Blam!—he hit me in the other leg. Blam! In the arm with his third shot."

All told, Roberto Martin-Perez took six bullets. "The last one finally hit me in the crotch." He smirks. "I don't really know if he was trying to kill me, or what. But he did shoot *one* of my testicles off. I suppose that's what he was aiming at, given my nickname at the time. But typical for these 'expert guerrilla warriors'—as the *New York Times* and, to this day, all the exalted college professors acclaim these idiots—he couldn't even hit a target from five feet away."

At sixty-six, Roberto Martin-Perez is hale, hearty, gregarious, and good-natured. He laughs loud and often. Incredibly, he laughs after almost *thirty years* in Castro's dungeons. Martin-Perez survived one of the longest political prison sentences of the twentieth century.

A Romanian journalist named Stefan Bacie visited Cuba in early 1959 and was fortunate enough to get an audience with the already famous Che Guevara, whom he'd also met briefly in Mexico City. The meeting between Bacie and Guevara took place in Che's office in La Cabana. Upon entering, the Romanian saw Che motioning him over to his office's newly constructed window.

Stefan Bacie got there just in time to hear the command of *"Fuego!"* and the blast from the firing squad and see the condemned man crumple and convulse. The stricken journalist immediately left and composed a poem, titled "I No Longer Sing of Che."[13]

"I no longer sing of Che any more than I would of Stalin," go the first lines.

Besides his demanding job in the La Cabana killing grounds, Herman Marks also served as "security director" at Havana's El Principe prison, already packed to suffocation with political prisoners. Within a year, stadiums, schools, and movie theaters throughout Cuba became makeshift prison camps also. The roundup of political prisoners required it.

On June 3, 1959, Captain Herman Marks took a break from his demanding profession to stand as witness at Che's wedding to Aleida March. Captain Marks was among the lucky few, and the envy of many revolutionaries. Che's wedding was the hottest ticket of Havana's social season. It would take until 1961 for the erratic Marks to finally run afoul of the revolution. He somehow slithered back into the country that had already revoked his citizenship. (Given his Castrophilia, it's a wonder Marks did not become a scholar for the Institute for Policy Studies, or CNN's Latin America correspondent.) The man who replaced Marks as the humanistic revolution's "security director" also had an impressive resume. He was Ramon Mercader, the Stalinist assassin who had driven an ice-ax into Leon Trotsky's forehead in 1940.

Castro's fervently "nationalist" revolution, widely hailed as eradicating humiliating foreign influences from Cuba, overran Cuba with rude, malodorous Russian communists. It had as its main executioners of Cuban patriots an Argentine hobo and a genuine American psycho.

Cuban Blood for Sale

Biographer Jorge Castañeda stresses that Che operated from an ethical and *humanistic* stance. Given the rate of firing-squad executions in Cuba in the early years of the Cuban Revolution, thousands of gallons of valuable blood were gushing from the bodies of young men and boys, soaking uselessly into the mud, washing into gutters, or getting licked up by Herman Marks's hound. What a waste, reasoned Cuba's new rulers.

Heaven knows that Cuba, then as now, had a crying need for some foreign exchange. And here was an ocean of fresh, plasma-rich blood freed from its confines by bullets and spilling in torrents daily. Let's collect it and sell it, reasoned the cash-hungry communist regime for which Che ministered.

Below is a court record from a lawsuit filed by the family of a U.S. citizen, Howard Anderson, murdered by a Cuban firing squad in April 1961.

Anderson v. Republic of Cuba, No. 01-28628 (Miami-Dade Cir. April 13, 2003): "In one final session of torture, Castro's agents drained Howard Anderson's body of blood before sending him to his death at the firing squad."

After the volley at La Cabaña's blood-spattered wall, Howard Anderson's sparse blood soaked into the same soil and bricks as that of Rogelio Gonzalez, Virgilio Campaneria, and Alberto Tapia, all Havana University students and members of Catholic Action. Like Howard Anderson, they refused blindfolds. These young men all died yelling, "Long Live Christ the King!"

Fourteen thousand young men would join them in mass graves shortly, on the orders of Ted Turner's chum Fidel and the icon of Burlington Industries' T-shirts, Che.

Herman Marks's hound might have found less blood to lap up, but Havana's birds were gorging on flesh. "Those firing-squad volleys rang like a dinner bell to the birds," recalls Cuban freedom fighter Hiram Gonzalez, imprisoned in La Cabana at the time of Anderson's murder, in the documentary *Yo Los He Visto Partir*. "Those firing squads had been going off daily since January 7, 1959, the day Che Guevara entered Havana. It didn't take long for the birds to catch on. Flocks of them had learned to perch atop the wall that surrounded La Cabana fortress and in the nearby trees. After the volley they swooped down to peck at the bits of bone, blood, and flesh that littered the ground. Those birds sure grew fat."[14]

Paul Bethel was press attaché for the U.S. embassy in Cuba during the anti-Batista rebellion and the first years of revolution. Later he worked as head of the Latin American division of the U.S. Information Agency, where he interviewed hundreds of the Cuban refugees then landing in South Florida. Bethel also kept hearing accounts of this blood extraction from firing-squad victims. Finally he was able to question Dr. Virginia de Mirabal Quesada, who escaped Cuba through Mexico and had actually fled, horrified, after witnessing the process. "It's absolutely true," she told the U.S. Information Agency. "Before being shot, the men are taken to a small first-aid room at La Cabana, where the communists extract between a quart and a quart and a half of blood from each victim. It is then placed in a blood bank. Some of it is shipped to North Vietnam. Sometimes the victims are so weak, they have to be carried to the execution stake. Others, not healthy at the time from the prison ordeal, or with bad hearts, die during the extraction."[15]

On April 7, 1967, the Organization of American States Human Rights Commission finally issued a detailed report on the humanistic Cuban revolution's long-practiced vampirism. The report was based on dozens of verified eyewitness accounts by defectors.

"On May, 27, 1966, from six in the morning to nightfall political prisoners were executed continuously by firing squad in Havana's La Cabana prison," the report read. "One hundred and sixty-six men were executed that day and each had 5 pints of blood extracted prior to being shot. Extracting this amount of blood often produces cerebral anemia and unconsciousness so that many had to be carried to the execution wall on stretchers. The corpses were then transported by truck to a mass grave in a cemetery outside the city of Marianao. On that day, the truck required seven trips to deliver all the corpses. On 13th Street in Havana's Vedado district Soviet medical personnel have established a blood bank where this blood is transported and stored. This blood is sold at fifty U.S. dollars per pint to the Republic of North Viet Nam."

Communist Cuba's innovative blood-marketing program has received no attention from the mainstream media and "scholars" in general, though Cuba's medical practices usually get no end of fawning coverage. Dr. Juan Clark, sociology professor at Miami-Dade Community College, Bay of Pigs veteran and former political prisoner, is the shining exception. His research included interviews with dozens of Castro's and Che's ex–political prisoners and defectors who confirmed the practice. Needless to say, in the thousands upon thousands of pages devoted to their subject, no Che "biographer" mentions Cuba's blood trade, yet they all play up Che's role as minister of industries starting in early 1961—*just when the blood-marketing campaign began.*

Henry Butterfield Ryan, diplomat and scholar, in particular laments that Che's glowing record as Cuba's export manager at the time has largely gone unheralded. "Where Guevara shone," he writes in his widely praised book *The Fall of Che Guevara,* "was in the role of a diplomat, especially on economic issues. He secured export and import deals for Cuba within the communist bloc on terms that no other countries received and that helped Cuba enormously."[16]

As we will see, Che was an economic disaster, wrecking every vestige of Cuba's flourishing capitalism. But history should not overlook this signal economic achievement, that *Cuban* blood had a ready market in Cuba's sister socialist republics on distant continents for ready cash.

A crowning irony: This was the same man who liked to proclaim that he helped free Cuba from the rapacity of those "bloodsucking Yankee imperialist exploiters!"

6

Murderer of Women and Children

Wearing a smile of melancholy sweetness that many women find devastating, Che Guevara guides Cuba with icy calculation, vast competence, high intelligence and a perceptive sense of humor.
—*Time* MAGAZINE, AUGUST 8, 1960

On April 17, 1961, a counter-revolutionary named Amelia Fernandez García had her young body destroyed by a firing-squad volley.

On Christmas Eve of that same year, Juana Diaz spat in the face of the executioners who were binding and gagging her. She had been found guilty of feeding and hiding "bandits" (the term for Cuban farmers who took up arms to fight the theft of their land). When the blast from that firing squad demolished her face and torso—remember, all ten executioners shot live ammo—Juana was six months pregnant.

Dr. Amando Lago has fully documented the firing-squad executions of eleven Cuban women in the early days of the regime. He documents a total of 219 female deaths, the rest listed as "extrajudicial." (And we've seen what even a "judicial" execution meant to Che—the verdict announced before the trial.)

Lydia Perez also died "extrajudicially," on August 7, 1961, while a prisoner at the Guanajay women's prison camp. Eight months pregnant at the time, she somehow annoyed a young guard, who bashed her to the ground, kicked her in the stomach, and walked off. Lydia and her baby were left to bleed to death. Olga Fernandez and her husband, Marcial, were both machine-gunned to death on April 18, 1961, while rushing to the Argentine embassy for asylum. Amalia Cora was machine-gunned to death along with five others for the crime of trying to exit Cuba in a boat on February 5, 1965.

Twenty-four-year-old Teresita Saavedra was a lay Catholic leader when the Che-trained militia arrested her in the town of Sancti-Spiritus in central Cuba. The Bay of Pigs invasion had just been crushed and a huge dragnet was sweeping Cuba for any who had sympathized with those abandoned freedom fighters. Teresita, who certainly qualified, was hauled away at Czech machine-gun point to the town's police headquarters. In the interrogation room she was repeatedly raped by five *milicianos,* who then released her. Teresita committed suicide that night. "Without Che the militias would not have been reliable," goes the refrain of Che biographer Jorge Castañeda. The recent foreign minister of Mexico is correct. The *milicianos* were unusually reliable. And diligent.

Two Catholic nuns were part of the "extrajudicial" massacre of women. Sister Aida Rosa Perez kept getting on the authorities' nerves with her anticommunist speeches. She was finally sentenced to twelve years at hard labor, despite her heart condition. Two years into her sentence, while toiling in the sun inside Castro's Gulag and surrounded by leering guards, Sister Rosa collapsed from a heart attack. The media are always ready to headline atrocities, such as the killing of Catholic nuns in El Salvador by "right-wing" death squads. When Salvadoran archbishop Romero was assassinated, it provoked a major Hollywood movie. Aside from independent efforts by brave loners, like Andy Garcia's *The Lost City,* few directors will touch a story that fairly portrays the victims of Che.

A good case can be made that Castro and Che preempted the Taliban by a good forty years. The stifling economic and social conditions created by the Cuban Revolution leave Cuban women today as the most suicidal in the world. This does not, however, prevent the United Nations from naming Cuba to its Human Rights Commission. Nor does the regime's treatment of women prevent UNICEF from naming an award in Castro's Cuba's honor.

Certainly, *Time* magazine did not report how "devastating" Che actually was for many Cuban women.

Evelio Gil Diez was seventeen years old when Che signed his death warrant and Marks blasted his skull apart in La Cabana's killing ground, with Che watching from his window. Luis Perez Antunez was also seventeen when he stared his executioners boldly in the face, seconds before the volley riddled his body and ended his young life.

Seventeen-year-old Calixto Valdes was found guilty of "crimes against the revolution" in the same mass trial that condemned his father, Juan. From his cell in La Cabana, Juan watched the guards stomp down the hall and enter the nearby cell that held his son. He heard a scuffle, then watched how they yanked his struggling boy from the cell in a chokehold. "Cowards!" yelled Juan in tears of rage, bashing the cell bars. "Miserable assassins!" While one guard bent his boy's arms back and bound his hands, two more guards came into play. One grabbed his furiously struggling son's hair and jerked his head back, trying to steady him. The other taped his mouth shut. (By then, the firing squads were becoming rattled by the defiant yells of "*Viva Cuba Libre!*" "*Viva Cristo Rey!*" and "Down with Communism!")

Juan watched helplessly as his son struggled. Three guards managed to drag him down the hall, and Juan tried to steel himself. A few moments later he shuddered at the blast that murdered his boy. A few seconds later he shuddered again at the coup de grace. Juan Valdes's sentence had been twenty-five years in prison. Would a sentence of death have been any worse?

Rigoberto Hernandez was also seventeen when Che's soldiers dragged him from his cell in La Cabana, jerked his head back to gag him, and started dragging him to the stake. Little "Rigo" pleaded his innocence to the end. But his pleas were garbled and difficult to understand. His struggles while gagged and bound to the stake were also awkward. The boy had been a janitor in a Havana high school and was mentally retarded. His single mother had pleaded his case with hysterical sobs. She had begged, beseeched, and finally proved to his prosecutors that it was a case of mistaken identity. Her only son, a boy in such a condition, *couldn't possibly* have been "planting bombs."

But there was no bucking Che's "pedagogy of the *paredon!*"

"Fuego!" and the volley shattered Rigo's little bent body as he moaned and struggled awkwardly against his bonds, blindfold, and gag. The revolutionary courts followed Che Guevara's instructions that "proof is secondary and an archaic bourgeois detail." Remember this, and remember Harvard University's rollicking ovation to honored guest Fidel Castro during the very midst of this appalling bloodbath.

The point lost on Harvard was the use of terror to cow the public, to let them know who was now in charge, and the fate that awaited any challengers. The more horrifying the murders, the better they served their purpose.

One mother, Rosa Hernandez, recalls how she begged for a meeting with Che in order to try to save her seventeen-year-old son, who was condemned without trial to the firing squad. Guevara graciously complied. "Come right in, *señora,*" said Che as he opened the door to his office. "Have a seat." Silently he listened to her sobs and pleas, then picked up the phone right in front of her. "Execute the Hernandez boy tonight," Che barked, and he slammed the phone down. His goons then dragged out the hysterical Mrs. Hernandez. This happened more than once. These grieving people can be found today, wiping their red-rimmed eyes, ambling amid the long rows of white crosses at the Cuban Memorial in Miami's Tamiami Park. It's a mini Arlington Cemetery, in honor of Castro and Che's murder victims. But the tombs are symbolic. Most of the bodies still lie in mass graves in Cuba.

Some of these Cuban Memorial visitors kneel, others walk slowly, looking for a name. Many clutch rosaries. Many of the ladies press their faces into the breast of a relative who drove them there, a relative who wraps his arms around her spastically heaving shoulders. Try as he might not to cry himself, he usually finds that the sobs wracking his mother, grandmother, or aunt are contagious. Yet he's often too young to remember the face of his martyred uncle, father, or cousin.

"*Fusilado,*" it says below the white cross. Firing-squad execution. The elderly lady still holds a tissue to her eyes and nose as they wait to cross the street, her grandson still has his arm around her. She told him how his freedom-fighter grandfather yelled, "*Viva Cristo Rey!*" the instant before the volley shattered his body.

Still escorted by her grandson, the woman crosses the street slowly, silently, and runs into a dreadlocked youth coming out of a music store. His T-shirt sports the face of her husband's murderer. They turn their heads in rage and toward the store window. Well, there's the murderer's face again, on a huge poster; $19.95 it says at the bottom, right under the poster's slogan: "Resist Oppression!"

The reason for the UNICEF award to Castro's Cuba was "the Cuban state's priority to assist and protect children."

"We Execute from Revolutionary Conviction!"

"Innocent people were not executed in significant numbers," goes the familiar assurance of Jorge Castañeda. "It is surprising that there were so few abuses and executions." It's an old lie. In an April 1959 issue of *Reader's Digest,* writer Dickey Chapelle comforted her readers with the observation that "the Cuba of Fidel Castro today is free from terror. Civil liberties have been restored."

In fact, the opposite was happening. Historians consider Hitler's enabling act, passed on March 23, 1933, among the foremost legal horrors of the century, a law that abolished legislative power and judicial guarantees, laying the groundwork for dictatorship. In Cuba, an almost identical law was passed on January 10, 1959, by Castro's cabinet that gave a legal veneer to Che Guevara's firing-squad massacres. This act was initially met by the liberal media as the restoration of the rule of law. Castro has "a deep reverence for civilian, representative, constitutional government," wrote Jules Dubois in the *Chicago Tribune* in January, 1959.

"Mr. Castro's bearded, youthful figure has become a symbol of Latin America's rejection of brutality and lying; every sign is that he will reject personal rule and violence," concluded the *London Observer* on January 9, 1959.

"Castro is almost Christ-like in his care and concern for his people," Edwin Tetlow of the *London Daily Telegraph* assured his readers.

"Humanistic" is the parroted term used by the *New York Times* for Castro and Che's *Revolución* innovations. Among them was this new law that *introduced* the death penalty to Cuba and made it apply *retroactively*. To cap it all, this new law—just passed by a government hailed worldwide as a paragon of justice—abolished habeas corpus.

Within months, Cuba's jails held ten times the number of prisoners that they had held under the beastly Batista.

Though Che Guevara was overall head of the prosecuting tribunals, many of the executed got no trial whatsoever. The few farcical trials horrified and nauseated all observers, even some of the revolution's earliest champions. Edwin Tetlow, Havana correspondent for the *London Daily Telegraph*, started having second thoughts as he watched the guilty verdicts and sentences of death announced almost mechanically. He was particularly rattled when he saw some of these verdicts posted on a board—*before the trials were held.*[1]

One day in early 1959 one of Che's revolutionary courts actually found a Cuban army captain named Pedro Morejon innocent. This brought Che's fellow *comandante,* Camilo Cienfuegos, to his feet. "If Morejon is not executed," he yelled, "I'll put a bullet through his head myself!" The court reassembled frantically and quickly arrived at a new verdict. Morejon crumpled in front of one of Che's firing squads the following day.[2]

"I went to one trial as a reporter for NBC," recalls New York radio legend Barry Farber. "The one for Jesus Sosa Blanco horrified me. I had to leave. Later I heard from a colleague that the prosecution—I really hate to dignify the proceedings with formal legal terms—but the prosecution asked one of the witnesses to point out the guilty—and she pointed to one of *their* guys! She couldn't recognize the so-called Batista war criminal they were trying. This type of thing went on for hours. No defense witnesses, at all. I'd been one of those young idealists who initially applauded the revolution, but right then, fairly early in the game, I knew something was very wrong—knew that Cuba was heading for major trouble."

"It was a dismal scene," wrote Havana's *New York Times* correspondent Ruby Hart Phillips about a trial she attended in early 1959. "The trial was held at night. The masonry walls were peeling and there was only a dim light. No defense witnesses were called . . . the defense attorney made absolutely no defense . . . instead he apologized to the court for defending the prisoner. The whole procedure was sickening. The prisoner was shot at two that morning."[3]

Equally sickened were some young attorneys who'd swallowed the rebels' claims about a democratic, just, and "humanistic" revolution and signed on with the regime's legal team, known as the *Comisión Depuradora* (Cleansing Commission), headed by Che. "What's the holdup, here!" Che Guevara barked at a commissioner, José Vilasuso, as he stormed into his office in La Cabana. Vilasuso, an honorable man, answered forthrightly that he was gathering and assembling evidence and attempting to determine guilt. Che set him straight. "Quit the dallying! Your job is a very simple one. Judicial evidence is an archaic and secondary bourgeois detail. This is a revolution! We execute from revolutionary conviction." José Vilasuso quickly fled.[4]

A rebel captain named Duque de Estrada was Vilasuso's immediate superior. "Let's speed things up!" Che turned and gave him the familiar bit of advice. "You people need to start working during the night. Always interrogate the prisoners at night. A man's mental resistance is always lower at night."

"Certainly, *Mi Comandante,*" responded Estrada.

"Besides, to execute a man we don't need proof of his guilt," continued Guevara. "We only need proof that *it's necessary to execute him.* It's that simple."

"Yes, of course, *Comandante.*"

"Our mission isn't to uphold legal guarantees," Che further clarified the matter. "It's to carry forth a revolution. For that we must establish the pedagogy of the firing squad!"

"Very well, *Comandante.*"

"Surely you're familiar with what Trotsky said, right, Estrada?"

"No, *Mi Comandante,* I'm afraid I'm not."

"Trotsky said that terror is an essential political instrument, and that only hypocrites refuse to acknowledge that. You can't teach the masses with good examples, Estrada. It just won't work."[5]

A respected Cuban lawyer named Oscar Alvarado joined Che's legal dream team with high hopes in early January. During these early revolutionary "trials," guilt was often determined by a "mother." She'd enter the courtroom dressed in solid black mourning garb, including a veil to shield the face, point at the accused, and exclaim, "Yes, that's him! I'm sure of it! That's the Batista criminal who killed my son!"

Alvarado started studying the female face behind the black veil. It seemed to be the same woman every day. One day he got one of his *barbudo* assistants to shave, dressed him in civilian garb, and put him up as the accused. "No doubt about it!" shrieked the woman as she circled him from close up and studied his face. "I'd recognize him anywhere! That's the Batista criminal who killed my son!"[6]

But even this process was wasting precious time. Soon Alvarado noticed little Xs next to the names of the men and boys to be tried and asked Che's legal adjutant about them. "Why, those are the death sentences," he explained, shrugging, as if the logic spoke for itself.

"We execute as a means of social prophylaxis," is how one of

Che's favorite henchmen and prosecutors, Fernando "Puddle of Blood" Flores-Ibarra, explained it a bit later. He'd gotten with the program much more quickly than Duque de Estrada.[7]

Yet we have it from scholarly Che biographer and *New Yorker* writer Jon Lee Anderson that "most were sentenced in conditions aboveboard, with defense lawyers, witnesses, prosecutors." And how is Anderson so certain? He interviewed the prosecutors themselves, while both he and his interviewees were living in Cuba. "We gave each case due and fair consideration and we didn't come to our decisions lightly," he dutifully quotes Duque de Estrada himself. "Che always had a clear idea about the need to . . . exact justice on those found to be war criminals."[8]

"Our paramount concerns . . . were that no injustice was committed. In that, Che was very careful," Orlando Borrego, an early Che henchman who served as a "judge" and later as Castro's minister of transportation, told Anderson.

And besides, according to Duque de Estrada (who lives in Cuba as a Castro minister today), the death toll was minimal. "We carried out about fifty-five executions by firing squad in La Cabana," he says.[9] Others, no longer associated with the regime, can attest to a different reality. "At a meeting in early 1959 Che was interrupted by an aide who walked in with a big stack of papers," recalls Jose Pujols, who served briefly as director of ports for the Castro regime. "Che grabbed the stack and just started signing away, without looking. These were the executions for that night."[10]

For a Cuban exile, reading the scholarly biographies of Che is like reading a Hitler biography in which the primary sources for the chapter on the Holocaust were Adolf Eichmann and Julius Streicher who scoff at Elie Wiesel and Anne Frank as embittered frauds. Or it is like reading a biography of Stalin that covers the purge trials and the Gulag using testimony mainly from Andrey Vyshinsky and Lavrenty Beria, who snort at Alexander Solzhenitsyn and Cardinal Mindszenty as fanciful cranks. Add to that the media that hails these books as "Superb! A masterly job in separating the man from the myth!" as the *New York Times Book Review* crowed about Anderson's Che biography, or "admirably honest and staggeringly researched!" as the *Sunday Times* hailed Anderson's work.

Armando Valladares, who somehow escaped the *paredon* but spent twenty-two torture-filled years in Cuba's Gulag, described his trial very succinctly: "Not one witness to accuse me, not one to identify me, not one single piece of evidence against me."[11] It was simply enough that he'd been arrested in his office for the crime of refusing to display a pro-Castro sign on his desk.

Evelio Rodriguez was murdered by Che's firing squad in February 1959. His daughter-in-law, Miriam Mata, scoffs at Anderson's account of Guevara's justice. "My father-in-law was a police officer in Cuba—not a 'Batista war criminal,'" she says, rolling her eyes. "He had served in democratically elected Cuban governments in the forties, and in 1952 he stayed on. His checks weren't signed by Batista, for goodness sake. In fact, he was relieved from his post by Batista's people. He couldn't for the life of him imagine what Che's people could possibly arrest him for. So he stayed in Cuba."[12]

Evelio Rodriguez was arrested and executed by Che within weeks of the rebel victory.

Again, there is a certain logic here. As in Stalin's Russia, being *related* to a "counter-revolutionary" qualified one for a death sentence in Che's Cuba. Pedro Diaz-Lanz had been Castro's personal pilot in the Sierra during the anti-Batista skirmishes. In January 1959, Castro appointed him head of Cuba's air force, where Diaz-Lanz saw Che's communist instructors indoctrinating the new air force cadets in Marxist-Leninist dogma. Soon Diaz-Lanz realized this indoctrination was going on from one end of Cuba to the other and involved all members of the military and police.

Diaz-Lanz resigned his post in May and tried to warn his close friends, the Cuban people, and U.S. officials of what was coming down the pipeline in Cuba. Pedro bundled his wife and kids onto a small boat and escaped to Miami. A few weeks later he rented a small plane and flew over Havana dropping leaflets warning Cubans of the communization Castro and Che planned for Cuba. Pedro Diaz-Lanz's brother, Guillermo, was immediately arrested in Cuba and thrown into a La Cabana dungeon. No evidence of any counter-revolutionary activity was ever presented, but a few months later he was jerked from his cell and bayoneted to death.[13]

At around the same time, a Cuban father of five named Juan Alvarez-Aballi received a visit from the Cuban police. "We'll only be gone an hour or so," the officer told Alvarez-Aballi's terrified wife. "Just bringing him down to the station to ask a few questions." What was his crime? Alvarez-Aballi had a brother-in-law named Juan Maristany who had slipped into the Venezuelan embassy just ahead of Castro's cops a few days before. He suspected it was something to do with that. "Don't worry, honey." Alvarez-Aballi kissed his wife. "I'll be right back."

He was in fact dumped into a La Cabana dungeon. The "humanistic" rebels were simply using him as a hostage to lure his brother-in-law from his refuge in the embassy. A few days later Alvarez-Aballi himself was dragged from his cell and subjected to Che's avant-garde judicial procedures. No charges were ever filed against him. But the sentence was pronounced promptly: death by firing squad.

Alvarez-Aballi had to pass a picture of Fidel and one of Che on his way to the stake. "Because of those two wretches," Armando Valladares recalls him saying as he walked past, "there will be five orphans!" The following day his bullet-shattered body was dumped in an unmarked grave in Havana's Colon Cemetery.

Idelfonso Canales was an interrogator for Cuba's Che-indoctrinated military police, the G-2. In 1961 he explained the workings of the system to Dr. Rivero Caro. "Forget your lawyer mentality," he sneered. "What you say doesn't matter. What proof you provide doesn't matter, even what the prosecuting attorney says doesn't matter. The only thing that matters is what the G-2 says!"[14]

To some, equating the young Cuban revolution with the young Nazi regime or Stalin's seems outrageous or fanciful, a typical stunt of those "Cuban exile hard-liners and right-wing crackpots." But the historical comparison is solid, not rhetorical.

Hitler, Stalin, and Che

Well before the outbreak of World War II, Nazi Germany had become the modern standard for political evil. By 1938, FDR was already calling Hitler a "gangster," and Winston Churchill was sputtering at Hitler as a "bloodthirsty guttersnipe." Even future ally Benito Mussolini denounced Hitler as "worse than Attila!"[15]

In 1938, according to both William Shirer and John Toland, the Nazi regime held no more than twenty thousand political prisoners. Political executions up to that time might have reached a couple of thousand, and most of these were of renegade Nazis themselves during the indiscriminate butchery known as the "Night of The Long Knives." The infamous Kristallnacht that horrified civilized opinion worldwide caused seventy-one deaths out of a total German population of 70 million.[16] The regime would, of course, go on to murder six million Jews and millions of others.

How does Castro's Cuba compare to Hitler's Germany before the war? The *Agencia de Informaciones Periodisticas* was an organization of exiled Cuban newsmen active in the 1960s in Miami. Their *Boletín Nacional de Noticias,* Vol. VI, No. 754, December 27, 1967, calculated that by 1966, some 7,876 men and boys had been executed by revolutionary firing squads—out of a population of 6.4 million.[17] Not that it stopped there. *The Black Book of Communism* has Castro and Che's firing squads' murdering 14,000 people by 1970.

At one point in 1961, 300,000 Cubans out of a total population of 6.4 million were crammed in prison. Anne Applebaum writes in her book *Gulag* that, all told, 18 million people passed through

Stalin's prison camps. At any one time, 2 million were incarcerated, out of a Soviet population of 220 million.

Apply your calculator to the figures for Cuba's population, and to Toland's and Shirer's figures for the Nazi execution and incarceration rate versus Germany's population at the time, as well as Applebaum's figures for Stalin's Soviet Union. In absolute terms, Castro and Che were outdoing the Hitler regime before World War II. In proportional terms, they were imprisoning more Cubans at one time than Stalin imprisoned in the Soviet Gulags.

Even the Nazi treatment of conquered France helps with perspective. The *HarperCollins Atlas of the Second World War* puts total French civilian deaths during the Nazi occupation at 173,260, out of a French population of 40 million. Cuban-American scholar-researchers Dr. Armando Lago and Maria Werlau, who head the Cuba Archive Project, meticulously documenting every death caused by the Cuban revolution, put the total of Cuban deaths by the Castro-Che regime conservatively at 107,805, including 77,833 desperate souls who died at sea while trying to escape. When it comes to generating refugees, Cuba also merits comparison with Nazi Germany. Between 1933 and 1937, 129,000 German citizens fled Germany, out of a population of 70 million.[18] Five years into the Castro-Che regime, *half a million* Cubans had fled Cuba, out of a population of 6.4 million. And the Cuban figure is for those who succeeded against enormous odds and were forced to abandon their every possession and last penny in the act. An easier trip from Havana to Florida, and a policy of unhindered emigration with property and family (as practiced in all civilized countries, including pre-Castro Cuba), in 1961 would have emptied the island in a fortnight. And don't forget: Before the Castro-Che liberation, Cuba's immigration pattern was in the exact *opposite* direction, with people from Italy to Haiti clamoring to *enter*.

Nelson Mandela once gushed, "Che Guevara is an inspiration for every human being who loves freedom." For all the suffering he endured on Robben Island, if Mandela had instead been sent to La Cabana, he would have never been heard from again.

Cuba's Death Squads

The Castro-Che bloodbath was hardly confined to La Cabana and the dozens of other official execution grounds. With the Cuban people promptly disarmed, Cuba's police, militia, and Communist Party toadies swaggered through the streets in search of *gusanos*, miscreants, and assorted "lumpen" (Che's favorite insult). Special targets were those who had somehow dissed them in the days prior to the glorious revolution, with its meteoric promotions of such worthies as themselves into positions of authority and eminence.

Ask anyone who's lived through such times—Cuban, Vietnamese, Pole, or Czech—this type of vengeance is the most characteristic feature of a communist revolution. "Che played a central role in establishing Cuba's security machinery," admits his hagiographer Jorge Castañeda.[19] As we've seen, it is not a huge mural of Justice adorning the compound of Cuba's Ministry of the Interior, or secret police. It is the likeness of Che Guevara gracing the secret police HQ, much like the statue of Feliks Dzerzhinski in Lubyanka Square, near the headquarters of the old KGB.

"What a Young Communist Should Be," Che had titled his exhortation in fall 1962 to the Union de Jovenes Comunistas. "The happiest days of a youth's life is when he watches his bullets reaching an enemy."[20] In the schoolyard of Havana's Baldor high school the chief of the local "Communist Youth" took Che Guevara's speech to his organization to heart.

On October, 7, 1962, fourteen-year-old Ramon Diaz was in the schoolyard during recess when he saw the local Communist Youth leader, gun in hand, approaching a friend of his. Ramon started yelling, pointing, and rushed up to help. But the communist didn't shoot. Instead, he started pistol-whipping Ramon's friend savagely.

Ramon rushed up and shoved the Communist Youth, who stopped the bashing for a second, looked over, and shot Ramon to death in front of his classmates. The revolution armed a schoolyard bully with a gun, and excused his act of murder.

On September 9, 1961, Cuba's secret police broke into the home of the Cardona family in the town of Esmeraldo in Camaguey province. The Cardonas were suspected of harboring "counter-revolutionary bandits." After bashing down the door, the police emptied their clips indiscriminately into whatever moved in the house. They murdered the entire family, mother and father along with the two Cardona boys, one five years old, the other six years old.[21]

That same month, fourteen-year-old Armando Gonzalez Peraza was picked up by police in Las Villas province. After days of desperate inquiries to the local authorities, Peraza's parents were finally informed that Armando had committed suicide. The identical news was imparted that year to the parents of Elio Rodriguez, who lived in Havana. Elio was thirteen years old when he was rounded up by the Che-trained militia. None of these boys had the slightest mental problem. "Committed suicide" was the Castro-Che counterpart to the infamous phrase "shot while trying to escape" generally used by the thuggish "right-wing" police that Hollywood, academia, and the mainstream media love to portray.

Lydia Gouvernier was a vivacious twenty-year-old University of Havana student who somehow annoyed the authorities. On November 12, 1959, she was hauled in by the police. Her parents recovered her dead body from the police station the following day. (*Always interrogate your prisoner at night. A person is easier to cow at night.*)

"Street murders by the police were rampant," recalls Ibrahim Quintana, "whenever somebody showed the slightest disrespect for the regime." Quintana was in a good position to know. Until escaping to the United States in 1962, he was a mortician at the Rivero Funeral Home in Havana. "The murder victim was always taken to a government first-aid station—*first.* Then a mortuary was telephoned to pick up the body. The reason for using the government aid station as an intermediary is so the government official there can make out a death certificate claiming the dead person was killed by means other than shooting. He or she was run over by a truck and the like. . . . The government always orders the mortuary not to permit the family to see the body. In 80 percent of the cases where the body came in with a death certificate saying it had died of something other than shooting—we found one or more gunshot wounds in that body."[22]

Unlike the corpses piling up in Cuba's police stations, the hundreds of bodies delivered from La Cabana required no bogus death certificates. After all, these had been executed "judicially" after a "trial." "Cause of death was internal hemorrhaging caused by firearm projectiles," read the official death certificates delivered by the regime to thousands of ashen-faced Cuban families.

"Some of the bodies from La Cabana would come straight to our funeral home accompanied by a man named Menendez," recalls Quintana. "They always arrived at night. Then at 6:00 A.M. the bodies would be stacked up in vehicles and moved out to Colon Cemetery. The dead had a small piece of paper with their names on their wrists. The cemetery attendant removed the tag and dumped the bodies in an unmarked grave. He had strict instructions to wait three days following the burial before reporting to his family that the body is somewhere in the cemetery."[23]

Not long after Che had fired up Cuba's Communist Youth with his spirited October 1962 speech, seventeen-year-old Armando Piñeiro was chatting with a group of friends in front of the La Perla Hotel in the town of Sancti Spiritus in central Cuba. These were all teenaged boys, hence rowdy, boisterous, and not exactly discreet. And somebody please break the news to Rage Against the Machine (who use Che Guevara as their band's emblem) that if *ever* any group of youths had cause for youthful angst and rebellion, it was Cuban youth from 1959 on.

The sassy gang (think a Spanish-speaking Delta House here) outside La Perla started complaining loudly about the sorry state of the country, the stifling regimentation, all the nit-picky rules, the idiots and scoundrels running the country into the ground, the rationing, and the forced labor "while chanting government slogans" as mandated by the illustrious minister of industries, Che. In the middle of their spirited confab a young communist militiaman strutted by cradling his prized Czech machine gun. Usually this was enough to quell such talk quickly. But this group either didn't notice him or didn't care.

The *miliciano* didn't like what he heard and stopped in front of the group. The teenagers finally stopped talking and looked at him just as the *miliciano* opened up with his machine gun, emptying an entire clip into their group.

Armando Piñeiro fell dead along with his friends Carlos Rodríguez, Ismael Lorente, and Rene Odales. Many more kids were on the ground writhing and moaning.[24]

Some might call this type of thing "collateral damage." But Che Guevara's own writings and exhortations help clarify the matter. He wrote, "The people's cooperation can often be coaxed by the use of systemic terror."[25]

This was a young Cuban militiaman who pulled the trigger. The Che-indoctrinated *miliciano* in front of La Perla Hotel was, as Castañeda observed, plenty "reliable."

An early revolutionary colleague once complained to Che of difficulties raising money for the anti-Batista rebellion in Cuba's Matanzas province. "It's understandable in a way," the revolutionary shrugged. "I mean, after all, what can I offer them except the chance to live democratically if we succeed?"

"Don't waste your time with that stuff," snorted Che. "That rarely works. Instead you offer them *terror*—you threaten them with *terror* for not contributing."[26] Extortion, blackmail, and death threats—these are traits you do not see in the Che of the Hollywood Left.

Researchers Maria Werlau and Dr. Armando Lago have documented 20,400 "extrajudicial" murders of Cubans by the Castro-Che regime. Every morning in school, Cuban kids recite the Castroite counterpart to our Pledge of Allegiance, which begins and ends with "We will be like Che!" Jon Lee Anderson writes with apparent pride how his own daughter dutifully recited the pledge every morning while they lived in Cuba. Even Herbert Matthews didn't go *that* far.

Che's Camps for "Delinquents"

"On October 9, 1967, the first news of Ernesto Che Guevara's alleged death reached the United States," recalls journalist John Gerassi, who taught at San Francisco State University. "I was approached by a nineteen-year-old coed. She had tears in her eyes and a 'Make Love Not War' button on her breast. 'Do you think it's true?' "[27]

Around the world, young idealists were in tears over a man who mandated perpetual war and universal military service for youth. "For me it was the most marvelous sight in the world," wrote Che about a supply of machine guns delivered to his guerrilla column in Cuba's Sierra mountains. "There under our envious eyes were the instruments of death!"[28]

An eighteen-year-old Cuban named Emilio Izquierdo got the news of Che's death on the same day as Professor Gerassi's class. But Emilio's reaction was markedly different from the San Francisco flower child's. "Oh, how I wanted to cheer!" he recalls from Miami today. "I wanted to jump up and down! To whoop with joy! To throw a party! To hug the very man who had given me the news!"

But that would have been very unwise. The news of Che's death had been imparted to Emilio by a machine-gun-toting guard. Emilio, you see, was in a UMAP prison camp for "delinquents" and "lumpen" in October 1967. This penal system had been the brainchild of Che Guevara (the hero of students who want "no rule from above") back in 1960 at a place called Guanahacabibes in extreme western Cuba.

Notice the Rolex watch peeking out from under Che's sleeve in this photograph. Many Westerners have swallowed wholesale the myth that Che Guevara was a saintlike defender of Latin America's underclass. In truth, he was a power-thirsty, materialistic ladder-climber, like so many communist figures who preceded and succeeded him in history.

Far from living like "one of the people," Che enjoyed the material life in a luxurious Havana mansion, which featured a waterfall, swimming pool, and giant television screen that would rival today's models.

Robert Redford, one of Hollywood's most reliable useful idiots, pals around with Che's daughter, the blonde Aleida, in 2004 at the Havana screening of *The Motorcycle Diaries*.

Che abandoned his first wife, Hilda, a Peruvian woman of Indian extraction, for a taller, blonder trophy wife (also named Aleida). Their 1959 wedding in Havana was the social event of the year and featured Raul Castro as "best man." After he married Aleida, Che would continue to "upgrade" his women, taking the worldly Tamara "Tania" Bunke, born of German parents in Argentina, as his mistress.

Carlos Santana, shown here on the red carpet with his wife, is a mindless Che-worshipper. "Che is all about love and compassion, man," he claims. Here he proudly displays his Che Guevara T-shirt, the uniform of the useful idiot.

Supermodel Gisele Bundchen demonstrates as little political sense as she has fashion sense, sporting this bikini donned with pictures of Che's face.

Actor Johnny Depp wears a Che medallion around his neck as though it's a religious medal. (Look closely, and you'll find it among his other wacky jewelry.)

Che probably would have condemned Depp as a "lumpen," and had him tossed into a work camp for his long hair, rebellious attitude, and artistic flair. Such attributes were not tolerated in Che's Cuba. The Left is delusional in believing Che represents a free, rebellious spirit.

Actor Benicio Del Toro stars as Che Guevara in two upcoming movies directed by Steven Soderbergh. Del Toro was photographed filming movie scenes in New York City, where Che addressed the United Nations.

Apparently Che didn't think much of New York. He told the *London Daily Worker* in 1962, "If the nuclear missiles had remained we would have used them against the very heart of America, including New York City."

Angelina Jolie sports a tattoo of Che, though she won't reveal where. How ironic that a winner of the U.N. Global Humanitarian Award for her work with refugees has such a close relationship with a man who deliberately provoked one of the biggest refugee crises in the history of the hemisphere and personally ordered the execution of hundreds without trial. In Che's 1964 U.N. speech he crowed: "Certainly WE execute!"

One woman, Juana Diaz, was six months pregnant when she was executed by the Castro/Che regime in 1961. An estimated 77,000 Cubans—young and old, male and female—have died in the Florida straits as refugees.

This giant mural of Che is a favorite photograph backdrop for silly European tourists visiting Havana. Guess which building it adorns? The Cuban secret police. Che Guevara is the mascot of a communist police state, but that fact doesn't seem to sink into the heads of useful idiots.

The writing on the building reads "*Hasta la Victoria Siempre!*" ("Until Victory, Always!")

Just what "victory" Che referred to has always mystified those aware of his genuine combat record, which was dismal.

A small country farmer, Jose "Macho" Piñeiro took to the hills in 1961 to fight against the Che-trained communist militia. One day Che's soldiers pulled up in front of Piñeiro's home and threw his body out of the back of their truck, riddled with fifteen bullet holes. "You're the wife of Piñeiro?" they asked his grief-stricken widow. "Well here's your husband!" They laughed and drove off as she sobbed unconsolably.

Cuba's rural rebellion lasted from 1960 to 1966 and saw tens of thousands of Cuban peasants herded into concentration camps or murdered during a communist reign of terror.

Aldo Robaina fought Che Guevara's army and militia down to his very last bullet (which is more than can be said for Che, who surrendered to his Bolivian captors with a full clip and pleas for leniency).

"My brother always said those communist SOBs would never take him alive," recalls Aldo's brother, Guillermo Robaina. Armed with only sixty-seven bullets— stolen from the Soviet-backed army Che liked to pretend he was running—Aldo was optimistic against the communists.

To this day, Aldo's family doesn't know where he is buried.

A colonel in Cuba's police, Cornelio Rojas (seen dancing here with his wife, Blanca), disappeared shortly after the Battle of Santa Clara. He was a pillar of philanthropy and public service in his community. Nevertheless, he was captured by Che's rebel troops, and his family was left to wonder what had become of him.

Che's firing squad executed him on live television one day, while his family was watching. The cameras zoomed in on his shattered skull for effect. His wife of forty years collapsed and suffered a fatal heart attack.

In this October 9, 1967, photograph, Che Guevara is held prisoner by his Bolivian captors. Che surrendered with a loaded pistol, begging them: "I'm worth more to you alive than dead." Hours later, the Bolivians would execute Che before he could stage a communist takeover of their country.

To his left in the photograph stands Felix Rodriguez, an exiled Cuban who became a CIA officer and helped the Bolivian Rangers capture Che. To this day, Rodriguez wears Che's Rolex watch—a minor plunder, considering what Che and his communist cohorts stole from the people of Cuba.

One of the longest and bloodiest guerrilla wars waged on this continent was fought against the Castro/Che regime by Cuban campesinos. Farm collectivization was no more voluntary in Cuba than in the Ukraine. And Cuba's kulaks had guns, a few at first, anyway. JFK's "solution" to the Missile Crisis required a U.S. pledge to stop supplying the Cuban freedom fighters. Completely strangled of supplies they continued waging their desperate and lonely anticommunist insurgency for years on America's doorstep.

Castro himself admitted that his troops, militia, and Soviet advisers were up against 179 different "bands of bandits," as they labeled these rural freedom fighters. Tens of thousands of troops, scores of Soviet advisers, and squadrons of Soviet tanks, helicopters, and flamethrowers finally extinguished the lonely Cuban freedom fight. The Kennedy-Khrushchev agreement that "solved" the Missile Crisis not only starved these freedom fighters of the meager aid they'd been getting from Cuban-exile freebooters (who were promptly rounded up on orders of the Kennedy administration for "violating U.S. neutrality laws"), it also sanctioned the 44,000 Soviet troops ocupying Cuba.

Castro and Che's "revolutionary justice" had made great strides in just one year. No bogus trials without defense counsel and with illiterate common criminals as judges condemned these prisoners, as they had thousands in 1959 to the firing squads and prisons. "We send to Guanahacabibes people who have committed crimes against revolutionary morals," announced Che himself. "It is hard labor . . . the working conditions are harsh . . ." And that was that.[29]

"Rehabilitation" was the professed goal at Che's forced-labor camps. Jon Lee Anderson uses the word without quotation marks and apparently with a straight face in his Che biography. Pol Pot and Ho Chi Minh preferred the term "re-education" for a similar process.

"Slave labor and torture" is the preferred term of Emilio Izquierdo and of the tens of thousands who suffered in similar camps before him, alongside him, and after him. Like Stalin's Gulags, the prisons of Cuba filled up with tens of thousands of social parasites, loafers, and unreconstructed men. If this sounds familiar, recall Ernesto Guevara's cheeky signature on his early correspondence as "Stalin II."

In time, all of Cuba became a prison. Che instituted a "progressive" labor program of "volunteer" weekend work and sixty-hour workweeks that galled Cuba's working class. Before their liberation by Che, Cuba's workers had become accustomed to such working hours and benefits as to make Lane Kirkland and George Meany gape in envy. In fact, in the 1940s and 1950s, Cuban labor was more highly unionized, proportional to population, than U.S. labor. And their leader, Eusebio Mujal, made Samuel Gompers and Jimmy Hoffa look like corporate lapdogs.

Professors and the mainstream media parrot the Castro-Che fable of pre-Castro Cuba as a pesthole of poverty and misery for workers. Susan Sontag bewailed Cuba's "underdevelopment" in her *Ramparts* screed. The *New York Times* referred to it as Cuba's "former near-feudal economy," and hailed Castro and Che's "promise of social justice which brought a foretaste of human dignity for millions who had little knowledge of it in [pre-Castro] Cuba."

By 1965 counter-revolutionary activity was winding down in

Cuba. The Kennedy-Khrushchev deal in October 1962 had pulled the plug on much of the anti-Castro resistance, including the bloody and ferocious Escambray Rebellion. Now the Castro regime—needing a new pretext for the mass jailings, the cowing of the population and, especially, slave labor—turned its police loose on "antisocial elements," on "deviants," "delinquents," and those branded "lumpen" by Che Guevara (the term is indicative of his famous hauteur). Youths were the target here, with special emphasis on longhairs, suspected rock and roll listeners, the incorrigibly religious, and—especially—homosexuals. "*Peligrosidad predelictiva*" was the favorite charge by the regime against these youths.

Your long hair, your snide look, your taste in music, your tight pants, your open practice of Christianity, your family background, your refusal to volunteer for "voluntary" labor on weekends—any of these would make you a violator of revolutionary morals.

Emilio's fellow prisoners also included Jehovah's Witnesses, active Catholics and Protestants, and children of political prisoners—all swept up in Cuba's mid-1960s dragnet. This system of prison camps that held Emilio Izquierdo and tens of thousands of other youths was called Unidades Militares del Ayuda de Producción (Military Units to Help Production). The official and euphemistic title, UMAP, did little to hide the pretext for the camps—forced labor. In Stalin's Russia, the initials GULAG stood for the same thing.

These camps were completely enclosed by high barbed wire and had machine guns in each watchtower and ferocious dogs keeping watch below. As we saw earlier, the camp for homosexuals had a sign, "Work Will Make Men Out of You," above the entrance gate, eerily reminiscent of the Auschwitz sign "Work Will Set You Free."

The UMAP camps featured brutal labor in the tropical sun and summary beatings and executions for any laggards. As at Guanahacabibes, none of the UMAP prisoners had been convicted, even in the sham Castroite courts, of any "counter-revolutionary" crimes. Military and police trucks would simply surround an area of Ha-

vana known as a homosexual pick-up place, or as a hangout for rock
and rollers, or near churches. Then every person in sight would be
herded into the military trucks at gunpoint. "Everybody in the
prison camp wanted to cheer when we heard Che had been killed,"
recalls Emilio Izquierdo, who survived to become president of the
UMAP Political Prisoners Association.

"You could see everyone trying to stifle their joy, because the
guards were watching us all *very* carefully right then, focusing on our
faces. They wanted desperately to detect the slightest sign of joy.
This would have been a serious 'crime against Revolutionary morals,'
as Che himself had described it—and right there the guards would
have an excuse to indulge their sadism.

"The Castro-Che regime hired hard-core sadists and
psychopaths—complete mental cases—as guards and wardens for
these camps," Emilio continues. "I suppose all totalitarian regimes
hire such people. I read books by Alexander Solzhenitsyn, by Elie
Wiesel, by the U.S. POWs in the Hanoi Hilton, and I think to myself: This sounds very familiar. Anyway, many of these guards—
despite all the regime's propaganda about its literacy campaign—were
virtually illiterate. They loved any excuse to beat us, to throw us in a
tiny punishment cell to roast half to death under the midday sun,
even to shoot us. I saw boys shot to death for simply being unable to
stand up to the workload. You try and explain these things to people
in this country and nobody believes it. They can't imagine these
horrors just ninety miles away—much less initiated by men whom
much of the international media portray as well-meaning reformers.

"But one poor boy was unable to disguise his joy at Che's
death," recalls Emilio. "He just couldn't. I don't think he was any
happier than the rest of us—just unable to effectively disguise it.
So the guards dragged him off and soon we heard the screams—
accompanied by the laughter. When they were in a playful mood,
some of the guards' favorite punishment was to rip all the clothes
off a prisoner and tie him up to the fence at dusk, totally naked,
totally immobile. The UMAP camps were in the countryside, not

far from the coast. And you know about Cuba's salt-marsh mosquitoes . . .

"Those things almost feel like a wasp when they first jab it in. Well, the guards loved to watch these bloodthirsty mosquitoes completely cover the bodies of the helpless naked prisoner, dig in for hours at a time, and drive the prisoner to the point of agonized insanity. The prisoner might hang on that fence for two days without food or water, too. Oh, how the guards would laugh!"[30]

"Another favorite game for those guards," recalls fellow UMAP prisoner Cecilio Lorenzo, "was to gallop up on one of their horses, throw a lasso over some prisoner whose attitude they didn't like, and drag him off. A friend of mine, seventeen years old at the time, was dragged for over a mile down country roads and through brambles and thickets. He came back unconscious and covered in blood."[31]

Che himself explains the matter in his *Socialism and Man in Cuba*: "For the masses to follow the vanguard, they must be subjected to influences and pressures of a certain intensity."

Che and Dogs

Che killed men, but rarely in combat. He also killed animals, but not as a hunter. Perhaps fittingly, he seemed to have a particular animus toward man's best friend. Che's own *Motorcycle Diaries* go into the gory details. Shortly after leaving on his famous motorcycle jaunt with his chum Alberto Granados, their motorcycle, La Poderosa, blew a cylinder and they stopped at a house of a country couple near the Argentina-Chile border. The kind couple took them in, gave them dinner, and even gave them overnight lodging in their barn's hayloft. During dinner, recounts Guevara, the couple warned them of a ferocious puma that roamed the area and often prowled near the houses at night.

While turning in that night, the motorcycle duo discovered that the barn door did not close securely. So Che slept with his trusty pistol loaded and within reach, as he wrote, "in case the Chilean lion, whose dark shadow filled our minds at the time, decided to pay us a midnight visit."

And sure enough, near dawn the itinerant Argentines were awakened by the sound of scratching on the barn door. As they were startled awake and sat there gathering their wits, "Alberto was locked in apprehensive silence beside me," recounts Guevara. Finally the barn door swung open. "My hand gripped the pistol and my finger was tight on the trigger" writes Guevara, "as a pair of luminous eyes gazed at me from the shadows!"

So Che leveled on the eyes and blasted away with this pistol. "The instinct of self-preservation is what pulled the trigger," he writes. Che *then* turned on his flashlight and saw he'd killed "Boby," the couple's pet dog, whom he'd met and petted during dinner. Che goes on about "the stentorian yells of the husband" and "the hysterical screams and moans of the lady" as she hugged the body of her murdered dog.

To those who later got to know Che in Cuba the whole account sounds like a rationalization, a fable that prettified the man's primal sickness. Why didn't Che turn on the flashlight *before* he shot the beast, asks former revolutionary Marcos Bravo? Probably because he *wanted* to kill the dog, he surmises.

Other passages in Guevara's own writings argue against the likelihood of his mistaking a puppy for a puma. While "fighting" in the Sierra, Che's "column" had befriended a stray puppy only "a few weeks old," according to Guevara himself. The little mongrel came by their campsite for scraps of food and to frolic and play with the men. He became the group's mascot, according to Guevara himself. One day as they marched off to plan an "ambush" of Batista's army, the dog followed them, happily bounding along and constantly wagging his tail.

" 'Kill the dog, Felix,' " Che ordered one of his men. " 'But don't shoot him—strangle him.' Very slowly, Felix pulled out his rope, made a noose, and wrapped it around the little animal's neck—then he started tightening," writes Che.

When Felix picked him up, the puppy's tail had been wagging happily. Naturally, the puppy had expected the usual petting and caresses. Now Felix grimaced as he tightened the noose on the agonized puppy. "That happy wagging of the tail turned convulsive," writes Che. "Finally the puppy let out a smothered little yelp. I don't know exactly how long it took, but to us it seemed a long time till the end finally came," recounts Che. "Finally after one little spasm the puppy lay still, his little head resting over a branch."[32]

During the Bolivian campaign, compatriot Dariel Alarcon heard Che screaming, "Move it! Move it! Move it! Goddammit!" Alarcon turned around and saw Che atop his little mule and kicking it savagely. The beast was unable to pick up speed. Che hopped off and pulled out his dagger. "I said move it! Move it! Move it!" he started shrieking again. This time, with every exclamation, he plunged the dagger into the little mule's neck until it fell dead.

As former political prisoner Roberto Martin-Perez says, "There was something seriously wrong with Che Guevara."

One wonders what this strangler of puppies and stabber of donkeys would have made of "The Che Café," an ultrahip student hangout in La Jolla, California. The owners deplore cruelty to animals, so the café proudly boasts a strictly vegetarian menu. "The Che Café is a great place to meet and hang out with other people who envision a better world," says the menu.

Papa Che

Jon Lee Anderson's *Che: A Revolutionary Life* contains many touching pictures of "Papa Che" with his darling little daughters in his lap. While describing Che's good-bye scene as he left Cuba in late 1966 for his Bolivian venture, *The New Yorker* writer tugs mightily at our heartstrings. "The last few days had been emotional for everyone," writes Anderson about the final family scene. "But the most poignant were Che's final encounters with Aleida and his children.

Che was in disguise for his clandestine trip to Bolivia and couldn't reveal himself even to his children. Papa Che was instead 'Uncle Ramon,' who was there to pass along their father's love and little pieces of advice for each of them. They ate lunch with *tio* Ramon at the head of the table like papa Che used to do."[33]

Orlando Borrego was the "judge" without legal training who presided over bogus trials during a time when hundreds of Cubans were sent to the firing squad at Che's orders in the first months of the revolution. He stayed on as a Castro henchman and sycophant, recently a Cuban government official. While in Cuba writing his "impartial" Che biography that "separates man from myth," Anderson apparently found Borrego among his most trusted and cooperative sources on Papa Che.

Borrego also was present for Che's teary Cuban farewell. "For Borrego, Che's final visit with his three-year-old daughter, Celia . . . was one of the most wrenching experiences he had ever witnessed," sighs Anderson. "There was Che with his child but unable to tell her who he was or to touch her and hold her as a father would."[34]

In the process of "separating man from myth," there is no mention by Anderson of the hundreds of mothers and daughters who would wait outside La Cabana prison for a final chance, not to touch, but perhaps merely to see or to say a few last words to their husbands and fathers condemned to death by Papa Che.

"One day we'd been waiting for hours in the hot sun," recalls Margot Menendez, who was hoping to see her condemned father. "Finally we see a car driving out and it's Che himself inside, so we start screaming and shouting for someone to let us in to see our loved ones. Che stopped the car and rolled down the window. 'You're all punished!' he yells. 'No visits this week!' and he rolls his window up. So we start screaming even louder. Then we see he picks up a radio and calls someone. A few seconds later gangs of his soldiers came rushing out of La Cabana with billy clubs and guns and started bashing us brutally until we dispersed."[35]

"'Until always, my little children,'" Anderson quotes Papa

Che's good-bye letter to his children, " 'a really big kiss and a hug from Papa.'

"The most Che could do was to ask his children to give him a little peck on the cheek," Anderson continues. Papa Che was leaving for Bolivia, so "tears welled up in Che's eyes. Aleida was devastated but managed to contain her own tears."[36]

A woman named Barbara Rangel-Rojas, who today lives in Miami, has a tough time commiserating with Borrego and Anderson about the sad parting of Papa Che from his children.

Shortly after the bogus battle of Santa Clara, her grandfather Cornelio Rojas disappeared. He was a beloved pillar of the community, well known for his public service and philanthropy. He was also a colonel in Cuba's police. "Naturally my mother, grandmother, and father all suspected he'd been arrested," says Barbara. "But we heard nothing and all our inquiries turned up nothing."

An entire week went by and the Rojas family was still in the dark about their patriarch's fate. "We were all worried sick—especially my poor mom, who was six months pregnant at the time. My grandmother kept up a stoic front, but we knew what was going on inside. She was going to pieces."

In 1959, most Cuban homes had three generations living in them at the same time. Families were very close. "Like most Cuban girls, I was extremely close to my granddad," says Barbara. "We ate dinner together every night. I sat on his lap in the living room every night. He spoiled me absolutely rotten with gifts and constant attention. I was only seven at the time, but I remember all this vividly."[37]

A week after her grandfather's disappearance, Barbara heard her mother calling excitedly from the living room. She rushed in and saw her mother pointing at the television and her grandmother staring wide-eyed and covering her mouth. There on the screen was her grandfather.

"And he was alive," she recalls, "walking apparently freely, without handcuffs or anything. My grandfather had been an important figure in the province for decades. Our family had fought prominently in all of Cuba's wars of independence. And this was a news show, so we thought nothing of it for a few seconds. We all looked at each other wide-eyed. My grandmother even put her hand to her chest and looked heavenward, apparently relieved. My grandfather as he appeared on the screen, didn't seem scared at all—or that he was under any type of coercion."

Then the camera angle changed and Rojas was seen standing and holding his hand aloft while saying something. "It took us a few seconds to realize that he was then standing in front of a thick concrete wall. My mother frowned. My grandmother squinted and leaned toward the television."

Then the camera moved back, the angle changed again, and some rifles came into view—rifles that were pointing at Rojas. " 'No! No!' My mother started screaming 'No!' My grandmother and my mom rushed to each other and hugged. My granddad was standing in front of one of Che's firing squads! But—typical for my grandfather—he'd refused a blindfold and was facing the firing squad head on. He was preparing to give the order. . . ."

"Fuego!" Colonel Cornelio Rojas gave the order and the firing-squad volley murdered Barbara's granddad in front of his family's eyes. It was a horribly graphic murder. The camera closed in to show the shattered head and body, blood oozing.

"My grandmother collapsed on the floor at the horrible sight," recalls Barbara. "My mother was screaming. I'm crying. We rush over to my grandmother—remember, my mom was six months pregnant at the time, so I'm helping out here. *'Abuela! Abuela!'* I'm crying. 'Wake up! Wake up!' "

Barbara's grandmother could not be revived. She had suffered a fatal heart attack from the diabolical vision she had just seen on Cuban national television. She joined her husband and constant companion of forty years.

"After a few minutes," recalls Barbara, "my mom, horribly traumatized, as you might imagine—goes into labor. She managed to contact some neighbors and they rushed over to help. She delivered my brother, prematurely, right there in her bedroom, with my grandmom's body still in the living room, with my grandfather's bloody body lying in front of that bullet-pocked wall. To this day we don't know where he was buried by Che's firing squad. A mass grave, we imagine, like so many others. The murdering Che Guevara didn't even give us the solace of a funeral, of allowing us to put a cross or flowers atop my murdered granddad . . . How can you expect someone to forget that? These things haunt me still."

Caridad Martinez was ten years old in March 1959 when a crew of Che's militiamen burst into her home carrying two crude wooden boxes roughly the shape of coffins and dropped them loudly on the floor of their humble living room. "That one's Jacinto" (Caridad's father), barked a bearded goon while pointing at a box. "And that one's Manuel" (Caridad's uncle). "We don't want to hear of any funeral and we don't want to hear of any major show of grief!"[38] They looked around at the ashen-faced women and the terrified children now clinging to them, then marched out and drove back to La Cabana, where lovable "Papa Che" had gleefully watched the executions of Caridad's father and uncle from his favorite window.

"Our family was never the same," recalled Caridad, now fifty-five but still weeping unapologetically at the memory. "My mother became a mere shadow of her former self, walking listlessly around until her death. I'd go in our patio to weep where no one could see me. I was a little girl and afraid Che's men would come back to harm us if they saw me crying."[39]

Much like al Qaeda's beheading of Nicolas Berg, Che's murders were staged to cow and terrorize. The televised murder of Cornelio Rojas was a pioneer version of what would later become an Internet specialty of professional terrorists. (The murder of Cornelio Rojas, Barbara

Rangel's grandfather, on Che Guevara's orders, can be viewed at http://www.aguadadepasajeros.bravepages.com/menu1/fusivista.htm.)

Thousands of other Cuban mothers, daughters, sisters, aunts, and grandmothers simply got an anonymous phone call saying the bodies of their formerly imprisoned menfolk were now in Colon Cemetery. These were usually unmarked mass graves. To visit and place a cross or flowers over them was to invite retribution from "Papa Che's" goons.

"I and thousands of other little girls in Cuba had the laps and kisses of our fathers and grandfathers stolen forever by that murdering Argentine coward," says Barbara Rangel-Rojas. "When I recall my granddad's and my uncle's courageous death—then I think of Che Guevara's famous words when he was captured: 'Don't shoot! I'm Che! I'm worth more to you alive than dead!' . . . Well, I'm torn between laughing and crying . . . not really . . . the truth is . . . I still cry."

Heartbreak wasn't over for the Rojas family after grandfather Cornelio's public murder. Two years later Barbara's seventeen-year-old uncle Pedro, who'd escaped to the United States, came back to his homeland by landing at the Bay of Pigs with a rifle in his hands, hell-bent on freeing Cuba from Che Guevara.

After three days of continuous ground combat on that doomed beachhead, Barbara's young uncle was grim-faced, thirst-crazed, and delirious. A CIA officer named Grayston Lynch had trained, befriended, and even fought alongside these men. On the third day of battle he was on his U.S. flagship thirty miles offshore and had just learned from Washington that they'd been abandoned. No ammo was coming—no air cover, no reinforcements, no naval support. He was enraged and heartsick as he radioed his brothers in arms and offered to evacuate them.

"We will *not* be evacuated!" yelled Pedro Rojas's commander into his radio, even as forty-one thousand communist troops and swarms of Soviet tanks closed the ring on him and his fourteen hundred utterly abandoned band of brothers. "We came here to *fight*! This ends *here*!"

"Tears filled my eyes," recalls Lynch. "Never in my thirty-seven years had I been so ashamed of my country."

After expending his last bullet on that bloody beachhead, seventeen-year-old Pedro Rojas was captured and murdered in cold blood by the Che-trained and -indoctrinated communist militia.

7

The "Intellectual and Art Lover" as Book Burner and Thief

Che is not only an intellectual, he was the most complete human being of our time—our era's most perfect man.
—JEAN-PAUL SARTRE

All Che biographers dwell on his affinity for matters intellectual and literary. "Che was interested in everything from sociology and philosophy to mathematics and engineering," writes former *Time* and *Newsweek* editor John Gerassi, "there were 3,000 books in the Guevara home."[1]

"The asthmatic boy spent long hours . . . developing an intense love of books and literature," writes Jorge Castañeda. "He devoured the children's classics of the time, but also Robert Louis Stevenson, Jack London, Jules Verne. He also explored Cervantes, Anatole France, Pablo Neruda. . . . He bought and read the books of all Nobel Prize winners in literature and held intensive discussions with his history and literature professors."

Jon Lee Anderson quotes a Che friend from the era of *The Motorcycle Diaries*, "For Ernesto Guevara everything began with literature." Then Anderson goes on to rhapsodize about Che's "voracious reading appetite" and immense "intellectual curiosity."

Certainly, one of this bibliophile's first acts after entering Havana in January 1959 was to stage a massive book burning.

We've all seen the newsreels of Nazi goons burnings books in Berlin's Opernplatz. Probably no two weeks go by without the History Channel or PBS graphically reminding us of this intellectual atrocity, with either a voiceover or subtitles of Joseph Goebbels gloating that "these flames not only illuminate the final end of an old era; they also light up the new!" Many have heard a somber voiceover quoting German philosopher Heinrich Heine: "If you burn books today, you burn people tomorrow." In Berlin today, a "Submerged Library" monument stands in Berlin commemorating that outrage.

This is, of course, good history, necessary to remember and retell. Liberals are especially sensitive—and in some cases, oversensitive. Let some rural school board today refuse to assign Darwin or James Joyce in its curriculum and liberals quickly trot out the Nazi book-burning episode as the obvious next step by officials in the dark hinterlands of Red State America.

But regarding the intellectual atrocity by Che in Cuba? "The portrait of Che is now as complete as it will ever be," says the *London Times Literary Supplement* about Anderson's book.

You'll search Anderson's book, along with all the other massive and "scholarly" biographies of Che, in vain for any mention of his biblio-pyre.

It happened. On January 24, 1959, in the street directly in front of 558 G Street in Havana's Vedado district—on Che Guevara's direct orders—three thousand books were doused with gasoline and set ablaze, to the cheers and whoops of his communist toadies.

"I contacted several foreign correspondents in Havana at the time," recalls Salvador Diaz-Verson, whose books, pamphlets, and files had fueled the blaze, and whose private office and library had been broken into and pillaged by Che's armed goons. "Jules Dubois of the *Chicago Tribune* and Hal Hendricks of the *Miami News* were among the dozens of correspondents who came with me to inspect the ruins of my library and the ashes which had become of my books. None of them attached any importance whatsoever to the incident."[2]

We can only imagine the U.S. media reaction had it happened a month earlier at the hands of Batista's unbearded and unfashionable henchmen.

The Nazi book burning was public and theatrical, a naked attempt at rabble-rousing. Joseph Goebbels and the SA hoodlums mocked the books' authors by name—Einstein, Freud, H. G. Wells—and displayed the book contents while scorning them and heaving them into the bonfire. Che's motives were different; they had nothing to do with totalitarian pageantry. Indeed, Che tried to keep his bonfire secret. The very *last* thing he and Castro wanted was more exposure of the contents of Salvador Diaz-Verson's library.

Diaz-Verson, a renowned Cuban journalist, scholar, and former public official, was president of Cuba's Anti-Communist League, a private research organization and an early version of a think tank. Since the mid-1930s—labeled by Eugene Lyons as the "Red Decade"—the league had devoted itself to the study of communism. In the course of their investigations Diaz-Verson and his staff compiled detailed lists of Communist Party members and agents (both card carriers and secret) and their assorted front groups. By 1959 they had accumulated information on 250,000 Latin American communists, agents, and accomplices.

During World War II, the league had also investigated the activities of Nazi agents in Latin America (remember, Nazis and commies were allies from September 1939 till June 1941). Early in the war, the Florida Straits crawled with German U-boats playing havoc with Allied shipping. Cuba herself had four of her merchant marine fleet sunk. Salvador Diaz-Verson and his people uncovered a cell of Nazi agents who were passing along details about the ships' schedules to their German masters.

The Nazi agents were rounded up and the problem nipped in

the bud. Cuba's death penalty, abolished in 1933, was very briefly reinstated just for the occasion. Diaz-Verson was often consulted on his work by a man who consequently became his friend, J. Edgar Hoover. The friendship and professional relationship had actually begun during the work against Nazis and grew afterward. The FBI chief began receiving reports from the Anti-Communist League every month.

Diaz-Verson's books and files—notably his just-published *Red Czarism*, three thousand copies of which helped fuel the massive fire in front of his office—posed a bigger threat to Castro and Che's plans for Cuba than anything written by Einstein, Freud, or H. G. Wells presented to Hitler and Goebbels's plans for Germany. Both the Castro brothers' and Che's communist contacts and affiliations were heavily documented by Diaz-Verson, hence their urgency on the matter.

"I have never been a Communist," the *New York Times* had dutifully quoted Ernesto "Che" Guevara as saying during an interview on January 4, 1959. "It gives me great pain to be called a Communist!"

At the time they were also parroting the line that "Castro himself is a strong *anti*communist." (Nary a note of apology or "Oops! We goofed," appeared afterward in the *New York Times* either. We're going on forty-eight years of the most unrelenting communist regime in history, and the "Newspaper of Record" has yet to do a mea culpa on this one.)

"Che Guevara never concealed his beliefs," stresses his hagiographer Jon Lee Anderson.

"Guevara had always spoken honestly about the aims of Castro's revolution. I have never heard anyone—even his most bitter foes—accuse Guevara of betraying his beliefs in Marxist revolution."[3] Well, this learned and universally acclaimed Che biographer might consult the January 4, 1959, edition of the *New York Times,* the very paper Anderson has written for.

"Che did not once betray his basic loyalties," wrote Ariel Dorfman in *Time.*

"Che's life demonstrates conclusively that he was not a hypocrite,"[4] wrote Christopher Hitchens in the *New York Review of Books*. Professor Dorfman and Hitchens might have a look at that *New York Times* edition themselves.

In early 1959, Diaz-Verson's work exposed Castro and Che's treachery with a brilliant spotlight. When the alarmed U.S. ambassador to Cuba in late 1958, Earl T. Smith, asked CIA Havana chief Jim Noel, "Is this Che Guevara a communist?" a cocksure Noel quickly replied, "Don't worry. We've infiltrated Castro's group in the Sierra. Castro has *no affiliations with any communists whatsoever*" (italics mine).[5]

The U.S. embassy's top political officer at the time was John Topping, described as "very able" by the CIA's inspector general, Lyman Kirkpatrick. Topping had snorted derisively at the rude and tacky inquiry of Ambassador Smith (a Republican interloper into that State Department circle) and heartily endorsed his trusted colleague Jim Noel.

Noel's CIA superior in Washington, Frank Bender, known as the agency's "expert" on Latin America, was equally on the ball. "Castro is a strong *anti*communist fighter,"[6] he declared after chatting up Fidel during his U.S. visit in April 1959. Bender was so impressed he planned on setting up an information exchange between the CIA and the Castro-Che government as a partnership in the joint fight against the spread of communism in the hemisphere. The CIA of George Tenet had many antecedents.

Even before he entered Havana, Che's Cuban Communist Party comrades had informed him of Diaz-Verson's diligent work. So just a week after entering Havana, Che dispatched an armed mob straight from his La Cabana headquarters to Diaz-Verson's office and library. At the door stood a friend of Salvador's named Vicente Blanco, who refused them entry. Che's mob pummeled Blanco into a near coma with their rifle butts, bound and gagged him, smashed down the door, and stormed in to rampage. They tore down pictures and slashed and smashed Diaz-Verson's furniture to splinters before carting out his books and files. Che—Sartre's intellectual, the most complete human being of our age—destroyed Diaz-Verson's property and had his men bash and bloody his associates with machine-gun butts. He also quickly condemned Salvador Diaz-Verson to death by firing squad, for the crime of publishing truth.

Luckily, and unknown to Che, a friend of Diaz-Verson's was involved in the revolutionary paperwork. He saw the charges and the death sentence on their way to the "public prosecutor" in La Cabana and secretly alerted his friend. Appreciating the speed and efficiency of Che's "revolutionary justice," of his "pedagogy of the *paredon*," Salvador Diaz-Verson jumped into the trunk of his friend's car the very next night and was driven to the docking point for the Havana-Miami ferry, which he boarded incognito, without even notifying his family.

"I arrived once more in the United States broke and minus a passport," recalls Diaz-Verson. "But at least I wasn't lying in a mass grave."

Notice the "once more." Just six years earlier, Diaz-Verson had come briefly to the United States on the strong advice of Batista's police, who'd been harassing him for his services as intelligence consultant to Carlos Prio, the Cuban president Batista ousted with his coup in 1952. Diaz-Verson hadn't actually feared for his life at the time and was able to keep all his property—and indeed return to Cuba the following year under a general political amnesty declared by Batista himself, the same amnesty that pardoned and released from jail a fellow named *Fidel Castro*!

But the point is, Salvador Diaz-Verson was anything but a Batistiano (Batista follower), the justification used by Che, his henchmen, and his biographers against the victims of his massacre.

"My father simply disappeared," recalls his daughter Sylvia, who lives in Miami today.[7] "And any day, any hour, any minute, we expected a call to go claim his body in Colon Cemetery. This was happening to families all over Cuba. Also, we knew that Che knew that my dad knew that he was a communist. So you can imagine what my poor mom was going through at the time—all of us, really. So when we find out a couple days later that my dad was in Miami, we were jubilant, as you can imagine.

"But we also knew we had to get out of Cuba ourselves—and fast. My dad was a lifelong researcher into communism. So naturally some of his knowledge and insights rubbed off on us. We knew very well that Che's people would soon be coming for us, if not overtly to grab us, at least secretly to watch for my father's return.

"Heck, you don't have to be an expert on communist tactics to know this," says Sylvia. "Just watch *Doctor Zhivago*, or read the book! So my mom and sisters and my brother and I, we all took off for Miami immediately. A few weeks later, my mom, who barely knew English, is trying to sell Avon products door to door, my dad's washing dishes and mowing lawns—we're all doing whatever we can to make ends meet."

On May 6, 1960, with Cuba already filling with Russians, with close to two thousand Cubans already massacred by Che's firing squads, with Castro's orientation much clearer, and with Che on Cuban television yelling, "Our road to liberation will be opened with a victory over U.S. monopolies!"—with this backdrop Salvador Diaz-Verson finally got his say in the United States, by testifying before the U.S. Senate at a hearing titled, "Communist Threat to the United States Through the Caribbean." We can imagine the nervous coughs behind the hand by the CIA's Latin American wizards at the time. But, amazingly, even at this late date, Diaz-Verson had much to teach. Many in Congress were still skeptical. From the session:

MR. SOURWINE. *Is it true that the Castro forces destroyed files on Cuban Communists?*

MR. DIAZ-VERSON. *Yes, sir.*

MR. SOURWINE. *How many such files?*

MR. DIAZ-VERSON. *I had an archive of 250,000 cards of Latin American Communists and 943 personal records. . . . The Communists have everywhere two lines of leadership: One that they show to the public, the other that acts underground—one visible; the other "invisible." In Cuba the "underground" is the one that operates at La Cabana prison, with Che Guevara at the head.*[8]

To this day, Western intellectuals remain utterly undisturbed by the fact that sixteen librarians languish in Castro's dungeons with twenty-five-year prison sentences for stocking such subversive literature as Orwell's *Animal Farm*, Martin Luther King's "I Have a Dream" speech, and the U.N. Declaration on Human Rights. "After sentencing the librarians, Castro's judges declared the confiscated library materials 'lacking in usefulness' and *ordered them burned.*"[9]

No less an authority on book-burning than *Fahrenheit 451* author Ray Bradbury was appalled. "I pled with Castro and his government to immediately take their hands off the independent librarians and release all those librarians in prison, and to send them back into Cuban culture to inform the people," Bradbury declared during the keynote speech at the American Library Association's annual convention in 2005.[10]

The Art Burglar

It's an oft-told story that the Nazis stole valuable paintings and assorted art holdings from the people they murdered, conquered, and exiled. Many private art galleries in Europe were visited by Nazi goons and "Aryanized," as they termed it. But the Nazis, Hermann Goering in particular, usually hogged the loot for themselves.

The Castroites were in this league, with "nationalized" the preferred term. Che's stolen palace at Tarara was crammed with gorgeous art. This luxury lasted as long as the Soviet sugar market paid the bills.

But when that transatlantic ATM machine went out of order in 1990, the suddenly desperate Cuban burglars started hocking their stolen wares on the international market. The Cuban American National Foundation estimates that since 1991, the Castro regime has sold off almost one thousand invaluable paintings, antiques, manuscripts, and other items stolen from their rightful owners.

From his first day in office as Cuba's exalted National Bank president, Che Guevara had been particularly keen on funding, staffing, and arming Cuba's newly created *Ministerio de la Recuperación de Bienes Malversados*, or Ministry for the Recuperation of Stolen Goods. This Orwellian ministry—as anyone familiar with communist terminology will immediately infer—was in charge of stealing. (The Nazis titled their ministry of theft "The Reichsleiter Rosenberg Institute for the Occupied Territories.")

The homes and bank accounts of anyone who fled Cuba to escape a firing squad were subject to seizure by the diligent and heavily armed agents of this ministry. The property of anyone who didn't display the proper revolutionary zeal was also subject to seizure. The property of anyone who might have had cross words with any of the newly minted *comandantes* and "ministers" when they had been purse snatchers, winos, hubcap thieves, and unemployed ambulance chasers—which is to say, before they were lionized by *Time* and the *New York Times*—were also subject to seizure. The injured parties were all accused of having been "Batista crooks and gangsters."

But even this farce gave way a year later to unabashed looting. In the immortal words of Che Guevara himself during his speech on March 23, 1960, as National Bank president: "In order to conquer something we have to take it away from somebody!"

And take they did—some $2 billion worth from U.S. businessmen and stockholders, and many times that amount from Cubans themselves, including many valuable art treasures.[11] Because of its history as the Spanish empire's crown jewel and its later prosperity as a U.S. business partner, Cuba had always been rich in private art collections. Many of these stolen art treasures have fetched handsome prices for the thieves at Sotheby's and Christie's in New York and London.

When the Cuban-exile Fanjul family started noticing many of their former art possessions in European museums and boardrooms, they began legal action to recover them. It was an utterly vain exercise, at least in Europe. Sure, these very European countries were the ones looted by the Nazis. Sure, these very Europeans raised a raucous and self-righteous hullabaloo about that looting in every international forum. But when it came time to apply the same scruples to looting by Castro and Che? Well, the Fanjuls have never retrieved a dime's worth of their property in Europe.

Cuban sugar magnate Julio Lobo had amassed one of the world's most extensive collections of Napoleon Bonaparte memorabilia, from weapons, to paintings, to furniture, to historic documents. Many now sit in French museums, which may seem appropriate, except that Julio Lobo was not a willing donor. An official in Havana's French embassy named Antoine Anvil facilitated the sale of the Lobo collection to a French museum for an undisclosed price.[12]

Not that all of Castro and Che's loot wound up in European museums and auction houses. On a recent visit to Cuba, Danielle Mitterrand, widow of former French socialist president François Mitterrand, squealed with undisguised glee when presented with a priceless porcelain vase by the Castro government.[13] Communists had looted this Sevres vase from a Cuban owner no less blatantly than the Nazis looted the Louvre.

No doubt as a token of Castroite appreciation, David Rockefeller, a steadfast behind-the-scenes bankroller of propaganda against the Cuban "embargo," had his private art collection enriched by stolen Cuban paintings. Former Mexican president Salinas, Colombian novelist Gabriel García Márquez, and Argentinean soccer star Diego Maradona have all been given various valuable art objects that caught their eye while visiting Cuba—every one of them stolen from their rightful owners during Che Guevara's stint as Cuba's economic minister.[14]

The plunder has not been entirely one-sided, however. The good guys have gotten in a few jabs of their own. Felix Rodriguez, the Cuban-American CIA officer who helped nab Che in Bolivia and was the last to question him, wears Che's Rolex to this day.

8

Academia's Rude Surprise

Ernesto "Che" Guevara is one of the most appealing figures of our century.
—UCLA PROFESSOR DAVID KUNZLE

Near the thirtieth anniversary of Che Guevara's untimely death, the Bolivian government of President Gonzalo Sanchez de Lozada invited representatives from Castro's regime to Bolivia to search for Che's bones.

In light of Che's prominent role in destroying Cuba morally, spiritually, economically, and even physically, his burial in Cuba seemed proper even to many Cubans outside the island. So with the help of Bolivian representatives, Castro's henchmen were taken to a grave near a rural airstrip and dug out the remains. These were carted back to Cuba, and on October 17, 1997, Che's remains were deposited in a mausoleum in Santa Clara, at the base of a giant statue of the gallant Guevara, rifle in hand.

It seemed a hugely humanitarian gesture to return the hallowed bones of Che to Cuba. But according to Mario Riveron, who headed the CIA team that hunted Che down in Bolivia in 1967, there's a little more to it. "Castro paid a princely sum—many millions—to various Bolivian officials for Che's remains," he says. "Not that it hasn't been worth it. Che's mausoleum is a major tourist attraction in Cuba. Castro has earned back his bribes many times, I assure you."

Much mawkish pomp and the usual deluge of Castroite cant characterized the funeral extravaganza. "His unerasable mark is now in history," Castro declared. "His luminous gaze of a prophet has become a symbol for all the poor of this world."[1]

One hundred thousand in the captive audience cheered and waved Che flags as a twenty-one-gun salute thundered in the background. "We are not here to say good-bye to Che and his comrades," continued Castro. "We are here to welcome them. I see Che and his men as a battalion of invincible combatants, who have come to fight alongside us and to write new pages of history and of glory."[2]

Castro ended the extravaganza with Che's most famous line: "*Hasta la Victoria Siempre!*" (Until Victory, Always).

Exactly what "victory" Che referred to has always mystified those who studied Guevara's military record with open eyes and a clear head. "Quite simply, in the military sense, there were *no* victories," says Felix Rodriguez, the man who played a key role in capturing Che. But a revolutionary song was composed for the state funeral occasion, "San Ernesto de la Higuera" (borrowing from the Christian lexicon to make a patron saint out of the communist martyr and the name of the little village where he met his end).

By a strange coincidence, the very week Che's bones were entombed in Santa Clara, Cuba hosted "the 14th World Festival of Youth and Students"—another orgy of Che homage. This festival included 771 "delegates" from the United States, which "embargoes" and "blockades" Cuba, compared to 520 from North Korea.

The hoopla was nonstop. Castro's captive press declared the entire year of 1997 "The Year of the Thirtieth Anniversary of the Death in Combat of the Heroic Guerrilla and His Comrades." Western media and academia were hardly outdone by that pithy proclamation. That thirtieth anniversary of Che's untimely death saw a blizzard of hype in American and European press and publishing circles to fully match Cuba's.

Major publishers released five massive Che Guevara biographies, including one by French-Algerian Pierre Kalfon, *A Legend of Our Century.* "Ernesto 'Che' Guevara was a pop icon of mythic proportions," proclaimed PBS in a forum titled "The Legacy of Che."

"He was the first man I ever met who I thought not just handsome but beautiful," Christopher Hitchens quoted the late *Nation* editor I. F. "Izzy" Stone, in a *New York Times Book Review* in 1997, as saying. "With his curly reddish beard, he looked like a cross between a faun and a Sunday-school print of Jesus." An alarmed Stone once wrote that "families are being broken up, long-time residents driven into exile, men face permanent detention on tenuous charges." Hundreds of thousands of people now living in South Florida have horrible memories of just such a place, right after Che Guevara assumed his official duties in Cuba. But I. F. Stone was instead describing conditions in the United States of the 1950s.[3] Stone, celebrated by his admirers today as a latter-day Socrates, a wizened old man who stood for freedom and fair play, looked at one of the worst violators of human rights in modern times and found only a mild, erotic charge.

On the thirtieth anniversary of Che's death, even compared to the media/academic heralding of Che throughout the world, the University of California in Los Angeles laid it on pretty thick and heavy in UCLA's October 1997 symposium, titled "Thirty Years Later: A Retrospective on Che Guevara, Twentieth-Century Utopias, and Dystopias." (The critical viewpoint of Che ended with the title.)

UCLA's Latin American Studies Center and the Fowler Museum of Cultural History were not to be outdone, running an exhibition of Che iconography entitled "Che Guevara: Icon, Myth and Message," and even issuing a book to commemorate the gala.

"The exhibition comprises some 200 works, mostly posters, with a few etchings, paintings and photographs, which demonstrate a gamut of artistic inventiveness among artists from Cuba and elsewhere," announced UCLA's campus paper. "Thematically the show divides into groups such as Che and Latin America, Che and Cuba, Che as Everyman, Che as landscape, *'Chesucristo'* and Che's message of solidarity with the poor of the Third World. At once cultural icon and romantic inspiration, Che was also used for political ends in demonstrations against the Vietnam War and U.S. imperialism everywhere."[4]

No Cuban-American survivors were invited to speak. But as proof of the event's evenhandedness, Che biographer, *Newsweek* writer, academic, and former Mexican Communist Party member Jorge Castañeda was among the prominent panelists. He was billed as being on the "con" side.

UCLA professor of political sociology Maurice Zeitlin was among the first panelists to commence the exultation. "Che's legacy is embodied in the fact that the Cuban revolution is alive today," he said, beaming, and the crowd concurred, clapping madly. "Che taught us all that freedom, democracy, and socialism are inseparable." More applause and more cheers acclaimed the professor's reverie.

"Bullshit!" suddenly erupted from the back of the hall. The professor stopped and craned his neck as the crowd and panel looked around in alarm.

Panelist professor Fabian Wagmister tried defusing the scene, interjecting, "As utopian as Che's dreams may have been, as utopian as a world of peace and plenty for all may seem, no social justice is possible without a vision like Che's."

"Complete *horseshit!*" erupted again from a little knot now moving through the flustered crowd toward the front of the room and the flustered panelists. "Complete crap!" blurted someone as the group bustled to the stage.

"Che Guevara was a *murdering* swine!" one shouted. "He was a *coward*, too!" barked another.

"Yes, a murderer—but also a *patsy* and a *fool!*" continued the first man in his heavily accented English.

"And just how is it that you know that, sir?" asked a professor from the panel.

"Because he murdered my father," answered the hard-faced man in front of the stage. "*Che Guevara murdered my father,* using his own pistol and *in cold blood* when my dad was *completely defenseless.*" The room fell suddenly quiet. The panelists looked at each other. Finally motions were graciously made for the heckler to continue. "My father was completely defenseless at the time. That was a Guevara specialty. Che had his men beat him savagely, then he shot my father in the back of the head and neck."

One of the panelists added that yes, okay, a few dozen men had been killed in the early weeks of the Cuban revolution, but these had been tried by courts and found guilty of horrible crimes while serving as Batista policemen and soldiers.

"Bullshit!" answered the man again. The inflamed protester was a Cuban American named Jose Castaño, who was accompanied by a dozen or so of his compatriots (many were Bay of Pigs veterans). Again Jose Castaño was graciously given the floor. "My dad never laid a finger on anyone. He was a researcher of communist activities in Cuba and Latin America, an intelligence analyst—and so he had the goods on Che as a communist at a time Che was denying it—and at a time idiots like reporters for the *New York Times* were spreading his lies word for word."

The panel and auditorium were humming with rude murmurs now, but Jose Castaño bulled ahead. "My father's trial was a complete *farce.* Even Castro was hesitant to execute my father." Many in the crowd and even some panelists seemed intrigued now, and they motioned Jose to continue.

Indeed, the reputation in Cuba of Castaño's father, Lieutenant Jose Castaño Quevedo, as a man of honor was such that even Fidel Castro was leery of executing him. When his death sentence by Che's prosecutors was made public, many in Cuba finally saw through Che's lies. Others had their worst fears confirmed. A flurry of protests from the Catholic Church, the U.S. embassy, and several still nominally free newspapers finally led Castro to call Che in La Cabana to call off the execution at the last moment.

"But Che told Castro that it was too late," Jose Castaño said. "The sentence had already been carried out. My father had already been shot." Castano looked around the UCLA auditorium and noticed a few raised eyebrows, a few people even nodding. He went on. "Che Guevara was *lying*. We learned from people on the scene that my father was still alive at the time. So Guevara knew he had to act fast. Heaven knows he wasn't one to disobey a Fidel order. So he hung up, had his men drag my father out of his cell and into his office where they beat and tortured him. Finally Che put his pistol to the back of my father's head and fired two quick shots."

"Well now . . . how?" The professors were a bit taken aback by this.

"How do we *know* this? . . . I'll tell you how. We snuck in and retrieved my father's body from a mass grave in Havana's Colon Cemetery—I was only fifteen at the time—and had an autopsy performed. My father's femurs were both broken. He had broken bones all over his body. His liver was demolished. His forehead was gone and he had entrance wounds in the *back* of his head and neck. That's not where a firing-squad volley hits one."

Some in the crowd were getting restive now, and the panelists were murmuring to each other. "This was early in the revolution," said Castaño. "Many people were defecting from Castro and Che's ranks. From them we got the details of the murder—details that the autopsy abundantly confirmed."

"And it wasn't 'a few dozen' that Che executed either," added Castaño's friend Hugo Byrne to the stuttering panel. "He and his courts and his firing squads murdered thousands! You people haven't done your homework—and you claim to be professors."

The professorial panel and crowd were getting surly by now, and some burly students started closing in on the vastly outnumbered Cuban Americans. A few were shoved. "Fine!" said Hugo, shoving back briskly. "But if that's what you people want, let's go outside and settle this!"

Leftist for all causes Ralph Schoenman had traveled to UCLA from his San Francisco offices of the "International Committee Against Repression" (another nice touch of Orwellianism). Schoenman entered the discussion and even aped Castro and Che's own jargon, calling Cuban Americans *gusanos,* or worms.

Hugo Byrne turned to face him and leaned in closely, "The only worm here is *you*! Don't like it? Fine. Let's go outside and we'll see who's the real worm!"

"Looking back on it," says Hugo, "that was a childish thing for me to do. Good heavens, I was a grown man. But I simply wasn't going to let this pack of leftists insult Cuba's heroes and martyrs— friends of mine who'd put their lives on the line, then gone down in front of firing squads yelling in defiance. No, I couldn't sit still for that. I simply lost it when I saw that complete piece of trash, Schoenman, trashing the memory of men I knew to be heroes. So I jumped in his face—literally. Here we're listening to these long eulogies to Che," snorts Hugo. "And I'm sitting there recalling that the men Che murdered didn't get family eulogies. Most got dumped in anonymous mass graves. And the families were warned not to hold any memorials—and were watched to make sure they complied. I was fuming. I wasn't gonna put up with those insults from these pasty-faced idiots."[5]

Jose Castaño Quevedo's "trial" in La Cabana on March 4, 1959, had been a pathetic joke, even by the standards of Che's legal dream team. Most in Cuba knew of Lieutenant Castaño's sterling reputation. He was a highly educated man who spoke five languages, including Russian, and he was renowned as being scrupulously honest. Far from being a "Batista police criminal," Castaño had never even carried a gun. Among other professions, he was a language instructor at Cuba's military academy and had worked as an intelligence analyst for the democratically elected governments of Ramon Grau and Carlos Prio, uncovering details of communist infiltration into Cuba's labor unions. The usual frame-up of a "Batistiano-sadist-torturer-murderer" would never fly against Castaño in

Cuba (though the *New York Times*, *Paris Match*, and CBS might buy it). So Che's prosecutors came up with the charge of rape.

"That was even more preposterous," recalls his son, Jose Castaño. "Here was perfect proof that Che knew nothing about Cuba, and that his half-literate prosecutors and judges were in no way familiar with my father's reputation. What made the thing even more absurd was the woman they picked to claim the role of rape victim. Good grief. All Cuba was laughing over this one."[6]

The woman who testified against the very handsome Jose Castaño was a failed actress, a failed radio personality, and a failed journalist named Alicia Agramonte. She was also—surprise!—a Cuban Communist Party member. Jose Castaño takes after his father. He's a true gentleman of the old school, who refuses to describe Alicia Agramonte's physical attributes.

The woman was hideous.

Of course, an ugly woman can be raped. But Cubans knew that even more hideous than her face and body was Alicia's soul. All those who have experienced the hijacking of their nations to communism—from Cubans, to Vietnamese, to Hungarians—know the archetype of the Communist Party member and activist: the failed professional who becomes the professional failure. They resent being bested by others who are more talented, industrious, or virtuous. So they nurture a malignant grudge against the world, or society, or "the system." Che himself was a failed physician. Castro was a failed lawyer. Behind them were legions of "*Los Resentidos*," the Resentful Ones.

Fifteen others "testified" against Jose Castaño Quevedo during his trial, enumerating a long list of fabricated crimes. Every one of these witnesses was a longtime Cuban Communist Party member (in a fair system of justice, that would be an odd thing, for Cuba was not yet officially communist at the time).

"My father had the goods on them," Jose Castaño repeats. "It was as simple as that. People like him and his colleague, Salvador Diaz-Verson, had stacks of files that could alert the nation to what was going on behind the scenes."

And much was. Indeed, almost everything important to Cuba at the time was scrupulously hidden from the public. A secret government was pulling all the strings. Castro himself, a few years later, finally boasted about how he did it. At Castro's luxurious house in Cojimar, and at Che's palatial estate in Tarara, these "spartan leaders" hatched and fashioned Cuba's *real* regime with members of Cuba's old-line Stalinist Communist Party. This bunch decided everything transpiring in Cuba at the time. Meanwhile a sap "president" and a sap "cabinet" in Havana gabbled, gave each other ornate titles, held meetings, shuffled papers, decreed documents, and imagined themselves to be accomplishing something, with Castro and his henchmen back in their palaces laughing themselves silly.

"All this behind-the-scenes stuff was hidden from the Cuban people and from the worldwide media at the time," recalls Jose Castaño. "My dad was murdered because he planned on making public something Castro and Che themselves proclaimed loudly and boastfully a short time later. 'I am a Marxist-Leninist and I will be a Marxist-Leninist to the last day of my life!' Fidel Castro said in October 1961.

"You hear about Che Guevara's 'idealism,' his 'pureness of heart,' his 'utter lack of pretense or guile,'" says Jose Castaño. "In fact, my dad's murder was a classic rubout in the time-honored gangster tradition. Che put a hit—and carried it out himself—on a defenseless witness who could bring his criminal plans to light, who could blow the whistle on his criminal and murderous scheme to Stalinize Cuba. So here I was listening to all these professors at UCLA expounding on Che's 'utopian visions' blah . . . blah. It was a little hard to take, especially while watching these professors' smug grins while flashbacks of my sobbing, grieving mother, my stricken family, and my father's broken and bullet-riddled body filled my mind. But I guess, in a way, Al Capone and Don Barzini were 'visionaries,' too. And Heinrich Himmler and Pol Pot certainly dreamed of a better world to come—after a little housecleaning."

"It's funny," Jose Castaño says while relating the UCLA incident.

"But the odds we few faced from Che fans in that auditorium were about the same as we faced from Che's militia and army during the Bay of Pigs—about thirty to one. We weren't intimidated then—and we sure as hell weren't intimidated by the gang at UCLA."[7]

Barely seventeen at the time, Jose Castaño got word of the recruitment for what came to be known as the Bay of Pigs invasion and promptly volunteered as a paratrooper. His father's murder was very fresh in his mind at the time. Young Jose yearned to see Che and his toadies up against *armed* men, for once—and even better, to be one of them.

9

Brownnoser and Bully

Few doubt Che's sincerity.

—David Segal, *Washington Post*

Che's decency and nobility always led him to apologize.

—Jorge Castañeda

Bravery, fearlessness, honesty, austerity and absolute conviction . . . he lived it—Che really lived it.

—Jon Lee Anderson

"It's literally true that Che never made one Cuban friend," says former revolutionary Marcos Bravo. "Deep down, he didn't like us. And we didn't like him. He was the typical haughty Argentine, didn't dance, didn't joke—and except when around Fidel, because he was always terrified of him, never smiled."[1]

The only pictures of Che Guevara smiling show him in Castro's presence. And these smiles look transparently phony. Sniveling behavior isn't usually associated with an archetypal "Heroic Guerrilla."

"I never thought I'd admit to feeling sorry for Che Guevara about *anything*," says former political prisoner and Bay of Pigs veteran

Miguel Uria, who witnessed a Fidel-Che meeting in early January 1959. "But when Castro ripped into him and I noticed the look on Che's face I *had* to. I cringed. You never heard such savage abuse as Castro yelled at Che in a fit of pique. And you never saw a little puppy tuck his tail in between his legs and start whimpering as quickly as Che did. This was a constant topic of conversation among those who saw Fidel and Che together. Nobody could miss it."[2]

Che actually entered Havana a few days before Castro in 1959. When the local rebels planned a twenty-one-gun salute to greet Fidel's glorious grand entrance into Cuba's capital, Che freaked. "Oh, no, please!" he told Antonio Nunez Jimenez. "I got here first and Fidel might think I've formed a rebellion against him and that we're shooting at him! Please!"

"Don't worry," Nunez Jimenez calmed Che. "It's a custom. Fidel is the revolution's chief. He'll expect it."

"Okay, okay," replied a still-nervous Che. "But please send a messenger to him first to explain that we're doing it. I don't want any misunderstandings."[3]

Reading Che Guevara's literary grovelings to Castro is almost embarrassing. "Song to Fidel" is the title of a poem Che wrote to Fidel shortly after meeting him in Mexico City. "Onward ardent prophet of the Cosmos!" goes the first line. "When your voice shouts to the four winds: agrarian reform, justice, bread, liberty, there at your side you will find me."

In the April 9, 1961 issue of *Verde Olivo*, the official paper of Cuba's armed forces, Guevara poured forth again: "This force of nature named Fidel Castro Ruz is the noblest historical figure in all of Latin America. . . . A great leader of men, boldness, strength, courage, have brought him to a place of honor and sacrifice that he occupies today."

Then, on October 3, 1965, came the mushiest ode of all, Che's famous "Farewell Letter to Fidel." "I have lived magnificent days at your side, and feel a tremendous pride in having served beside you," Che wrote. "Rarely has statesmanship shone as brilliantly as yours . . . I am also proud of having followed you without hesitation, identifying with your way of thinking. I thank you for your teachings and for your example. My only mistake was not to have recognized your qualities as a leader even earlier," on and on, in an unrelenting obsequiousness that would shame a court eunuch.

The shameless apple-polishing reinforced Castro's conviction that in Che, he had a handy and dependable—and malleable— puppet. The brilliant longshoreman-philosopher Eric Hoffer comes to mind here. "People who bite the hand that feeds them," he wrote, "usually lick the boot that kicks them." The Soviet Union fed Che Guevara, while Fidel Castro kicked him.

Che's notorious sneer and cruelty were his habitual manner of dealing with *defenseless* men. Against armed men on an equal footing, his behavior was markedly different.

A few months into the Sierra skirmishes, Castro had ordered Che to take command over a guerrilla faction led by a fellow July 26 Movement rebel named Jorge Sotus, who had been operating in an area north of Fidel and Che, and had actually been confronting and fighting Batista's army. Che and a few of his men hiked over to Sotus's command station and informed him that Che was now in command.

"Like hell," responded Sotus.

"It's Fidel's order," responded Guevara. "We have more military experience than you and your group."

"More experience in running and hiding from Batista's army, perhaps," Sotus shot back. Che dithered and looked around. "Besides, me and my men aren't about to take orders from a foreigner," Sotus added. "I don't even know you. You're not even Cuban. Forget it."

"Well, I came on the *Granma* with Fidel," whimpered Che.

"I don't give a shit," snapped Sotus. "I'm in command here!"[4]

Sotus walked away, and the minute Che thought he was out of sight and earshot Che started mingling with his men, trying to get them to come over to him. It was all on Fidel's orders, of course. And surely they had to listen to Fidel? He was, after all, the . . .

"Listen here, *Argentino*!" Sotus had snuck around, seen Che, and stomped in front of his face. "You keep this shit up and I'll blow a hole in you. Now scram!"[5]

And Che did just that, back to Fidel where he whined about Sotus's insolence. "You're not worth a damn, Che!" Castro shouted at him. "I didn't tell you to *ask* him to give you command. I told you to *take* it from him! You should have done it by force!" The problem, of course, had been that Sotus was armed. Che, who was armed, too, quailed before him.[6]

A few weeks after Batista's flight and Castro's triumph, Sotus was arrested without warning and shoved into the Isle of Pines prison. The intrepid Sotus managed to escape, made his way to the United States, and joined an exile paramilitary group, taking part in many armed raids against Cuba from South Florida until the Kennedy-Khrushchev deal nixed them.

"That Sotus was a hell of a guy," recalls Carlos Lazo. "We became friends in prison." Lazo was a Cuban air force officer who had bombed and strafed Sotus during the rebellion. They both found themselves jailed by the Castroites.

Che Guevara also had a run-in with a rebel group named the Second Front of the Escambray. These operated against Batista in Cuba's Escambray mountains of Las Villas province. When Che's column "invaded" the area in late 1958, he had orders from Castro to bring these guerrillas under his command, much as he'd attempted with Sotus. But again he ran into trouble, especially from a *comandante* named Jesus Carreras who knew of Che's communist pedigree and basically told him to go piss up a rope. Again, Guevara didn't press the issue.

A few weeks into the January 1959 triumph, Carreras and a group of these Escambray commanders visited Che in La Cabana to address the issue of how they'd been frozen out of any leadership roles in the new regime. On the way in, Carreras ran into a rebel he'd known in the anti-Batista fight and stopped to chat while the rest of the group entered Che's office. Once the others were inside,

Che immediately ripped into Carreras as a drunkard, a womanizer, a bandit, and a person he'd never appoint to any important position.

Midway into Che's tirade, Carreras had finished chatting with his old buddy and entered the office, having overheard much while outside. "Che went white," recall those present. An enraged Carreras jumped right in his face and Che backed off. Finally, Carreras challenged Che to a duel, "right outside in the courtyard!" he pointed. "Let's go!"[7]

"How is it possible," Che said, smiling, "that two revolutionary *compañeros* get to such a point simply because of a little misunderstanding?"[8]

The subject was dropped and they turned to other issues, but a year later an unarmed Jesus Carreras was ambushed by Che's men and shortly found himself a prisoner in a La Cabana dungeon. A few months later, he found himself bound and facing a firing squad.

Fuego! The volley riddled him, and the coup de grace blasted his skull to pieces while Che watched from his favorite window.

10

Guerrilla Terminator

One of the longest and bloodiest guerrilla wars in the Western Hemisphere was fought not *by* Fidel and Che, but *against* Fidel and Che—and by landless peasants. Farm collectivization was no more voluntary in Cuba than in the Ukraine. And Cuba's Kulaks had guns, a few at first, anyway, until the Kennedy-Khrushchev deal cut off potential supplies.

It's rarely reported, but Che Guevara had a bloody hand in one of the major *anti*-insurgency wars in this hemisphere. "We fought with the fury of cornered beasts," was how one of the few lucky who escaped alive described these guerrillas' desperate freedom fight against the Soviet occupation of Cuba through the Soviet proxies Castro and Che.

Of course, slaughtering resisters was not an ideological departure for Che, who, as we saw, justified the extermination of Hungarian freedom fighters by Soviet tanks as early as 1956.

Che got a chance to do more than cheer from the sidelines in 1962. "Cuban militia units [whose training and morale, remember, Jorge Castañeda insists we credit to Che] commanded by Russian officers employed flame-throwers to burn the palm-thatched cottages in the Escambray countryside. The peasant occupants were accused of feeding the counter-revolutionaries and bandits."[1] Though it raged from one tip of the island to the other, most Cubans know this war as "the Escambray Rebellion," for the mountain range in central Cuba where most of the bloodiest battles raged. Cuba's country folk went after the Reds with a ferocity that forced Castro and Che to appeal to their Soviet sugar daddies for help. In the countryside, these Cuban rednecks often faced the firing squads untrussed, shoved in front of a recently dug pit with their hands free. "Aim right here!" was a favorite among some of these as they reached below the belt, "'cause you ain't got any!"

"I was a poor country kid," says Escambray rebel Agapito Rivera. "I didn't have much, but I had hopes and aspirations for the future. And there was abosolutely no chance that I'd go work like a slave on one of Cuba's state farms. I planned on working hard, but on my own, for myself, getting my own land maybe. Then I saw the Castro communists stealing everything from everybody. They stole my hopes. I had no choice but to fight them."[2] Agapito Rivera had two brothers and nine cousins who took up arms in the anticommunist guerrilla war. He was the only survivor.

"It was hard to sleep in those days," recalls Emilio Izquierdo, who was twelve at the time. He lived in the Pinar del Rio province of western Cuba where, in 1961, a fierce rural rebellion also raged. Cuba had been divided into three military zones, each with a member of the Holy Revolutionary Trinity in command. The eastern provinces were Raul's, the center was Fidel's, and the western, including Pinar del Rio province, was Che's.

"All those Russian helicopters flying over day and night— *whomp-whomp-whomp*. I still remember the sound, almost like thunder. It was constant. And Russian trucks loaded with troops constantly passing in front of our house. They were all headed to the hills to fight the freedom fighters. It was a terrible thing to watch, because we knew the rebels got no support from anywhere, not from the Americans. They fought on a shoestring with very little ammunition and supplies. It's amazing how they held out and the damage they caused the communists. Very few people on the outside know about this terrible fight. My family lost many friends in that fight."[3]

One of these was Aldo Robaina. "My brother always said those communist SOBs would never take him alive," recalls Aldo's brother, Guillermo Robaina, who would bring the guerrillas supplies from time to time. "I remember the time I brought them a supply of bullets I'd managed to steal from Castro's army. My brother's little band of rebels divided them up right there—and it came to sixty-seven bullets per person. They were ecstatic. 'Now we'll see!' they said, and everybody was slapping backs. They regarded it as an enormous amount of ammo. The following week my brother and his band were wiped out. One who made it out of the encirclement said they simply ran out of bullets but refused to surrender. They literally fought to the last bullet. My brother kept his vow—the communists never took him alive. We don't know where he's buried."[4]

Lazaro Piñeiro was only seven at the time, but the memories are still vivid.

"My father took to the hills of Pinar del Rio as a rebel in 1961. We knew what he was up against because we could see the Russian helicopters and the convoys of Russian trucks constantly taking troops into the hills to pursue them. My mother, as you can imagine, was going through a living hell. But my father said he'd fight those communists as long as he had a breath in his body and a bullet in his gun. We lived in the country, had a small but comfortable house. We didn't have a sugar mill or anything like that. When we came to the U.S. that's all we heard, 'Oh you people must be those millionaire plantation owners that lost your fortunes to Castro, huh?'

"We were very surprised by the ignorance, and even today we still hear much of the same things. One day I was out in front of the house playing and one of the Russian trucks braked to a halt in front of me. 'Get your mother!' some guy yelled from the window. I ran inside and my mother opened the door and peeked out. She was, of course, terrified. 'You the wife of Piñeiro, right?' the soldier shouted from the truck. My mom stood there stunned, but she nodded.

"Then two guys in back of the truck hoisted a body like if it was a butchered animal. 'Well here's your husband!' and they threw my father's body out of the back of the truck into a ditch in front of our house and roared off, all of them laughing. All the neighbors came running to console my mother who was . . . well, as you can imagine, sobbing and shaking uncontrollably. My father had over fifteen bullet holes in his body. He fought to his last bullet. He had always told my mother the communists would never take him alive. They certainly didn't."[5]

The Maoist line about how "a guerrilla swims in the sea which is the people" fit Cuba's *anti*communist rebellion perfectly. Raul Castro himself admitted that his government faced 179 bands of "counter-revolutionaries" and "bandits" at the time.[6]

In a massive "relocation" campaign—reminiscent of that of the Spanish general Valeriano "The Butcher" Weyler at the turn of the century—Castro's armed forces ripped hundreds of thousands of rural Cubans from their ancestral homes at gunpoint and herded them into concentration camps on the opposite side of Cuba. One of these Cuban wives refused to be relocated. After her husband, sons, and nephews were murdered by the gallant Che and his minions, she grabbed a tommy gun herself, rammed in a clip, and took to the hills. She became a rebel herself. Cubans know her as *La Niña del Escambray*.[7]

For a year she ran rings around the communist armies sweeping the hills in pursuit of her. Finally she ran out of ammo and supplies and was captured. La Niña suffered horribly in Castro's dungeons for years, but she survived to live in Miami today. Her tragic story would make ideal fodder for Oprah, for the professorettes of "Women's Studies," for Gloria Steinem, for a Hollywood movie, perhaps a Susan Sarandon role. Feisty female leads are big in Hollywood. They don't come much feistier than Zoila Aguila, her real name. Had she been fighting, say, Somoza or Pinochet, or U.S. forces in Iraq, Hollywood and New York would be all over her story. But she fought the most picturesque poster boy of the left, so her story is deemed uninteresting.

The skirmishing of Castro and Che that set them up to occupy the vacuum of the Batista regime lasted two years. The anticommunist rebellion lasted six years, and involved *ten times* as many fighters as the Castro-Che rebellion against Batista. But you'll search the *New York Times*, *Look*, *Life*, CBS, and *Paris Match* in vain for any stories on *these* rebels. In fact, you will not find any mention whatsoever of this fierce guerrilla war that raged for six years within ninety miles of America's borders.

Che's hagiographers aren't much help either. Jon Lee Anderson's eight-hundred-page biography devotes two hundred pages of hyperventilating prose to Che's puerile skirmishes in the Sierra and Las Villas. Anderson covers Cuba's six-year, islandwide, *anti*communist rebellion—that, again, according to Che's accomplice Raul Castro, saw 179 different bands of *anti*communist "bandits" and cost the Castroites six thousand casualties—in two sentences. Jorge Castañeda skips the anticommunist rebellion altogether, though he was clear that Che was technically Cuba's second-in-command at the time.

In 1987, the Cuban regime's own press hailed Che Guevara's role in the glorious slaughter of rural rebels. "*Presencia del Che en la Lucha Contra Bandidos y Limpia del Escambray*," crowed the Castroite press ("Che's Role in the War Against Bandits and the Escambray Clean-Up"). The Castroites were "cleaning" the area, you see, of counter revolutionary vermin and "bandits," also known as brave peasants who took up arms and took to the hills to defend their humble family farms against the genuine bandits—Cuba's Stalinist regime.

"With his great moral authority, tenacity and fine example," says one of the Che-trained bandit exterminators quoted in the article, "Che came into our camp and compelled our combat spirit. He pored over all the battle maps. He pointed out the main points of bandit resistance. Che inquired about all of our recent actions. He instructed and investigated and greatly fortified us. He spurred us on to whip and whip the enemy until defeating him. Che's lessons, his visits and his inspiration contributed much to the victory of the War Against the Bandits. When he was leaving our camp he turned around pointed to the hills and shouted, 'The mountains are now ours!' "[8]

Indeed they were. According to evidence presented to the Organization of American States by Cuban-exile researcher Dr. Claudio Benedi, four thousand anticommunist guerrillas were summarily executed during this rural rebellion.

Here was a genuine rebellion with true battles. Cuba's *genuine* Bravehearts, Davy Crocketts, and Patrick Henrys fought a desperate and lonely war against a Soviet-backed enemy, against outrageous odds. They died unknown to the world, many summarily by firing squad. Those interested in plugging this yawning gap in their historical knowledge should forget the mainstream media and academia. Consult Enrique Encinosa's superb book, *Unvanquished*.

11

"The Brains of the Revolution" as Economic Czar

Che Guevara's *Socialism and Man in Cuba* is one of the great documents in the history of socialism.

—FORMER *Time* AND *Newsweek* EDITOR AND *New York Times* WRITER JOHN GERASSI

Eleanor Clift has the power to make the worldly and garrulous John McLaughlin—host of the eponymous political chat show—gape in astonishment. Clift said on national television, "To be a poor child in Cuba may be better than being a poor child in the U.S." McLaughlin had to ask her to repeat that to make sure he had heard her correctly.

Few myths are more persistent, or more rotten, than the myth of Cuban economic progress and egalitarianism.

In late 1959, Castro appointed Che as Cuba's "Economics Minister." Like a true child of the French Revolution, Che set out to refashion human nature, with hapless Cubans as his guinea pigs. His task was to create a "new man," diligent, hard-working, obedient, free from all material incentives—in brief, lobotomized. And any shirkers, or smart-alecks who offered any lip, would quickly find themselves behind the barbed wire, watchtowers, and guard dogs of the prison camp Che christened at the harsh Guanahacabibes peninsula in extreme western Cuba.

"This multifaceted being is not, as it is claimed, the sum total of elements of the same category (and moreover, reduced to the same category by the system imposed upon them)," writes Che in his riveting and pithy *Socialism and Man in Cuba*. "The past makes itself felt not only in the individual consciousness—in which the residue of an education systematically oriented toward isolating the individual still weighs heavily—but also through the very character of this transition period in which commodity relations still persist, although this is still a subjective aspiration, not yet systematized.

"It is still necessary to deepen his conscious participation, individual and collective, in all the mechanisms . . . and to link this to the idea of the need for technical and ideological education, so that we see how closely interdependent these processes are and how their advancement is parallel. In this way he will reach total consciousness of his social being, which is equivalent to his full realization as a human creature, once the chains of alienation are broken." Jon Lee Anderson hails this pile of turgid, Marxist gibberish as Che's "opus," as "the crystallization of Che's doctrinal message." For once, Anderson is probably right.

"Man is an unfinished product," Che wrote, "who bears the flaws of the past."[1]

Within months of Che's appointment, the Cuban peso, a currency historically equal to the U.S. dollar and fully backed by Cuba's gold reserves, was practically worthless. In 1958, Cuba had 518 million pesos in circulation. A year later, 1,051 billion pesos were in circulation. A few months later 1,187 billion were in circulation and suddenly declared worthless, whereupon a new 477 million were printed up and distributed as replacements.[2]

Talent like this begs for promotion. Castro promptly appointed Che as Cuba's "minister of industries." Che quickly wrecked Cuba's formerly robust sugar, cattle, tobacco, and nickel export industries. Within a year, a nation that previously had higher per capita income than Austria, Japan, and Spain, a huge influx of immigrants, and the third-highest protein consumption in the Western Hemisphere was rationing food, closing factories, and hemorrhaging hundreds of thousands of its most productive citizens from every sector of its society.

The customary observation that this was "communist misman-agement" is wrong. In the service of the goal of absolute power, the Cuban economy was *expertly* managed in the tradition of Lenin, Mao, Uncle Ho, Ulbricht, Tito, and Kim Il Sung.

A less megalomaniacal ruler might have considered the Cuban economy a golden goose. Castro, through Che, wrung its neck. He methodically wrecked Latin America's premier economy in order to disallow any other centers of power from developing. Despite a del-uge of tourism and foreign investment from Canada, Latin America, and Europe for over a decade, Cuba is as essentially communist in the early twenty-first century as it was in 1965. The Castro brothers are very vigilant in these matters.

Castro's rationale was simply to run Cuba as his personal ha-cienda, and the Cuban people as his cattle. His minister of indus-tries, however, seemed to actually *believe* in the socialist fantasy. When Che pronounced in May 1961 that under his tutelage the Cuban economy would boast an annual growth rate of 10 percent, Che seemed to *believe* it.

This is where libertarian-free-market ideologues got it wrong. They insisted that with the lifting of the embargo, capitalism would sneak in and eventually blindside Castro. All the proof was to the contrary. Capitalism didn't sweep Castro away or even co-opt him. He swept *it* away. He wasn't a Deng or a Gorbachev. In 1959, Castro could have easily left most of Cuba's economy in place, made it obedient to his whims, and been a Peron, a Franco, or a Mussolini. He could have grabbed half and been a Tito. He could have demanded a piece of the action from all involved and been a Marcos, a Trujillo, a Mobutu, or a Suharto. But this wasn't enough for him.

Castro lusted for power on the scale of a Stalin or a Mao. And he hired a sadistic and pretentious true believer named Ernesto Guevara de la Serna y Lynch to help him get it; first as chief executioner of his enemies (real, imagined, and potential), then as economic wrecking ball. The task accomplished, Ernesto Guevara was himself liquidated as routinely and cleverly as Castro had liquidated many other accomplices, rivals, and even a few true enemies.

One day, Che decided that Cubans should learn to play and like soccer (*futbol*) like the citizens of his native Argentina. A sugar plantation named Central Macareno near Cienfuegos had recently been stolen from its American owners (contrary to leftist mythology, barely a quarter of sugar plantations were U.S.-owned). The plantation also included a huge orchard of mango, avocado, and mamey trees that were just starting to give fruit. Che ordered them all cut down and the ground leveled in order to construct a soccer field.

A year later the field was weed-grown, potholed, and unusable. The decaying trunks of the fruit-yielding trees were still piled up around the edges of the field even as most Cubans scrambled for fresh fruit on the new black market. It seemed that—the threat of Guanahacabibes notwithstanding—Che's Cuban subjects simply didn't take to Che's *futbol*.

Che also believed he could "industrialize" Cuba by fiat, just as he believed his role model Stalin had "industrialized" the Soviet Union. In fact, Che's decrees ended Cuba's status as a developed, civilized country. In one of his spasms of decrees, he ordered a refrigerator factory built in Cienfuegos, a pick and shovel factory built in Santa Clara, a pencil factory and a shoe factory built in Havana.

Supply? Demand? Costs? Such "bourgeois details" didn't interest Che. None of the factories ended up yielding a single product.

Che railed against the new Coca-Cola plant's chemists because the Coke they were producing tasted awful. Some of these flustered chemists responded that *he'd* been the one who nationalized the plant and booted out the former owners and managers, who took the secret

Coca-Cola formula with them to the United States. This impertinence was answered with the threat of Guanahacabibes. During Che's ministry, he also bought a fleet of snowplows from Czechoslovakia—surely a parable of communism, if ever there was one. Che had personally inspected them and was convinced they could easily be converted into sugarcane harvesting machines, thus mechanizing the harvest and increasing Cuba's sugar production. The snowplows in fact squashed the sugarcane plants, cut them off at the wrong length, and killed them. This was just one reason Cuba's sugar production in 1963 was *less than half* of its Batista-era volume.[3]

Che's famous Havana shoe factory turned out a product that was good for about two blocks of brisk walking before disintegrating. Che Guevara, naturally, couldn't figure out why the shoes his pet factory manufactured just sat on shelves. In 1961, most Cubans still wore their prerevolutionary shoes, constantly repairing them, constantly polishing them—anything but wearing the product from Che's showcase factory. This enraged him, and he finally stormed down to the factory.

Knowing his "humanistic" reputation, all the factory workers were on their best behavior. "What's the problem here!" Che barked at the factory foreman. "Why are you turning out shoes that are pure shit!"

The factory foreman looked Minister of Industries Guevara straight in the face. "It's the glue, it won't hold the soles to the shoe. It's that shitty glue you're buying from the Russians. We used to get it from the U.S." This really stung Che. So he went off on one of his habitual tirades as the factory workers quaked, fearing the worst. Many had lost relatives in La Cabana, or had relatives behind the barbed wire of Che's pet concentration camp in Guanahacabibes.

"Okay, here," and the foreman handed Che a shoe fresh from the assembly line. "See for yourself."

Che grabbed the sole, pulled, and it came right off like a banana peel. "Why didn't you report this slipshod glue to anyone at our Ministry of Industries!" Che snapped.

"We did," shot back the foreman, "repeatedly, but nothing happened!" Che ordered his ever-present henchmen to grab the insolent foreman. "Now you people figure out how to make these shoes better." Che glared. "Or the rest of you will get it!" He spun away and stomped off with his captive, who was not seen again.[4] Yet Jon Lee Anderson assures us that "it was social change, not power itself, that impelled Che."

It was Guevara, of course, who threw out the prerevolutionary manager of that factory, and banned glue imports from the United States.

The Russians Say "*Nyet!*"

By late 1964, the Minister of Industries had so badly crippled Cuba's economy and infrastructure, had so impoverished and traumatized its workforce, that the Russians themselves were at their wits' end. They were subsidizing the mess, and it was getting expensive—much *too* expensive for the paltry geopolitical return. "*This* is an *underdeveloped* country?!" Anastas Mikoyan had asked while looking around on his first visit to Cuba in 1960. The Soviets were frankly tickled to have a developed and civilized country to loot again, as they had done in Eastern Europe after World War II.

Alas, the looting went in the *opposite* direction. Castro was no chump like Ulbricht or Gomulka. A French socialist economist, Rene Dumont, tried advising Castro as the wreckage of Cuba's economy spiraled out of control. "The Cuban Revolution has gone farther in its first three years than the Chinese in its first ten," he counseled.[5] But Guevara was allergic to criticism, however well-meaning.

In 1964, the Soviets themselves finally told Castro that Che had to go. Castro knew who buttered his bread. He had never much liked Che. And with power thoroughly consolidated, Castro no longer needed his Robespierre.

Here we come to another hoary myth spun by Che's hagiographers, that of his "ideological" falling out with the Soviets. Che's pureness of revolutionary heart, we're told, led him to clash with the corrupt Soviet *nomenklatura*. In fact, this was a purely *practical* conflict. The Soviets simply refused to bankroll Che's harebrained fantasies any longer. When Che finally realized this, he knew he was on the way out. He decided to retaliate. So in December 1964, right after his visit to the United Nations, Che visited his friend Ben Bela in Algeria and delivered his famous anti-Soviet speech, branding them "accomplices of imperialist exploitation."

To many it looked like Che was setting the stage for a role as the Trotsky of his generation. For Che, it was just a new role to play. When he touched down in Havana after the speech, the regime's press was absolutely mute regarding both his speech and his recent return. Soon, he was invited to visit the Maximum Leader and Raul. Raul had just returned from Russia, where Che's Algeria speech had caused quite a stir. As soon as he got within earshot, both Castros ripped into Guevara as undisciplined, ungrateful, and plainly stupid.

"Fidel!" Che stuttered back. "Please, show me some respect! I'm not Camilo!" Che's wife, Aleida, was forced to jump in between the men, exclaiming, "I can't believe such a thing is happening between longtime *compañeros*." [6]

The quaking Che finally went home, where he found his telephone lines cut. Much evidence points to Che's undergoing house arrest at this point. And it was under that house arrest that a seriously chastened and apparently frightened Che composed his famous "farewell letter to Fidel," in which he groveled shamelessly.

"I deeply appreciate your lessons and your example . . . my only fault was not to have had more faith in you since the first moments in the Sierra, not having recognized more quickly your qualities as a leader and a revolutionary. I will take to my new fields of battle the faith that you have inculcated . . ." and on and on in unrelenting obsequiousness. [7]

Che's few public appearances between his return from Algeria and his departure for the Congo always found him in the company of state security personnel. His Cuban adventure had come to an end.

What Che Had to Work With

In 1957, a UNESCO report said: "One feature of the Cuban social structure is a *large middle class*. Cuban workers are more unionized (proportional to the population) than U.S. workers . . . the average wage for an eight-hour day in Cuba 1957 is higher than for workers in Belgium, Denmark, France, Germany. Cuban labor receives 66.6 per cent of gross national income. In the U.S. the figure is 68 per cent. In Switzerland 64 per cent. 44 per cent of Cubans were covered by social legislation, a higher percentage than in the U.S. at the time."[8]

In fact, Cuba had established an eight-hour workday in 1933—five years before FDR's New Dealers got around to it. Forty-eight hours of pay were due for that forty-hour week, with one month's paid vacation. The lauded social democracies of Western Europe didn't manage this until thirty years later. Many Cubans enjoyed nine days of sick leave with pay, compulsory unemployment insurance paid by management, and—get this, Maxine Waters, Medea Benjamin, and all you feminist Castro groupies—*three months' paid maternity leave*. This was in the 1930s.[9]

Pre-Castro Cuba's labor laws led to a frequent lament in Havana's Yacht Club: "It's easier to get rid of a wife than an employee!" (This yacht club, incidentally, denied membership to the mulatto Batista himself—Cuba's president!)

In the 1950s the average farm wage in "near-feudal" Cuba, as the *New York Times* described the nation in 1959, was *higher* than those of France, Belgium, Denmark, or West Germany. According to the Geneva-based International Labor Organization, the average daily wage for an agricultural worker in Cuba in 1958 was $3.00. The average daily wage in France at the time was $2.73; in Belgium, $2.70;

in Denmark, $2.74; in West Germany, $2.73; and in the United States, $4.06.[10]

With the term "near-feudal," the *New York Times* also implied a Cuban countryside monopolized by a tiny number of millionaire absentee landlords, their vast estates worked by stooping legions of landless serfs. Jon Lee Anderson also describes Cuba's "wealthy class of land barons . . . consigning the workers to lives of endemic poverty."[11]

Actually, the average Cuban farm in 1958 was *smaller* than the average farm in the United States, 140 acres in Cuba versus 195 acres in the United States. In 1958, Cuba, a nation of 6.4 million people, had 159,958 farms—11,000 of which were tobacco farms. Only 34 percent of the Cuban population was rural.

In the 1950s, Cuban longshoremen earned the highest wages in Latin America and among the highest wages *in the world* for their trade, higher than those in New Orleans at the time. In 1958, Cubans owned more televisions per capita than any other Latin Americans, and more than any other continental Europeans. And Cubans owned more cars per capita than the Japanese and half of the countries of Europe.[12]

In short, Cuban workers had purchasing power. In 1958, Cuba had the hemisphere's lowest inflation rate—1.4 percent. The U.S. rate that year was 2.73 percent. The Cuban peso was historically equal to the U.S. dollar, completely interchangeable one to one.[13]

Cuba had its two top years economically in 1957–58, when, according to the *New York Times* and leftists in general, Cuba was not only "near-feudal," but in the midst of a ferocious "guerrilla war" at the hands of the masterful guerrilla chieftain, Che Guevara.

"Cuba is not an underdeveloped country," concluded the 1956 U.S. Department of Commerce guide for businesses. After Che became economic czar, Cuba was soon in a league with the poorest nations.

The country that in 1958 had the third-highest protein consumption in the Western Hemisphere would soon be on government rations.[14] And what were these rations? It is instructive to compare the daily rations imposed on Cubans by the brilliant Argentine's ministry to the daily rations of Cuban slaves as mandated by the Spanish king in 1842.[15]

	Slave rations, 1842	Castro rations since 1962
Meat, chicken, fish	8 oz.	2 oz.
Rice	4 oz.	3 oz.
Starches	16 oz.	6.5 oz.
Beans	4 oz.	1 oz.

Cuban slaves actually ate *better* than Cuban "citizens" under Ernesto "Che" Guevara's economic overlordship. These levels of rations persist to this day. Lincoln once said, "Whenever I hear anyone arguing for slavery, I feel a strong impulse to see it tried on him personally." Undoubtedly, many Cuban Americans watching *The McLaughlin Group* had an impulse to see Eleanor Clift have to choke down her daily ration of beans and starch, with a little stringy meat.

People never vote as candidly as when they vote with their feet. In the twentieth century, before Castro and Che marched into Havana, Cuba took in more immigrants per capita than any other country in the Western Hemisphere—more than the United States, including the Ellis Island years. In 1958, the Cuban embassy in Rome had a backlog of twelve thousand applications for immigrant visas from Italians *clamoring* to emigrate to Cuba. From 1903 to 1957 Cuba took in over 1 million immigrants from Spain and sixty-five thousand from the United States.[16]

Jamaicans and Haitians jumped on rafts trying to *enter* Cuba. Now, not only do people risk their lives to flee, 2 million as of 1992, but half-starved Haitians a mere sixty miles away turn up their noses at the place. People used to be almost as desperate to *enter* Cuba as they are now to escape.

Here's another example of actions speaking louder than statistics: When Castro's rebel movement called for a "National Strike" against the Batista dictatorship on August 5, 1957—and threatened to shoot workers who reported to work—the "National Strike" was completely ignored. Another was called for April 9, 1958. And again Cuban workers blew a loud and collective raspberry at their "liberators," reporting to work en masse.

The anti-Batista rebellion was staffed and led overwhelmingly by college students and professionals. Unemployed lawyers were prominent, beginning with Fidel Castro himself. "Workers and peasants" were conspicuous by their scarcity. The Castro Che regime's initial showpiece cabinet consisted of seven lawyers, two university professors, three students, one doctor, one engineer, one architect, one former city mayor, and one captain who defected from the Batista army.[17] They were a notoriously "bourgeois" bunch, as Che himself might have put it. By 1961, it was the workers and *campesinos,* or country folk, who made up the overwhelming bulk of the *anti*-Castroite rebels, especially the guerrillas in the Escambray Mountains.

No discussion of Cuba is complete without mentioning Cuba's vaunted "health care." Colin Powell himself, at the same time he was making his case against Saddam Hussein at the United Nations, was quoted as saying that "Castro had done some good things for Cuba."[18] Chances are he was anticipating some comment on Cuba's "health care" from the reporter and answered on reflex.

So again, some facts. In 1958, Cuba had the lowest infant mortality in Latin America and the *thirteenth lowest in the world.* Cuba ranked ahead of France, Belgium, West Germany, Israel, Japan, Austria, Italy, and Spain.[19] Today (and this if you believe the figures issued by Castro's propaganda ministry), Cuba ranks *twenty-fifth from the top.* So relative to the rest of the world, Cuba's health care has *worsened* after forty-seven years of Stalinism. Another thing: Castro's Cuba's staggering abortion rate of 0.71 abortions per live birth makes it—by far—the highest in the hemisphere and among the highest in the world. This reduces infant mortality by "terminating" high-risk pregnancies. Yet even with this harrowing statistic, Castro's Cuba of today ranks relatively worse in infant mortality than Batista's Cuba of half a century ago. Also, in 1957, Cuba had more doctors and dentists as a percentage of population than the United States and the United Kingdom.[20]

A report snuck out of Cuba by a dissident reporter reveals that tuberculosis, leprosy, and dengue—diseases long gone from Cuba in 1958—are making a strong comeback in the Cuba of 2005.[21]

Another left-wing truism is that Cuba was nothing but a corrupt and prostituted "playground" for American tourists. In 1957, Cuba hosted a grand total of 272,265 U.S. tourists. In 1950, there were more Cubans vacationing in the United States than Americans vacationing in Cuba. (In 2002, by the way, smack in the middle of the nefarious U.S. "embargo"—nay, the diabolical "imperialist blockade!"—approximately 203,000 Americans visited Cuba, by hook or by crook.[22]) Biloxi, Mississippi, today has three times as many gambling casinos as all of Cuba had in 1958.

Of course, we can't discuss Cuba without an account of her exploitation and humiliation by the rude and rapacious Yankee businessmen and gangsters who dominated her economy. Cuba's Mayari province was a "virtual vassal state of United Fruit," claims Che biographer Jon Lee Anderson. Cuba itself was "a virtual semicolony of the United States," claims Jorge Castañeda. Che Guevara himself berated the United Fruit Company as "the Green Octopus."[23]

In fact, in 1958—after only fifty-five years of independence following an utterly devastating war against Spain—only 9 percent of Cuba's invested capital was American, and less than *one-third* of Cuba's sugar production was by U.S. companies. Of Cuba's 161 sugar mills, only 40 were U.S.-owned. And only a *fraction* of these were owned by United Fruit.[24] Some "octopus."

"I think there is not a country in the world, including all the regions of Africa and any other country under colonial domination, where the economic colonization, the humiliation, the exploitation have been worse than those which ravaged Cuba." Those words were not spoken by Che Guevara on the stump at the United Nations. That was John F. Kennedy in an interview with French journalist Jean Daniel in 1963. "The result, in part, of the policy of my country," added JFK for good measure.[25]

In choosing the advisors who would inform his Cuba policy, President Kennedy once said, "You can't beat brains."

The U.S. Embargo—Che Begged for It

That the U.S. embargo of Cuba was a preemptive, unwarranted, and malicious "punishment" of Cuba by the arrogant Bully to the North has become enshrined in worldwide academic/leftist folklore. For fifteen years straight now, the U.N. General Assembly has voted every year almost unanimously to denounce it, even aping Cuba's eunuch of a foreign minister, Perez Roque, by terming it a "blockade." Only the United States, Israel, and the Marshall Islands buck the vote. Iran's U.N. ambassador, Javad Aghazadeh, was particularly vocal in favor of his Cuban friends at the last vote, climbing the stump to blast the "U.S. blockade" as "intolerance toward other political, economic, and social systems, that runs counter to protecting human rights and dignity!"[26] This lecture on intolerance and human rights issues from the delegate of a nation that wants Israel "wiped off the map."

History tells a different story, one in which U.S. policymakers had little choice. Che Guevara, as president of Cuba's National Bank, repeatedly raged against Cuba's business ties to the United States. Even though the United States bought Cuban sugar above the world price, Che denounced America for "economic slavery"!

Okay, fine, said Ike. So Americans stopped buying Cuban sugar. Well, according to Che, this response was now Yankee "economic aggression"! When Jean Paul Sartre called Fidel, Raul, and Che "the children in power," he meant it as a compliment. It was, in fact, a painful truth, for Cuban economic policy was a tantrum. Che Guevara *asked for the embargo.* In a hysterical speech televised on March 23, 1960, Che Guevara declared, "In order to conquer something we have to take it away from somebody. That something we must conquer is the country's sovereignty. It has to be taken away from that something called monopoly. It means that our road to liberation will be opened up with a victory over the U.S. monopolies!"[27]

Che was ordering mass larceny directed at U.S. businesses. As economic minister, Che ordered the theft of almost $2 billion from U.S. businessmen and stockholders. Some 5,911 businesses were stolen—lock, stock, and barrel—from their hard-working, capital-risking, rightful owners at gunpoint. This remains the biggest heist in history. In two weeks, and using a few bands of machine-gun-toting goons, Castro and Che swiped more from American business-men than all the other "nationalizations" (lootings) by all other nationalist (looter) regimes on earth, combined.

Castro crowed about it gleefully into a phalanx of microphones and shrieked that he'd never repay a penny. And he hasn't. A few who resisted the plunder were executed. One was American citizen Howard Anderson, who had his Jeep dealership stolen. (Anderson, the reader will recall, was one of the victims of Che's vampirism.) Another was Robert Fuller, whose family farm was stolen. Like An-derson, Fuller was bound, gagged, and shoved in front of a firing squad.

Europeans, especially the French, gloated while watching Che and Castro loot Uncle Sam. Then they scooted in themselves, rub-bing their hands. The Europeans, however, were surprised to miss their windfall. Cuba was more than willing to borrow, but found re-payment of foreign commercial and bilateral debt with all nonso-cialist countries decidedly inconvenient. It stopped payment in 1986. The Paris Club of creditor nations found Cuba simply unin-terested in talking to them.

What about the $5 billion a year Cuba received from its Soviet sugar daddy?

Fidel repudiated those debts, too. Once again, history absolved him when his creditor—the Soviet Union—no longer existed. How could he repay a legal entity that no longer existed?

"Che Lives"—the Squalid Legacy

"We arrived in Cuba without political prejudices, intent on seeing the country outside the much-lauded tourist areas," says Spanish backpacker tourist Isane Aparicio Busto. "The blow was shocking. We left with our perceptions about the reality of the Cuban revolution—and even with our prior social and political principles—demolished."

Isane had returned from a trip to Cuba in late 2005. Like so many "hip" European tourists, Isane might have been expected to sport Che Guevara's face on her backpack or T-shirt. I suspect she won't now.

"We saw police everywhere. And it soon became obvious that Cubans are the victims of the 21st century's version of apartheid. Hotels for foreign tourists, stores for foreign tourists, buses for foreign tourists—a world set apart from the Cubans themselves as they are prevented by the police from entering. . . . The Cuban people's personal aspirations seemed completely mutilated. I've never felt such anguish about a nation and a people in my life. If I were a Cuban, I'd certainly be on a raft."[28]

It sounds so easy. Why, just hop on a raft. Soon you're drinking café con leche with your cousins in Miami. Nothing to it! Except that up until very recently only one in three rafters lived through the ordeal.

Varadero, where Isane stayed, is a gorgeous beach east of Havana where millions of Cubans cavorted every weekend, at least during Cuba's stint as a racist-fascist U.S. satrapy terrorized by crooks and gangsters.

In 1959, Fidel and his vanguard of the downtrodden rose in righteous fury. Inflamed by a patriotic fervor, they ended foreign humiliation of Cubans. Of this we're assured by everyone from Charles Rangel, to Noam Chomsky, to Robert Redford, to Jesse Jackson, to Norman Mailer, to virtually any Ivy League history professor.

Now, after almost fifty years of this fervently nationalist revolution, the best of Varadero beach is barricaded against Cubans by armed police and reserved for rich foreigners, their local footservants, and prostitutes.

Jimmy Carter, Barbara Boxer, and high-rolling trade delegations from Nebraska, Louisiana, California, or Maine are welcome, as well as many Isanes. But let a nongovernmental Cuban citizen try to enter and he's bludgeoned with Czech machine-gun butts.

And I suspect Isane didn't know the half of it. She probably didn't know that before the glorious revolution, Cuba had a standard of living higher than the Venezuela and Mexico she'd visited, and higher than half of Europe, and boasted almost double her native Spain's per capita income.

Revolutionary Cuba's early minister of industries and bank president Che Guevara had quite a base to work with. It usually requires an earthquake, volcano, tsunami, or atom bomb to match Che's industrial and economic achievements in Cuba. Indeed Tokyo, Pompeii, and Hiroshima have all recovered. Havana, richer in the 1950s than Rome or Dallas, now resembles Calcutta, Nairobi, or Phnom Penh. One place where Cuban exiles agree wholeheartedly with Castro is regarding his exalted post as a Third World leader. He and Che certainly made Cuba into a Third World country.

In January 2006, supermodel Helena Houdova, who had also been crowned "Miss Czech" in 1999, visited Cuba. She followed in the footsteps of Naomi Campbell and Kate Moss, who had visited in 1998—but not in their exact footsteps. Campbell confined herself to the sparkling tourist enclaves and to the regime-approved sites, dutifully following the regime's helpful "guides" to La Plaza de la Revolución dominated by its huge portrait of Che Guevara. She came away smitten with everything around her.

"I'm very nervous!" Campbell twittered after arriving late at a press conference held at Havana's Hotel Nacional. "I just spent an hour and a half talking with your president, Fidel Castro! But he told me there was nothing to be afraid of. Fidel knew who we were from reading about us in the press, but he said that it wasn't the same as meeting us in person. We had also read so many things about Fidel. It is a great pleasure to be in Cuba," she gushed. "I've enjoyed myself, and I plan to come back. . . . Fidel Castro is a source of great inspiration for me, an intelligent and impressive man who fought for a just cause."[29]

Campbell was right about one thing: Fidel Castro indeed knew a lot about her. But not from perusing stories in *Cosmo* or *Elle* (more on this in a minute).

Czech supermodel Helena Houdova tried to shake her government "guides" and venture into the interior of Havana. She heads a charity called the Sunflower Foundation that assists poor, handicapped, sick, and orphaned children worldwide. The Castro regime could have told her not to waste her time looking for such things in Cuba. Everyone from Naomi Campbell to Eleanor "to be a poor child in Cuba is better than being a poor child in America" Clift could have told Helena Houdova that nothing remotely of the sort afflicts Cuban children.

But Ms. Houdova was born and lived in Czechoslovakia, a nation overrun by Soviet tanks in 1945 and again in 1968. Unlike Ivy League and Berkeley professors, and all those hard-nosed investigative reporters from Dan Rather to CNN's Lucia Newman, she knew better than to believe the proclamations from the propaganda ministry of a Stalinist regime—especially those of its multitude of agents and useful idiots. "It is almost impossible to provide any assistance through official means because the Communist authorities refuse to admit anything in their country does not work," Houdova told the *Prague Daily Monitor* before visiting Cuba.[30]

The intrepid model visited several Havana hospitals (not the ones for tourists and foreigners, the ones for Cubans) and came away disgusted. She then started snapping pictures of the dreadful slums around her in downtown Havana. And that's when the cops walked up and ripped the camera from her hands. "They screamed at us," said Houdova. "We were afraid, but we grew up under communism and know what it is like."

Castro's goons tore open the camera and stole the roll of film, but somehow Houdova managed to conceal the memory card of her digital camera inside her bra. Houdova and her friend, psychologist and fellow model Mariana Kroftova, were dragged off and detained for eleven hours without being allowed to contact the Czech embassy, and without being able to communicate with their captors in English. They were finally released after signing a document pledging they would refrain from joining any "counter-revolutionary activities."

"The revolution's watchmen rose up because I was taking pictures of something they do not like," she summed it up after arriving back in Prague.[31]

Now let's see how Castro learns such charming conversation points about such visitors as Naomi Campbell and Kate Moss—and Jack Nicholson. "Fidel Castro is a genius!" gushed Jack Nicholson after a visit to Cuba in 1998. "We spoke about everything," the actor rhapsodized. "Castro is a humanist like President Clinton. Cuba is simply a paradise!"[32]

Jack Nicholson has been saying such things for years now. Many of his Hollywood cohorts follow suit. Francis Ford Coppola, Steven Spielberg, Woody Harrelson, Leo DiCaprio, Chevy Chase, Robert Redford, and many others have waxed euphoric on Castro and his island prison. Bill O'Reilly called these celebs "Hollywood pinheads." But there might be more to these celebrity plugs.

"My job was to bug their hotel rooms," says high-ranking Cuban intelligence defector Delfin Fernandez. "With both cameras and listening devices. Most people have no idea they are being watched while they are in Cuba. But their personal activities are filmed under orders from Castro himself." And according to some sources, Havana, given the desperation of its brutalized and impoverished residents, has recently topped Bangkok as the world mecca for child sex. It's a blackmailer's bonanza.

"He [Delfin Fernandez] has not only met some of the most famous men in the world," says the *London Daily Mirror* about the Cuban defector, "he's also spied on them and been witness to some of their most innermost secrets."

"When the celebrity visitors arrived at the hotels Nacional [where Campbell and Moss stayed], Melia Habana, and Melia Cohiba," says Fernandez, "we already had their rooms completely bugged with sophisticated taping equipment. . . . But not just the rooms, we'd also follow the visitors around, sometimes we covered them twenty-four hours a day. They had no idea we were tailing them."[33]

Famous Spanish filmmaker Pedro Almodóvar was a special target for this bugging, but nothing of value came of it for Castro. "Everybody already knows I'm a *maricón*!" Almodóvar laughed at Castro's blackmailers. "So go right ahead! Knock yourselves out!"

"Fidel Castro is a special connoisseur of these tapings and videos," Fernandez says. "Especially of the really famous." Not even Castro's closest "friends" are safe from this bugging. The best example is Nobel Prize–winning novelist Gabriel García Márquez. In what appeared as a touching act of generosity and friendship, Castro gave his friend "Gabo" his very own, stolen mansion in Havana. "We had remodeled it right before," remembers Fernandez, "and we installed more cables for bugging devices than for the normal electrical appliances. We taped everything. Fidel doesn't trust anyone."

Castro's top intelligence people would gather for the screenings of these tapes almost like Hollywood types for the screening of an upcoming movie. "Hummmm, these scenes are more scandalous than anything in any of her movies!" Fernandez recalls a top intelligence officer chortling while watching the nighttime cavortings of a famous Spanish actress. "Now, it really seems to me, *compañeros*," the Castro intimate chortled as he looked around the room, "that this *señora* should be making more respectful comments about our regime, right?"

"But famous Americans are the priority objectives of Castro's intelligence," says Fernandez. "When word came down that models Naomi Campbell and Kate Moss were coming to Cuba, the order was a routine one: twenty-four-hour-a-day vigilance. Then we got a priority alert, because there was a rumor that they would be sharing a room with Leonardo DiCaprio. The rumor set off a flurry of activity and we set up the most sophisticated devices we had.

"The American actor Jack Nicholson was another celebrity who was bugged and taped thoroughly during his stay in the hotel Melia Cohiba," states Fernandez.[34]

Turns out, however, that at least one visiting dignitary foiled Castro's intelligence. On his visit to Cuba in 1998, Pope John Paul's assistants discovered and removed several bugging devices from His Holiness's hotel room. Perhaps Castro had a grudge against the papacy. Most don't recall, but in January 1962, Pope John XXIII excommunicated Fidel Castro from the Catholic Church. It seemed fitting, considering the hundreds of Cuban men and boys crumpling to Castro's firing squads while yelling, "Long Live Christ the King!" during their last seconds on earth.

Desperate Prostitutes

A good example of Che's ability to deny plain facts was on display during a state visit to Czechoslovakia in 1960, when his Cuban companions pointed out the numerous prostitutes on the streets, and in the very hotel where they stayed. Che nodded wearily. Back in Cuba when one of these winked and brought up the prostitutes, Che flared indignantly, "I didn't see any prostitutes there!"[35] The Cubans looked at each other, shrugging, but knew better than to press the issue. Che didn't *want* to remember the sight of prostitutes in a glorious socialist nation.

The Cuba that Castro and Che built has since become a global brothel, one in which women are exploited with shocking ease for "sex tourists."

"Since she is usually desperate," writes one Dr. Julia O'Connell Davidson, "he can secure sexual access to her very cheaply."[36] O'Connell Davidson, professor of sociology at Britain's University of Nottingham and author of *The Rights and Wrongs of Prostitution,* conducted a thorough study of contemporary Cuban prostitution.

"A Cuban prostitute can often be beaten down to as little as U.S. $2 to $4," O'Connell Davidson writes. "Inexperienced women and girls can be persuaded and/or tricked into spending a whole night with a client for the cost of a meal, a few drinks or small gift. Sex tourists state that it costs them less to spend two weeks indulging themselves in Cuba than it does in other centers of sex tourism, such as the Philippines and Thailand. This is partly because competition between so many Cuban women lowers the price.

"Girls aged 14 and 15 are even more desperate for dollars and therefore more vulnerable. We met 14- and 15-year-old prostitutes working in Varadero who reported that a number of their Italian, Canadian and German clients make between three and five trips to Cuba per year. More disturbing still, such tourists are paying older Cuban women and men, often prostitutes themselves, to procure 14- and 15-year-old girls for them."[37]

Professor O'Connell Davidson found that what she termed the "hostile sexuality" of many of Cuba's visiting tourists "can be encapsulated in the motto 'Find them, feed them, f**k them, forget them' . . . A U.S.-based company that publishes a book and electronic newsletter entitled Travel & the Single Male identifies Cuba as a new 'hot destination for the adventurous single male.' One British tourist explained that his Cuban 'girlfriend' (he had traded in another woman for her the previous day) had suggested that he move out of the hotel where he was paying $20 per night, and stay in her flat where she would do all his washing and cook his meals for him. For all this, plus acting as guide and interpreter and granting him sexual access, she asked only $5 a day plus the cost of the food.

At home, this man could not even buy a pack of cigarettes for this sum, far less obtain the services of a maid/prostitute."[38]

Professor O'Connell Davidson also discovered something of interest for Charlie Rangel, Jesse Jackson, Maxine Waters, Danny Glover, Harry Belafonte, Naomi Campbell, Kweisi Mfume, Che tattoo wearer Mike Tyson, and Che T-shirt wearer and rapper Jay-Z. "Cubans face many of the same 'racialised' barriers that oppress Black people elsewhere in the world. Groups that face this kind of structural disadvantage are often over-represented in prostitution. Our initial impression was that there were more Black than 'mixed' or white *jiniteras* (prostitutes). As one Canadian said to me, 'You can call a nigger a nigger here [in Cuba], and no-one takes it the wrong way.'"

Professor O'Connell Davidson concluded that in Cuba racists "find opportunities for satisfying a sexual appetite for others they both despise and desire. For them, Cuba is 'paradise.' Cuba presently has a great deal to offer the sex tourist. Such men can contemptuously command Cuban women and girls with the same ease that they order cocktails."[39]

These are not the words of embittered Cuban exiles, but a reading from a feminist European college professor.

But, lest we get the wrong idea and lump her with that tacky Miami bunch, Professor O'Connell Davidson closes with the following: "Their power [to command Cuban women] rests not only upon the obscene disparity in wealth between the developed and underdeveloped world, but also upon *American foreign policy*. Under Batista, the U.S. indirectly organized Cuba as its brothel and gambling house. Today, its *punishment* of Cuba is helping to recreate the conditions under which Cuban women and girls must become the playthings of the economically advantaged."

Once again, it's the Americans' fault. Well that's more like it, especially in view of Professor O'Connell Davidson's academic standing. At least she documents well what she saw in front of her eyes and heard with her ears in Cuba.

In 1958, Cuba enjoyed a higher standard of living than (I'm

looking at the professor's last name) Ireland. As we have seen, Cuba under Batista was *not* part of the "underdeveloped" world, much less "a brothel and gambling house for the U.S." In 1958, Cuba had approximately 10,000 prostitutes. Today 150,000 women ply their desperate trade on the island.[40]

Professor O'Connell Davidson's University of Nottingham is ranked among Britain's ten best universities by the *London Sunday Times*. So we can't expect them to teach accurate Cuban history, any more than Berkeley or Yale or Princeton teaches it. The "obscene disparity in wealth" between Cuba (today) and the developed world that Professor O'Connell Davidson documents has *nothing* to do with U.S. policy and everything to do with Castro's policy—especially his appointment of Ernesto "Che" Guevara as president of Cuba's National Bank and Cuba's minister of industries in quick succession.

Blacks in Cuba

Institutionalized racism was abolished in Cuba thirty years before Rosa Parks was thrown off that Montgomery bus. The government Che Guevara helped overthrow had included blacks as president of the Senate, minister of agriculture, chief of the army, and *head of state*, Fulgencio Batista himself.

Batista grabbed power in a (bloodless) coup in 1952, but in 1940 he had been elected president in elections considered scrupulously honest by U.S. observers. So whatever racial barriers existed in Cuba at the time did not prevent a country that was 71 percent white from voting in a black president—and electing him almost twenty years before Eisenhower sent federal troops into Little Rock to enforce integration.

Today, Cuba's jail population is 85 percent black. The regime Che Guevara cofounded holds the distinction of having incarcerated the longest-serving black political prisoner of the twentieth century, Eusebio Peñalver, who was holed up and tortured in Castro's jails *longer than Nelson Mandela languished in South Africa's*.

Peñalver was bloodied in his fight with communism but un-bowed for thirty years in its dungeons. "Nigger!" taunted his jailers. "Monkey! We pulled you down from the trees and cut off your tail!" snickered Castro's goons as they threw him in solitary confinement.[41]

His communist jailers were always asking Eusebio Peñalver for a "confession," for a signature on some document admitting his "ideological transgressions." This would greatly alleviate his confinement and suffering, they assured him.

They got their answer as swiftly and as clearly from Peñalver as the German commander who surrounded Bastogne got his from the 101st Airborne. Eusebio scorned any "re-education" by his Castroite jailers. He knew it was *they* who desperately needed it. He refused to wear the uniform of a common criminal. He knew it was *they* who should don it. Through thirty years of hell in Castro's dungeons, Eusebio Peñalver stood tall, proud, and defiant.

Ever hear of him? He lives in Miami. Ever see a CNN interview with him? Ever see him on *60 Minutes*? Ever read about him in the *New York Times*? The *Boston Globe*? Ever hear about him on NPR, or during Black History Month? Ever hear the NAACP or Congressional Black Caucus mention him?

He was a *Cuban* political prisoner. And as we all know, with the mainstream media and academia, that form of oppression doesn't count. Today, Castro's police bar black Cubans from tourist areas. Cuba's most prominent political prisoner, Elias Biscet, is black (I won't bother asking if you've heard of him). And exactly .08 percent of Cuba's communist rulers are black. In other places they called this "apartheid."

12

Che in Africa

[The Congo] was the path that would lead [Che] to glory.
—Jorge Castañeda

Che Guevara's campaign in Africa came to a comic end because Che could not begin to match his opponents' skill in organizing and inspiring African troops.

In a radio interview shortly after he entered Havana, Che Guevara gave a good clue to what lay ahead for Cuban blacks. A prominent Cuban businessman named Luis Pons, who happened to be black, called and asked Che what the revolution planned on doing to help blacks.

"We're going to do for blacks exactly what blacks did for the revolution," snapped Che. "By which I mean: nothing."[1] Today Pons is a prominent Cuban-American businessman in New York, and one of the founders of the Cuban American National Foundation. His mother was denied permission to leave Cuba, precisely because she was black.

"When we were training in Mexico before landing in Cuba," recalls Miguel Sanchez, who did much of the training, "Che delighted in belittling the Cuban black guerrilla named Juan Almedia. He always sneered at him as 'el Negrito.' Almedia would get furious at Che so I finally told him, 'Look, Juan, when Che calls you el Negrito call him *El Chancho* (the pig) because that guy never, but never takes baths.' And it worked for a while. But Che soon found other targets for his innate racism, sneering at all 'these illiterate Indians in Mexico.' "[2]

Did this attitude hobble Che in dealing with African troops? By April 1965, Che was in Tanzania with a contingent of Cuban military officers and troops. Code-named "Tatu," Che and his force entered the Eastern Congo, which was convulsed at the time by an incomprehensible series of civil (mostly tribal) wars. Leave it to Ernesto Guevara to size up this madhouse conflagration as a "people's war" against "capitalist oppressors" that demanded "proletarian brotherhood."

Tatu's self-appointed mission was to help the alternately Soviet- and Chinese-backed "Simbas" of the Congolese Red leader, Laurent Kabila, those of Pierre Mulele, and several other bands of rapists, cutthroats, and cannibals. All these "liberation" groups were busy hacking their way through the Congolese followers of Moise Tshombe, along with many of the defenseless Europeans still left in the recently abandoned Belgian colony.

The Simbas' sack of Stanleyville was particularly gruesome. Among those hacked to death during the murderous melee were American missionaries Dr. Paul Carlson and Phyllis Rine. U.S. Consul Michael Hoyt and his entire consulate staff and their families, though captured by the Simbas, who shrieked "*Ciyuga! Ciyuga!* [Kill! Kill!] Kill them all! Have no scruples! Men, women, children—kill them all!" while parading them through downtown Stanleyville, managed to escape alive. The Simbas had just herded their hostages into Stanleyville's main square under the Patrice Lumumba statue and were moving in to comply with the command "*Ciyuga!*" when Belgian Foreign Legion paratroopers literally dropped in. They jumped from Hercules C-130s flown by U.S. pilots from bases in France. The Simbas scattered in panic.[3]

Soon the Belgian legionaries linked up with the mercenary forces of "Mad" Mike Hoare, with Congolese who opposed Kabila, and with some Cuban Bay of Pigs veterans sent by the CIA. The Cubans were mostly pilots who provided close air support for Mad Mike with North American T-28 Trojans and Douglas B-26 Invaders. A small force of Bay of Pigs veterans also formed part of Mad Mike's Fifth Commando on the ground. They were soon making short work of the cannibal Simbas, to the lasting gratitude of Stanleyville's terrorized residents.

Around this time Che—the mighty "Tatu"—made his entrance.

Che's first military mission as an ally of these Simbas was to plot an attack on a garrison guarding a hydroelectric plant at Front Bendela on the Kimbi River in eastern Congo. An elaborate ambush of the garrison, it was meant to be a masterstroke. No sooner had Tatu's ambushers blundered into position than the ambushers became the ambushed. They fell under a withering rain of mortar shells and machine-gun fire. In this first military masterstroke, *Comandante* Tatu lost half his men.

Che's African allies started frowning a little more closely at his resume and asking a few questions (but in Swahili, which he didn't understand). Victor Colas was a Cuban *comandante* attached to Che. "I finally decided to give the order to retreat," he recounts about the next confrontation with Mad Mike and the CIA Cubans. "I turned around—and found I was alone! Apparently I'd been alone for a while. Everyone had fled. I'd been warned about this."

A few more routs followed, and soon Che couldn't get an audience with any African leader. "I tried to talk to Major Kasali," records Che. "But he refused to see me saying he was suffering from a headache."[4]

For weeks, Simba head Laurent Kabila himself pointedly refused to answer any of Tatu's correspondence. Finally he answered one missive brusquely, and Che was jubilant, responding like a neglected puppy to a man he had met only once, and briefly. "Dear Comrade," Tatu wrote him back. "Thank you so much for your letter. I await your arrival here with impatience because I consider you an old friend, and I owe you an explanation. Also be assured: I put myself unconditionally under your orders. I also ask you a favor. Give me permission to join the fight with no other title than political commissar of my comrades."[5] Obviously, Che's battlefield fame was spreading in Africa.

Some Simbas spoke halting French and were able to communicate with Che. "One of the first Congolese I met, a chief named Lambert," recalls Che in his diaries, "explained to me while pounding his chest how he and his troops merely laughed at the enemy planes. Lambert explained that the planes were completely harmless, their bullets had struck him many times and simply bounced off and dropped to the ground. The reason was because he and his troops were completely protected by a *dawa* applied by a local *muganga,* or witch doctor, a very powerful one at that. This consisted of many magical herbs sprinkled over them before battle. The only problem came if the combatant either touched a woman before battle or experienced any fear during it. Then he would lose the *dawa* protection. The power of the particular *muganga* was also important."[6]

Che, avowed Marxist theoretician that he was, seemed unfazed by this disclosure, reporting it in the same languid tone as the rest of his writings. Many of the Simbas' "helmets" were manes of monkey fur and chicken feathers.

After one of the very few successful ambushes of Mad Mike's Fifth Commando column, Che's troops discovered that the ambushed truck contained a major stash of whiskey. Having evaded a complete stomping that day, Tatu was in proud form. His victory discourse on "proletarian internationalism" and "imperialist exploitation" was louder and longer than usual. Not that anyone ever listened particularly closely to Tatu's promulgations. But that day his soldiers were truly distracted as they fell upon the captured truck's contents. Soon the revelry started.

For the full picture here, let's recall that "Tatu," when known as "Che" in Cuba, had decreed a ban on liquor, dancing, and cockfighting when he marched into Santa Clara. (This might come as something of a surprise to all the spring break revelers in Cancun who bear his image.)

It didn't take long for the ambush site to become a madhouse of yelling and laughing as Tatu screeched hoarsely and futilely from the sidelines about "proletarian internationalism." Alas, the Simbas had plenty of ammo left in their weapons, and soon the fireworks started, at first into the air. But soon aiming became difficult, and several Simbas ended up shooting themselves and each other in the festive melee. A poor peasant was quickly mowed down. The man was clearly a "spy of the mercenaries," explained a soused Simba.[7] (Richard Pryor's famous skit where he played a pistol-packing Idi Amin Dada comes to mind here.)

Tatu soon hit upon a familiar solution to such problematic behavior by his troops. He proposed setting up a "Congolese Military Academy," to properly indoctrinate his "African Liberation Army" in "proletarian brotherhood, and revolutionary consciousness," much as he'd done with the militia recruits in Cuba.

The Cubans under Che Guevara's command weren't quite as sanguine. "This whole thing is a stupid pile of sh*t!" one complained. As rout followed rout for the Congolese rebels and their Cuban allies at the hands of Mad Mike Hoare, the Belgians, and the CIA Cubans, morale plummeted. "Many revolutionary comrades are doing a dishonor to their pledge as revolutionaries," is how Tatu described this outburst of common sense among the Cuban troops in his *Congo Diaries.* "Their actions are the most reprehensible that can be imagined for a revolutionary. I am taking the most severe disciplinary measures against them."[8]

So Che/Tatu hit upon the disciplinary measure of *threatening to send his Cuban colleagues home!*

"We had no idea why we were in the Congo," recalls Dariel Alarcon, who as a teenager was recruited into Che's column in Cuba's Sierra and accompanied him on every catastrophe from then on. "That Congo thing was very hasty and reckless. We were simply soldiers following orders. But it was impossible to tell Che anything. We were very immature at the time, and Che treated us like marionettes. Whenever he called a meeting it was to browbeat us. No one dared contradict anything he said or offer an opinion. 'You there— shut your mouth!' was all he'd say."[9] (Recall Castañeda's statement that "Che's decency and nobility always led him to apologize.")

Che didn't have anything like that leverage over his African charges, who usually laughed at him. One day Tatu finally put his foot down with the soldiers of his "African Liberation Army." They had refused to dig trenches, to carry any supplies, to do any work whatsoever. "We're not trucks," they said, laughing at Che as he thundered his commands. "And we're not Cubans" (here referring to the ones doing all the grunt work). Che finally lost it.[10]

"In my fury," writes Che in his diaries, "I yelled at them that they were behaving like women. That I'd have to put aprons on them and baskets on their heads so they could carry yucca around like women."

But Che's tirade had to first pass through an interpreter. A French-speaking African would stand close to Che and translate his exhortations for the troops. This meant a slight time lag until his grandiloquence hit home. First the troops turned to face the sputtering Che. Then they turned to the interpreter, who would disclose what all that red-faced sputtering was about.

When the message finally sank in, "they started cackling hysterically," Che writes, "and in a very ingenious and disconcerting manner." It never seemed to occur to the shrewd Che, who didn't understand a word of Swahili, that his interpreters might deliberately mistranslate, thus framing the mighty Tatu as an even bigger jackass than his local fame already proclaimed.

Weeks and months went by and finally one of Che's Cubans, a high Cuban Communist Party official, Emilio Aragones, burst out: "Che!—*que cojones!* [roughly, "what the fuck"] are we doing here!" Che responded with his standard rhetoric about international proletarian solidarity and anti-imperialism. His comrades rolled their eyes, nodded, and walked off.

The Cubans on the other side of the battlefield had a very different experience. Mad Mike Hoare, after watching his allies, noted: "These Cuban CIA men were as tough, dedicated, and impetuous a group of soldiers as I've ever had the honor of commanding. Their leader [Rip Robertson] was the most extraordinary and dedicated soldier I've ever met. Those Cuban airmen put on an aerial show to compete with any. They'd swoop down, strafing and bombing with an aggressive spirit that was contagious to the ground troops who then advanced in full spirit of close-quarter combat."[11]

Gus Ponzoa is a Cuban-American pilot who flew near-suicidal missions over Cuba during the Bay of Pigs invasion, where half of his pilot brothers in arms were killed in action. Gus inflicted dreadful damage on his communist enemies at the Bay of Pigs. Four years later he itched to fight those enemies again and ripped into them in the Congo.

"I really hate to laugh about what we did against Che Guevara in the Congo," he says. "And I'm honored that Mad Mike Hoare thinks highly of us. We certainly think highly of him. That man was a fighter! He was a tank commander against Rommel at El Alamein, then in southern Africa he was a brave and resourceful commander again. But when I think back at those African cannibals we were up against, the ones Che—the mighty 'Tatu'—supposedly led, good grief! . . . I'd fly air cover over Hoare's Fifth Commando, which also included Cuban Americans, Bay of Pigs veterans and friends of mine. That was a thick jungle in the Congo, as you can imagine. We had to fly low—very low, usually following the roads. That was the only way to navigate over that jungle area. I'd spot the enemy and I'd radio down to Hoare's men: 'Throw a smoke grenade, let us know where you are.' And we'd see it—me and my wingmates Luis Ardois, Rene Garcia, and the others, all of us Bay of Pigs vets—we'd swoop down blasting with our fifty-calibers and shooting rockets . . . what a mess down there![12]

"Then Hoare would radio up. 'We're down here! You guys are gonna hit us! You're too close!'

"'We know you're down there, Mike,' we'd shout back. 'We know exactly where you are. You've got enemy close to you and we're taking them out.'" It took a couple of missions before Hoare felt comfortable with the Cuban CIA air support. He'd never had any that was quite *that* close before, certainly not in the expansive deserts of North Africa. But this was jungle; any air support *had* to be close."

Gus goes on to recall, "But after a couple of missions, Hoare loved us. He saw that we knew how to fly—and how to shoot. From then on, he couldn't do without us. He was always slapping us on the back when we met, all smiles."

When Ponzoa and his fellow pilots dove on a strafing run with guns and rockets blazing, they were often flabbergasted to see their African enemies standing in the road or in the few jungle openings, calmly looking skyward. They behaved more like spectators at an air show than targets. "Some would even wave at us right before we blasted them to smithereens," he recalls.

Soon the Cuban-American pilots learned of the magical *dawa,* or protection, that the local *mugangas,* or witch doctors, bestowed upon the mighty Tatu's troops and allies. "The African leader's name in our area was Pierre Mulele," says Ponzoa. "He told his soldiers that if they drank the magic water he was giving them—that a very famous and powerful witch doctor had concocted—then bullets would bounce off their bodies."[13]

Not that all of Che's allies fell for such transparent poppycock. Many remained skeptical. But Mulele had a way to quickly bring around the malcontents and assorted others of little faith. "Mulele would have a few of his soldiers drink the witch doctor water," says Gus Ponzoa. "Then he'd have his officers grab them, tie them up, and stand the poor bastards up to be shot—Pow! Pow! And they'd be shot—but with blanks. 'See?' He'd beam at the troops he'd gathered. 'See! There's the proof!' Now go drink your witch doctor water so we can go into battle against those imperialist mercenaries!'"

Pierre Mulele, by the way, was *education minister* under the

Congolese regime of Patrice Lumumba, who was described by Cornell University's John Henrik Clarke as "A Black Messiah," "the best son of Africa," and "the Lincoln of the Congo."

The heralded author of "Guerrilla Warfare: A Method," the man scholars hoist on the same pedestal with Giap, Mao, and Lawrence of Arabia, the founder of Cuba's Revolutionary Military Academy, the official trainer of Cuba's militia, the subject of the Hollywood hagiography *Guerrilla!*—this mighty Tatu might have persuaded his Congolese troops that fifty-caliber bullets and forward-firing aircraft rockets that opened German Tiger tanks like sardine cans do indeed penetrate human skin.

Tatu's final clash with the mad dogs of imperialism came at a mountaintop town called Fizi Baraka. Che's ally here was "General Moulana," who dressed in a motorcycle helmet draped in a leopard skin and was nicknamed "General Cosmonaut" by the other Cubans. When Che visited his headquarters, Moulana put on his splendid motorcycle helmet battle garb. Then, to display his formidable defenses, he had his troops in all their chicken feather and monkey fur finery parade before Tatu. Needless to say, General Cosmonaut's resident witch doctor had made them all bulletproof.

Hoare's Fifth Commando soon burst upon the scene—literally, with Gus and his partners flying cover with their machine guns and rockets. The result was another hideous slaughter and a complete rout. Tatu scrambled for his life between explosions. Another witch doctor nervously concocted excuses for his somewhat faulty *dawa*.

The whole comic-opera operation finally impressed itself even on Tatu. "History of a disaster," he titles his Congo diaries. But he blames it all on his allies. "The Congolese were very, very bad soldiers," he finally confided to Felix Rodriguez during his last hour alive. Yet, for some reason, the Congolese on Hoare's side seemed to fight rather well.

Tatu's Congo mission was soon abandoned. Che and the Castro Cubans made a humiliating retreat, across Lake Tanganyika. They abandoned their allies and possessions in a frantic retreat, barely escaping Africa with their lives. Che now set his sights on Bolivia for his next guerrilla adventure, for living his dream of turning the Andes "into the Sierra Maestra of the continent," for creating "two, three, many Vietnams."

Castro, as usual, drew valuable lessons from experience. He would soon get out of the business of guerrilla wars and "people's wars." In the mid-1970s, when Castro was serious about a client regime in Africa, he sent fifty thousand troops, hundreds of Soviet tanks, and squadrons of MIGs. They used saturation barrages of 122mm Soviet howitzer shells, hails of Katyusha rockets, and sarin gas against unarmed villages. Force at this level explained the Cuban "victory" in Angola, one unhampered by witch doctors and their *dawa*. (The Clark Amendment passed by Democrats in the U.S. Congress, which cut off all U.S. aid to Angolan anticommunists, also made things easier for Castro.)

One thing that *did* impress the Simbas about Tatu was that "he never went down to the river to wash."

13

Che's Final Debacle

Che died a martyr's death in 1967.
—DAVID SEGAL, *Washington Post*

Che Guevara . . . was young and charismatic and brutally murdered with the support of the CIA.
—GUGGENHEIM MUSEUM CURATOR TRISHA ZIFF

In a way, 1968 began in 1967 with the murder of Che.
— CHRISTOPHER HITCHENS, *The Guardian*

It would be difficult to imagine a more cockamamie plan for Bolivia than the one Che devised. Under President Paz Estenssoro in 1952–53, Bolivia underwent a revolution of sorts, with an extensive land reform that—unlike Che and Fidel's—actually gave ownership of the land to the peasants, to the tillers of the soil themselves, much like Douglas MacArthur's land reform in postwar Japan. Even stranger, Che himself, during his famous motorcycle jaunt, had *visited* Bolivia and *witnessed* the positive results. Still, his amazing powers of self-deception prevailed.

Che convinced himself that in a section of Bolivia where the population consisted not of landless peasants, but of actual *home-steaders*, he'd have the locals crowding into his recruitment tent to sign up with a bunch of foreign communists to overthrow the government that had given them their land, rural schools, and considerable freedom to manage their own affairs. These Indians were highly suspicious of foreigners and especially of white foreigners. Che was undaunted by any of these facts. *Hasta la victoria siempre!* as he liked to say. At this stage in his life Che was probably as deluded as Hitler in his bunker.

"The only place where we have a serious structure," a confident Che told the Bolivian Communist Party head, Mario Monje, "is in Bolivia. And the only ones who are really up to the [anti-imperialist] struggle are the Bolivians."[1]

Monje, a Bolivian native and a shrewd and veteran communist, must have wondered what planet Che Guevara had been inhabiting lately. The local Indians seemed equally mystified. "Their silence was absolute," wrote Che in his diaries about confronting the residents of a Bolivian village named Espina, "as though we were in a world apart."[2] This unnerved Che. In keeping with this principle, he had diligently prepared his guerrillas by having them learn some of the Quechua dialect spoken by most Andean Indians.

The problem was, the Indian population living in the area of Bolivia he had chosen for his glorious guerrilla campaign spoke Guarani, a completely different dialect.

There is no evidence that Castro took the Bolivian mission seriously except as a means to rid himself of Che Guevara. His Soviet patrons were certainly not behind it. They knew better. They'd seen every guerrilla movement in Latin America wiped out. The only thing these half-baked adventures accomplished was to upset the Americans, with whom they'd cut a splendid little deal during the Cuban Missile Crisis to safeguard Castro. Why blow this arrangement with another of Che's harebrained adventures? Much better to work within the system in Latin America, reasoned the Soviets at this time, subtly subverting the governments by using legitimate communist parties. A few years later Salvador Allende's victory in Chile bore fruit for the Soviet strategy.

The Bolivian Communist Party itself had very clear instructions regarding Che's Bolivian adventure. Its head, Mario Monje, was a faithful follower of the Soviet party line who wanted nothing to do with Che, except to help him fail. As soon as Che entered Bolivia, Monje visited both Havana and Moscow for instructions. According to former CIA officer Mario Riveron, who headed the CIA group that tracked down Che in Bolivia, Monje was gratified to learn that he and Castro were in full accord. Fidel's advice to Monje on helping Che was very explicit: "Not even an aspirin."[3]

The Bolivian communist leader's lack of commitment was so obvious that even the numbskull Guevara finally sensed it, but without at first grasping its origins in Moscow and Havana. After meeting with Monje in December 1966, Che wrote in his diaries, "The party is already against us, and I don't know where this will lead."[4]

It would lead, of course, to doom, to betrayal at the hands of Castro himself. That the "ardent prophet of the Cosmos," "the noblest historical figure in all of Latin America" had secretly sent out word that the Heroic Guerrilla would soon "sleep with the fishes" wasn't conceivable for Che—just yet. It would culminate in October 1997, with Castro shedding crocodile tears over his "very best friend" at Che's reinterment and funeral extravaganza in Santa Clara.

According to Mario Riveron, as early as 1964 Castro was already grooming Che for the same fate as his revolutionary comrade Camilo Cienfuegos, who had come across in the *Granma* and stood shoulder to shoulder with the Castro brothers and Che. "Castro's ego simply will not allow anyone to upstage him, even temporarily, even slightly," according to Mario Riveron. "Because of Che's fame by that time, eliminating him would be a more delicate matter than getting rid of Camilo. But get rid of him he would."

Who was Camilo Cienfuegos?

Camilo had entered Havana a day before Che on January 3, 1959, where, acting on Castro's orders, he promptly took command of Cuba's military headquarters at Camp Colombia. Camilo was handsome and charismatic, and in the eyes of many, actually outshone Fidel and Che at early revolutionary rallies, often stealing the limelight with his ready smile and humor. *Simpático* is the term Cubans use for Camilo Cienfuegos's personality. Castro seemed to recognize this and actually turned to Camilo on the podium during his first mass rally in Havana. *"Voy bien, Camilo?"* Fidel asked (am I doing OK, Camilo?). Such deference was—to say the least—not a Castro trademark.

A few months later, Camilo flew from Havana to the eastern province of Camaguey for the hateful task of arresting his friend and revolutionary comrade Huber Matos, who was being devoured by the revolution he helped seat at the table. On the flight back to Havana after he dutifully arrested Matos, Camilo Cienfuegos disappeared without a trace. His plane crashed and vanished, said the authorities, though the evening had excellent weather, according to all records. The Castro brothers made a big show of a search and rescue, but nothing turned up. To many, including Huber Matos himself, Camilo's death seemed much too convenient.

Two of Camilo's loyal lieutenants also died in "accidents" within days of their commander's disappearance. The head of Camaguey's small airport, from which Camilo had taken off on his doomed flight, was also suspicious and started to ask questions about the rescue effort. Two weeks after Camilo's disappearance, this airport official was found with a bullet through his head. His death was ruled a "suicide."

Always the true believer, Che Guevara swallowed Castro's version of Camilo's death without a hiccup. (Che's first son, Camilo, was named in honor of his deceased friend.)

Just two months after arriving in Bolivia and setting up camp in Nancahuazu, Che decided to leave a small crew at the camp and take his guerrilla band on a "conditioning" and "reconnaissance" trek through the surrounding area. "We'll be back next week," he told the others.

Not two miles from the camp, Che's outfit lost its bearings. Two weeks later, they ran out of food. A month later, they were still stumbling around totally lost, eating monkeys and parrots for sustenance and constantly bickering. Several had caught malaria. Then two men drowned while trying to cross a river with a load of six rifles and ammo. Forty-eight days later, the rest stumbled back to the main campsite, with their masterful guerrilla chieftain at their head, demoralized, sick, and half-starved. Here they learned that the few Bolivian guerrillas in their band were already deserting and ratting them out, and that the local peasants had already alerted the army to their "liberators' " presence.

Che, the author of the century's best-selling guerrilla guidebook, had gone into the jungle having learned the wrong local language and apparently lacking the ability to correlate a compass to a map. Che might have tried celestial navigation, or "steering by the stars," a reliable form of guidance used since the Upper Paleolithic. He did not.

The only Bolivians Che managed to recruit into his doomed group were renegade communists and Maoists. Most of these were tricked into joining. Che's guerrilla force, which averaged about forty-five members, was pompously titled the "National Liberation Army." Yet at no point during its eleven-month venture did Bolivians make up more than half of its members. And these few Bolivians all came from the cities, tin mines, and universities far distant from the guerrilla base. The rural population shunned their "National Liberation Army" like a band of lepers. On March 25, 1967, Bolivia's National Confederation of Peasants (as Latin American, as rural, and as indigenous an outfit as there is) *mobilized its entire membership against Che Guevara,* "against the intervention of foreign elements in our country's internal affairs."

Long before the Gap- and Birkenstock-clad tourists from Chelsea, Manhattan, and Malibu arrived on their Che tours, these Bolivian peasants were "on the trail of Che Guevara," as the tourist brochures advertise their junkets—but with machetes, pitchforks, and a hangman's noose.

Six hundred peasants from Bolivia's rural department of Cochabamba volunteered to form a militia to fight Che. This was *three times* as many guerrillas as Castro and Che's rebel army *ever* numbered in Cuba, and over *ten times* as many as Che's own Bolivian "National Liberation Army," counted at its peak, including the snookered miners. Sweetest of all ironies—all of these six hundred Bolivians willing to fight Che *were actually peasants,* not unemployed lawyers, bored college students, and cashiered philosophy professors.

Yet Bolivian peasants did not scorn and resent *all* foreigners. When U.S. Army major Ralph "Pappy" Shelton of the Green Berets arrived in Bolivia with his sixteen-man crew to train the men who would hunt down and extinguish Che and his "National Liberation Army," Bolivian peasants mobbed him at every turn. Everywhere "Pappy" and his men ventured in the Bolivian countryside the locals showered them with food, drink, song, and fond salutations.

"You hate to laugh at anything associated with Che, who murdered so many," says Felix Rodriguez, the Cuban-American CIA officer who played the key role in tracking him down in Bolivia and was a friend of "Pappy" Shelton. "But when it comes to Che as guerrilla you simply have to. In Bolivia he was unable to recruit *one single campesino* into his guerrilla ranks!—not *one!* I fought the Viet Cong, El Salvador's FMLF, the Sandinistas, and *with* the Nicaraguan Contras. So I know about guerrilla movements. All of those—especially the Contras—recruited heavily from the rural population.

"In fact, the few Bolivians Che managed to recruit were actually tricked into joining the guerrilla band. I interviewed several of them," says Rodriguez. "Che had told them to make their way to his camp and meet with him and he'd see to it that they'd be sent to Cuba—and even to Russia and China—for schooling and training. Then when they got to the camp. 'Cuba?' Che would frown. 'Russia? What are you talking about? Who said anything about going *there?*' Then Che would hand them a gun and say, 'Welcome! You're a guerrilla now. And don't you dare try to escape or the army will kill you.' That's why Che had so many deserters. And we took good advantage of those deserters. They were constantly feeding us information about the guerrilla group's whereabouts. They felt they'd been duped, tricked. I took advantage of that feeling of betrayal in my intelligence work."[5]

Leave it to Che Guevara to then complain about his Bolivian "recruits." "They do not want to work," he whined in his diaries. "They do not want weapons; they do not want to carry loads; they feign illness." On top of all this, one Bolivian, named Eusebio, was also a "thief, liar and hypocrite."[6]

"The peasant base has not yet been developed," wrote Che in his diaries for early May. "Although it appears that through the use of planned terror we can neutralize some of them. Their support will come later."[7]

It never did. It was the *campesinos* themselves who kept reporting the guerrillas' whereabouts to the army, with whom they were generally on good terms, and for an obvious reason: The Bolivian army was composed mainly of Bolivian *campesinos*, not bearded foreigners who stole their livestock. "Not one Bolivian enlistment has been obtained," wrote Che, the liberator of Bolivian peasants.

The East German female guerrilla Haydee Tamara Bunke, or "Tania," who went to Bolivia a year ahead of Che to do advance work for his grand entrance, was actually a KGB-STASI-DGI (Cuba's General Intelligence Directorate) agent sent to keep on eye on Che. The two had met on Che's trip to East Germany in 1960 when Tamara acted as his translator. Much translating, they say, took place in bed. Bunke, born in Argentina of German communist refugee parents, a woman who fancied herself quite sharp, bookish, and worldly, hit it off immediately with Che. Their relationship continued during Tania's lengthy stints in Cuba in the early sixties. Naturally privy to all this, Tania's intelligence chiefs recognized her as the ideal person to keep them informed on Guevara.

"Some claim Tania was a triple agent working also for the CIA," says former CIA officer Felix Rodriguez. "But that's untrue. She had been a longtime agent for the KGB and their allied East-bloc intelligence services. Castro knew this well. She was even a member of the Cuban Communist Party."

Alas, poor Tania (whose name would later become Patty Hearst's Symbionese Liberation Army moniker) was originally slated to remain primarily in the Bolivian capital of La Paz and act as Che's liaison with Havana and the city's guerrilla network, such as it was. In March 1967 she made a trip to Che's guerrilla camp at rural Nancahuazu to deliver the French journalist Regis Debray and the Argentine Ciro Bustos. Both were parlor leftists in thrall to the Cuban revolution and seemed poised to do for Che in Bolivia what the *New York Times*'s Herbert Matthews had done for Castro in Cuba. They were also ready to act in more official capacities as recruiters and messengers for the guerrillas.

Bustos, in particular, was instructed to pay close attention to the Bolivian setup, because promptly after the Bolivian triumph he was to set up a similar brilliant operation in Argentina. From there the mighty Che would lead nothing less than the "liberation" of the entire South American continent! "The struggle in Latin America will acquire, in time, continental dimensions," wrote Che. "It will be the scene of many great battles by humanity [no less!] for its liberation."[8]

And as this glorious conflagration spread like a wildfire across the Western Hemisphere, Che would ultimately lead "humanity" in battle against "the great enemy of the human species: The United States of America!"[9] The whole project should have sounded eerily familiar to Bustos, who had tried infiltrating Argentina to start a guerrilla war at Che's behest back in 1963. Now he was back with Che, escorted by Tania and ready for another go-round.

"Che planned on setting a Mount Olympus in the Andes with himself at the very top—with Che himself positioned higher than Fidel." This according to Dariel Alarcon, a Cuban guerrilla who had fought with Che in the Sierra and Congo, and was one of the three guerrillas who managed to survive the Bolivian debacle.[10]

Not a month into his Olympic venture, the few Bolivian "recruits" to Che's band had already started deserting. These ingrates had notified the Bolivian army about Che's camp just as Tania arrived with Debray and Bustos. Tania had also left a Jeep in the nearby town of Camiri full of guerrilla documents, photos, and her ID papers, complete with aliases. The Jeep and all its contents were found by the police, and were soon in the custody of the Bolivian army's intelligence division, which tracked down and nabbed all of Che's urban contacts (there weren't many) in La Paz.

Thanks to her incompetence as a spy, Tania was now stuck as a guerrilla. But Debray and Bustos schemed to sneak their way out of Che's camp in clever disguises, Debray as a foreign journalist and Bustos as a traveling salesman who took a wrong turn during his business calls. The always-on-the-ball Che Guevara had even vouchsafed Debray and Bustos several important messages for the outside world.

One was a bombastic "War Communiqué, No.2." Another was a request to his friends Bertrand Russell and Jean Paul Sartre to start whooping up his Bolivian cause. And one more was a summons to Fidel to send him a new radio, more money, and to please, for God's sake, hurry up and open that "second front" in Bolivia he'd long promised with all the Bolivian communists then training in Cuba.

Mario Monje's reaction to Che's second-front message to Fidel is not on record. And chances are, as a communist, his sense of humor was severely atrophied. But still, we can assume he had to laugh. Not half a day out of Che's camp, Debray and Bustos were nabbed by the Bolivian police and promptly turned over to Bolivian army officials, who gleefully pistol-whipped them. Within minutes, they were betraying Che's whereabouts. Bustos, briefly reverting to his original calling as an artist, even helpfully drew likenesses of the men he saw at the guerrilla camp for his interrogators. Perhaps Bustos was acting out of terror. Or, perhaps having been sent now on two suicide missions, Bustos felt he should reap a little payback on Che.

Bustos's drawings confirmed to the CIA suits what the lower-level Cuban-American CIA men like Mario Riveron had long known—that Che was in Bolivia. The training of the Bolivian army by Shelton and the Green Berets then began in earnest, now with clear targets in mind. Felix Rodriguez convinced the Bolivian military to stop summarily executing guerrilla prisoners. Questioned properly and treated decently, they could provide valuable information and help close the net on Che.

According to Dariel Alarcon, Che was at first furious with Tania for having shown up at the camp. "What the hell do I tell you things for!"[11] he screamed at her as she burst into tears. But Che was soon making good use of her presence. The two were often noticed sneaking down to the swimming hole on many afternoons—not that Che ever got wet. Among the bourgeois debauchments most disdained by Che were baths. Tania and Che were also noticed slinking into Che's tent many a night. This didn't sit well with the rest of the guerrillas, who were utterly famished in that department.

The erotic encounters with Tania revealed a new dimension of Che's hypocrisy. From his Sierra days through the Congo, and into Bolivia, Che closely policed and attempted to thwart his men's libidos, meting out harsh penalties for miscreants. His pathological despotism demanded it. "I have no home, no woman, no parents, no brothers, and no friends," wrote Guevara. "My friends are friends only so long as they think as I do politically." Now the friendless Che had, as his men saw it, brought a woman into the camp to comfort him.

Tania soon fell ill with a high fever. Che assigned her to his guerrilla "rear-guard" group, headed by the Cuban "Joaquin," which he divided from the "vanguard" group, which he headed. Within days of this decision, both groups were hopelessly lost from each other, and from their camp. During their groping about in the jungle, they bumped into a couple of inexperienced Bolivian army patrols and scored a couple of successful ambushes. Better luck was not to come. Both groups continued to bumble around—half-starved, half-clothed, and half-shod—without any contact *for six months,* though they were often within a few miles of each other. Lacking even World War II vintage walkie-talkies, the two groups never knew how close they were to each other.

Che's diary entries for early May are unintentionally comical. "We walked effectively for five hours straight, and covered from

12–14 kilometers, and came upon a campsite made by Benigno and Aniceto." These were men in Che's own vanguard group, evidence they had been walking in circles. "This brings up several questions," Che asks in his diaries. "Where is the Iquiri River? Perhaps that's where Benigno and Aniceto were fired upon? Perhaps the aggressors were Joaquin's people?"

In other words, they were not only walking in circles. They were shooting at one another.

Che's masterful *Guerrilla Warfare: A Method* gives no explanation for these sly guerrilla tactics. But his diaries are often astonishingly frank. "A day of much confusion about our geographic position," he wrote on May 2. Before he could liberate the continent, Che would have to figure out where he was. This is the same man who, in the words of *Time,* "waged a guerrilla campaign where he displayed outrageous bravery and skill," the man whom some scholars equate with Mao Zedong, and his thirty-eight-hundred-mile Long March.

Now separated from Che, Tania's rear-guard comrades found themselves in a position to vent their long-simmering resentment. They constantly tormented her. The Cuban guerrillas, in particular, liked to strip naked and surround her, laughing and gesturing lewdly. Tania was no delicate little flower, far from it. Her liaisons in amour ran from Che, to Cuba's tough intelligence officer, the black Ulises Estrada, to Bolivian president René Barrientos.

But the sexual threats and constant abuse from her revolutionary comrades wore Tania down. "Wait till we get back!" she'd cry. "I'm gonna report all this to Che!"[12] But Che was nowhere around, as both groups circled each other, eating tree roots and armadillos while racked with dysentery and constant vomiting. Toward the end of her Bolivian misadventure, reports fellow guerrilla Dariel Alarcon, Tania would often explode in tears at the men's crude insults and run off shrieking in rage. "Just shoot me—why don't you!" she yelled.[13]

The Bolivian army soon obliged her. After four months in the jungle, racked by fever, and rapidly starving to death, the "rear guard" blundered into an ambush by a Bolivian army patrol while crossing a river. There was more galling news for Che. An obviously unenlightened Bolivian peasant, Honorato Rojas, had set up the massacre.

A few weeks earlier, Che's own group had run into Rojas, who gave them some food and directions. In Che's own words, Rojas gave them "a good welcome and a lot of information." Heaven knows, this didn't happen often. So they were elated. This peasant obviously recognized his benefactors! Sure, if they triumphed, their "revolution" would steal his meager holdings, and murder him if he resisted, as they'd done to thousands of similar country folk in Cuba. But how was *he* supposed to know that?

In late August, Tania and the rear guard found Rojas again and asked him to point out a good place to cross the nearby Masicuri River. Once again, he obliged them. Rojas then scurried over to the headquarters of Bolivian army captain Vargas Salinas and gave him the precise location of the crossing. Honorato said he'd be wearing a white shirt to distinguish him from the guerrillas, so please be careful when they were mowing them down. Rojas went back home and waited for Che's rear guard, which managed to arrive punctually.

"Right this way, *amigos*!" and Honorato led them over to the shallow river crossing at the appointed time, bade them godspeed, and sat on a ridge with a clear view for the show. Only the popcorn was missing. When all ten members of the rear guard were sloshing through waist-deep water, Captain Vargas Salinas took the first shot. His soldiers had set up several machine guns. The ensuing crossfire was deafening and murderous. The water churned and frothed from the fusillade. Tania fell into the river, her body washed away by the current, along with the others.

Only a Bolivian guerrilla code-named "Paco" survived the slaughter. Upon questioning him later, Felix Rodriguez learned that Paco was quite eager to rat out the location of his guerrilla group's "vanguard" led by Che. Paco felt snookered and was bitter. Che, it appeared, had brought him on board, not as a proposed guerrilla at all, but with the bogus offer to send him to Cuba for schooling. As with others, as soon as Paco showed up at the guerrilla camp, Che reneged, virtually kidnapped him, and started treating him like a slave.

But finding Che's group wouldn't be easy, explained Paco. Che's location wasn't a mystery only to the Bolivian army—it was a much *bigger mystery* to Che himself, and to everyone under his command. (For once, Che's obtuseness was working in his favor.) Rodriguez, a veteran intelligence man, sensed that Paco was telling the truth. But nonetheless, the ring started closing on Guevara.

"Dear mother," Tania had written only a few weeks before she was mowed down in the Bolivian ambush, "I'm scared. I'm always frightened and am always crying. My nerves are shot. I'm not a woman. I'm a girl who would like to hide myself in some corner where no one can find me. But where can I hide?"[14]

The terror and despair of her last days would certainly have been tinged with the realization that her fate was tied to that of a man who was increasingly delusional and certainly doomed. "The legend of our guerrilla group is growing like a huge wave," Che wrote in his diaries for July. "We are already the invincible supermen."

Perhaps she also finally grasped the nature of Che's idealism. "*Animalitos,*" was how Che referred to the Bolivian peasants in his diaries. "The peasant masses do not help us in any way."[15] (Two years later, Rojas was captured at his home and murdered in front of his wife and children. This method of "fighting" was in complete keeping with Che Guevara's legacy, as many a peasant family in Cuba's Sierra Maestra could attest.)

Dariel Alarcon reports how, while lost and starving, Che was obsessed with posing for photos. One was of Che atop a (presumably stolen) horse on a ridgeline, where he was strategically silhouetted against the bare sky. Che handed Alarcon his Pentax and had him back off just the right distance to capture the entire scene. Che nodded, then plucked out a machete and waved it high over his head, shouting, "I am the new Bolivar!" as Alarcon dutifully clicked away.[16]

Meanwhile, Che's men blundered around, lost, constantly bickering with each other, constantly losing recruits, terrorizing peasants, now eating cats, condors, and armadillos. This was not guerrilla war as Castro had "fought" it, amassing weight, feted by fawning reporters and duped financial backers, who paid bribes to keep Batista's army from firing.

Dariel Alarcon also remembers Che browbeating him savagely. "One day I was cooking at the camp," he recalls, "and Che walks up. 'What you doing?'

" 'I'm getting ready to cook.'

" 'Well, what are you going to cook?'

" 'I think I'm gonna rustle up some boiled potatoes and a little meat.'

" 'No!' snapped Che. 'Don't cook any meat. Cook some rice and beans with some sardines.'

" 'Fine, whatever you command, Che,' I replied, and for some reason that set him off.

" 'It's not whatever I command, Chico!' Che raved. 'It's whatever comes out of my goddamned balls to command! You got that?'

" 'Yes, but wait a minute now. I have not insulted you in any way, *comandante*? Why are you raving at me like this?'

" 'I said *you got that?* ' "

Che spun around and stomped off.[17]

In his diaries, Che recounts Alarcon's committing a major blunder by allowing himself to be seen by a peasant family fishing. "Benigno [Dariel Alarcon's guerrilla name] let himself be seen, then let the peasant, his wife and kid all escape. When I found out I had a major tantrum and called it an act of treason. This provoked a fit of crying and bawling by Benigno." Apparently, Alarcon should have murdered the family.

This entry is typical. Che's diaries seem to revel in the punishment he doles out to his peons, along with the trivial infractions that provoked them. "Today there was an unpleasant incident," Che wrote in September. "Chino came to tell me that Nato had roasted and eaten a whole piece of meat in front of him. So I yelled and stormed at Chino."

"Every time Che sent for you it was to pull your ear about something or other," said his former Cuban bodyguard Alberto Castellanos.[18]

Dariel Alarcon, who'd dutifully fought alongside Che from the Sierra Maestra through the Congo and into Bolivia, managed to escape Che's final Yuro firefight, enter Chile after weeks of hiking, and eventually make his way back to Cuba (much to Castro's apparent discomfiture). It took a little while, but Alarcon finally came to his senses. He defected in 1996 and lives in Paris today. He has no doubt Che's fate in Bolivia was a deliberate setup by Castro, which provoked a resentment that fueled Alarcon's flight to exile. Back in Cuba he even heard it from Che's bodyguard, Alberto Castellanos, a friendly Cuban intelligence officer. "I'll tell it right to your face," Castellanos confided to Alarcon. "You people were dumped in the Bolivian jungle the same way someone throws a used bone into the garbage can."

"Well before the final ambush and Che's death it looked to us like Cuba had abandoned us," recalls Alarcon about a campfire discussion among the guerrillas one night.

"Forget about any help!" snorted Alarcon's fellow guerrilla Antonio Olo Pantoja. "Forget about it! Dammit! I'm telling you that over there in Cuba what they want *is to get rid of us*. It's obvious!"[19] And Antonio was in an excellent position to know. He was a veteran Cuban intelligence operative who knew full well how these things worked. He'd planned the offing of many fellow revolutionaries himself. Now he recognized that his turn had come.

While Che was posing for snapshots by Dariel Alarcon, neither he nor anyone in his group had any way to communicate with Cuba. By late summer, their antique tube radio had finally sputtered out. Castro had sent an agent named Renan Montero to La Paz to keep in touch with Che, but Montero abruptly left Bolivia in July and returned to Cuba. Significantly, just a week earlier, Aleksey Kosygin had visited Cuba and met with Castro.

Kosygin had just come from a meeting with Lyndon Johnson, during which the U.S. president complained about what he saw as "Castroite subversion" in Latin America. (If he'd only known the real motive.) This "Castroite subversion" was a clear breach of the deal the United States and the Soviets had cut back in October 1962, which had left Castro unmolested. Now this mischief in Bolivia might force the United States into an agonizing reappraisal of that deal, LBJ explained.

Hearing this from Kosygin, Castro concluded that the time had come to speed things up and finally rid himself of Che. Within days, Montero came home and Che was cast completely adrift. Barely two months later, the "National Liberation Army" was wiped out and Che was dead.

On September 26, a Bolivian patrol, alerted by those chronically unenlightened peasants, ambushed Che's vanguard near the village of La Higuera and killed three guerrillas. Felix Rodriguez, who had been getting a wealth of valuable information from the captured Jose Castillo Chavez, or "Paco," identified one of the dead guerrillas as "Miguel." This was a Cuban named Manuel Hernandez, a captain in Castro's rebel army who was second-in-command of the "vanguard" right behind Che. Felix sensed that Guevara was nearby and advised the Bolivian military to send their U.S.-trained ranger battalion to the area.

"But their training isn't complete," replied the Bolivian commander.

"No matter!" answered Rodriguez. "I think we've got Che pinpointed! Send them in!" Barely a week later Che was yelling his pitiful plea to those Bolivian rangers. "Don't shoot! I'm Che, I'm worth more to you alive than dead!"

Che's capture merits some clarification after the romanticization of his last day by his hagiographers. Che was defiant, they claim. Che was surprised, caught off-guard, and was unable to properly defend himself or to shoot himself with his last bullet, as was his plan. Jon Lee Anderson is particularly obsessed with this version. Jorge Castañeda has a machine-gun burst not only destroying Che's carbine, but actually "blasting it from his very grip and wounding him in the process."[20] Christopher Hitchens has written of Che's "untamable defiance."

In fact, Che, after ordering his men to fight to the last man and the last bullet, surrendered enthusiastically. His famous "wound" was a bullet graze near his calf that missed bone and most muscle. Che surrendered voluntarily from a safe distance, and was captured *physically sound and with a full clip in his pistol.*

"Che could not shoot back," claims Castañeda. "His pistol had no clip."[21]

"Che fired his M-2 carbine but it was soon hit in the barrel by a bullet, rendering it useless," writes Anderson. "The magazine of his pistol had apparently already been lost; he was now unarmed."[22]

And where did Che's diligent and hard-nosed biographers get this heroic version of events? Their source reads: "We have been able to precisely determine that Che had been battling even while wounded until the barrel of his M-2 carbine was damaged by a shot that made it totally useless. And his pistol was without a clip. These incredible circumstances explain why Che was captured alive."[23]

The above passage is in the prologue to Che's Bolivian diaries, published in Havana. This prologue had been written by *Fidel Castro.*

After all, PBS, in its 1997 special on Che commemorating the thirtieth anniversary of his death, informs us that "Mr. Anderson . . . gained unprecedented access to both Che's personal archive through his widow and to formerly sealed *Cuban government archives.*" Aleida March, of course, is now a Castro regime official who chairs the Ernesto Guevara Research Center in Havana. Anderson received unprecedented access to the propaganda of one of the world's most censored societies. It's as if historians were to uncritically accept neo-Nazi claims that Hitler had died battling Soviet troops, instead of commiting suicide.

What really happened? Castro, obviously, wasn't at the scene. The three Cuban guerrillas who escaped Bolivia were nowhere near Guevara at the time of his surrender. Willy, a Bolivian miner and guerrilla captured with Che, was executed along with Che the following day.

Why not consult the *full* records of the Bolivian officers actually *on the scene of the capture?* We know perfectly well why. The truth isn't pretty.

Bolivian army officers Captain Gary Prado and Colonel Arnaldo Saucedo Parada both inspected and listed all of Che's personal effects upon his capture. Both list his Walther PPK 9mm pistol as containing *a fully loaded clip.*[24]

More tellingly, though he was in the bottom of a ravine during the final firefight and could have made a fighting escape in the opposite direction like a few of his men, Che actually moved *upward* and *toward* the Bolivian soldiers who had been firing, ordering his comrade at the time, the hapless Willy, along with him. Yet Che was doing *no firing of his own* in the process. Then, as soon as he saw soldiers he made that yell, "Don't shoot! I'm Che! I'm worth more to you alive than dead!" and came out of the brambles completely unarmed, having dropped his fully loaded weapon.

"We represent the prestige of the Cuban Revolution!" Che had thundered to his men hours before. "And we will defend that prestige to the last man and to the last bullet!"[25] But he himself was ready to do no such thing.

"If he had wanted to die he could have stayed further down and kept fighting," says Captain Gary Prado. "But no, he was trying to get out."[26]

Che was surprised by "concealed soldiers who popped up a few feet away," writes Anderson, who got this version straight from Castro's sources while living in Havana itself.

"Che was surprised . . . caught off guard," claims Castañeda.

Again, these unattributable stories conflict with those from the men *who were actually there.* "Che made his position known to our soldiers well in advance so that they would stop firing," writes Colonel Saucedo Parada, "yelling, 'Don't shoot! I'm Che!' Then he came out unarmed."[27]

"Che raised his carbine from a distance," says Bolivian general Luis Reque Teran, who commanded the Fourth Division. "Then he yelled: 'I surrender! Don't kill me! I'm worth more alive than dead!'"[28]

"When captured all of Che's and Willy's weapons were fully loaded," writes Colonel Saucedo Parada, further demolishing the media's titillating fantasy of Che's "untamable defiance."[29] Also overlooked by his hagiographers is that the fully armed Che and Willy were confronted by only two Bolivian soldiers. That makes *two* Bolivian rangers against *two* armed guerrillas. But then, even odds were never to Che's liking.

What about Che's "damaged" carbine? Castro's account has Che armed with an M-2 carbine, as were all Cuban guerrilla officers. Captain Gary Prado lists a damaged carbine, but it is a damaged *M-1* carbine, which may have been that of Willy, Che's partner in the final firefight. Naturally, none of Che's diligent biographers care to speculate on the above discrepancies.

Immediately after his capture, Che's demeanor was even more telling. "What's your name, young man?" Che asked one of his captors. "Why what a lovely name for a Bolivian soldier!" he blurted after hearing it.[30] The firefight was still raging after Che's surrender. His men, unlike their *comandante*, were *indeed* fighting to the last bullet. Soon a wounded Bolivian soldier was carried by.

"Shall I attend him?" Che asked his captors.

"Why? Are you a doctor?" asked Captain Gary Prado.

"No, but I have some knowledge of medicine," answered Guevara, resuming his pathetic attempt to ingratiate himself with his captors, and admitting on the record that he was not, in fact, a doctor.[31]

"So what will they do with me?" Che asked Captain Prado. "I don't suppose you will kill me. I'm surely more valuable alive."

A bit later, Che asked again, "What will you do with me? I'd heard on the radio that if the Eighth Division captured me the trial would be in Santa Cruz, and if the Fourth Division captured me, the trial would be in Camiri."

"I'm not sure," responded Captain Prado. "I suppose the trial will be in Santa Cruz."

"So Colonel Zenteno will preside. What kind of fellow is Colonel Zenteno?" asked an anxious Che.

"He's a very upright man," answered Prado, "a true gentleman. So don't worry."

"And *you*, Captain Prado," said Che quickly. "You are a very special person yourself. I've been talking to some of your men. They think very highly of you, captain. And don't worry, this whole thing is over. We have failed." Then to further ingratiate himself, "Your army has pursued us very tenaciously . . . now, could you please find out what they plan to do with me?"[32]

A young Bolivian schoolteacher named Julia Cortes from the village of La Higuera had brought the captured Che some food on his last day alive. "He seemed to think he'd come out of it alive," she recalls. "They might take me out of here," Che told her. "I think it's more in their interest to keep me alive. I'm very valuable to them."[33]

Like an actor, Che was warming up to his new role as captured hero. In fact, he was captured wearing his famous black beret, sporting a bullet hole, yet those on the Bolivian mission with him, such as Dariel Alarcon, attest that Che *never once* wore that beret during the Bolivian campaign. Che had always worn a military cap. All pictures of him in Bolivia back this up. Marcos Bravo, an anti-Batista operative now in exile who knew many of Che's Cuban revolutionary comrades, speculates that Che put on his famous black beret (and even shot a hole in it) to make a dramatic celebrity surrender and impress his captors. Che probably expected a few snapshots in the process.

After a peaceful capture, Che expected a celebrity trial erupting into a worldwide media sensation. Bertrand Russell and Jean Paul

Sartre would issue eloquent pleas for his freedom. Norman Mailer and Susan Sontag would lend their voices from New York. Joan Baez, Country Joe McDonald, and Wavy Gravy would hold a concert and candlelight vigil in Golden Gate Park. Ramsey Clark would take a leave of absence as LBJ's attorney general to assist William Kunstler in Che's courtroom defense. And above all, college students around the world could be counted on to protest, riot, and disrupt their campuses until Che was released.

Here is what happened.

"Finally I was face to face with the assassin of thousands of my brave countrymen," recalls Felix Rodriguez. "I walked into the little schoolroom and he was tied up lying on the ground. My boots were next to his face—just like Che's boots had been next to my friend Nestor Pino's face after he was captured at the Bay of Pigs. Che had looked at Nestor with that cold sneer of his and simply said, 'We're going to shoot every last one of you.' Now the roles were reversed, and I was standing over Guevara."[34]

Both CIA officers involved in his capture, Felix Rodriguez and Mario Riveron, affirm that—leftist legend to the contrary—the agency happened to agree with Guevara. They wanted him alive and made strenuous efforts to keep him that way. "Handled decently, a prisoner talks sooner or later," says Riveron, "a dead prisoner, obviously, won't."

Despite attempts by Felix Rodriguez to dissuade the Bolivian high command, the orders came through to shoot the prisoner. Rodriguez reluctantly passed them on to his Bolivian colleagues. "I was their ally in this mission, an advisor," he says. "I wasn't the one who gave the final orders. But I operated the radio at that location and had the official rank of captain. The orders came to me: Che to be executed."

Felix passed the order along as he was duty bound, but kept trying to change the Bolivian officers' minds. "Felix, we've worked together very closely and very well," replied the stern Bolivian Colonel

Zenteno. "We're very grateful for the help you and your team have given us in this fight. But please don't ask me to disobey a direct order from my commander-in-chief. I would be dishonorably discharged."

Now that Che was gone from his command post, the fight by his guerrillas back at Yuro was *really* raging, and the Bolivian rangers were taking casualties. Unlike their gallant commander, Che's men were holed up and defiantly blasting away to the last bullet. So Colonel Zenteno had urgent business at his own command post.

"Felix, I have to go back to my headquarters now," Colonel Zenteno said. "But I'd like your word of honor that the execution order will be carried out by two this afternoon. We know the terrible damage Guevara has done to your country, and if you'd like to carry it out personally we'd certainly understand."

Instead, Felix kept trying to change the colonel's mind. Finally he saw it was futile. "You have my word, colonel."

"Actually, I knew that execution order was coming a little before I got it," says Rodriguez, "when I heard on the Bolivian radio station that Che Guevara had been killed in combat. So I asked Sergeant Teran to shoot Che below the neck to simulate combat wounds. Then I walked back into the little schoolhouse to break the news to Che. 'Look, *comandante,*' I said. 'I've done everything in my power to try and save . . .' At that moment Che turned white. He knew what was coming. So I asked Che if he had any last words he'd like me to pass along.

"He told me: 'Yes, tell Fidel that the armed rebellion will eventually triumph,' but Che said this very ironically, with a sad smirk on his face. I'm convinced that Che finally—at long last—realized that Castro had deliberately sold him down the river. For some reason, here I was finally face to face with one of my bitterest enemies, yet I felt no hate for Che Guevara at the moment . . . It's hard to explain.

"I walked outside the little schoolhouse and heard the shots. I looked at my watch and it was 1:10 P.M., October 9, 1967." Ernesto "Che" Guevara was dead.

Che's biographers, basing their accounts on Castro's fictions, tell a different, more edifying story. When it comes to heroism, perhaps it is better to remember the courageous and defiant yells of Che's firing squad victims.

"I kneel for no man!"

"Viva Cuba Libre!"

"Viva Cristo Rey!"

"Abajo Comunismo!"

"Aim *right here*!"

EPILOGUE

The History Channel Heralds Che

In October 2007 the A&E Network produced a *Biography* show on Ernesto "Che" Guevara. Years back they produced one on Senator "Tail-Gunner" Joe McCarthy. The contrast in these depictions is eye-catching.

The second of these historical figures was a freely elected official who campaigned to remove Stalinist agents that had infiltrated the government of a representative republic. Joe McCarthy launched his congressional inquiry into Communist penetration of the U.S. government at a time when Stalin's regime had already murdered more people, conquered more nations, and enslaved more of their citizens than Hitler's regime had managed at its murderous apex. On top of this, Stalin's regime had recently developed the atomic bomb.

In 1950 Senator McCarthy claimed to know of fifty-seven Stalinist agents in the employ of the U.S. government. Not a single one of these alleged agents suffered so much as a day in jail, though some lost their cushy government jobs.

Ernesto "Che" Guevara was second in command, chief executioner, and chief KGB liaison for a regime that outlawed elections and private property. This regime's KGB-supervised police—employing the midnight knock and the dawn raid among other devices—rounded up and jailed more political prisoners as a percentage of population than Stalin's and executed more people (out of a population of 6.4 million) in its first three years in power than Hitler's executed (out of a population of 70 million) in its first six.

Can you guess which show the History Channel titled "Epidemic of Fear"?

The regime Che Guevara cofounded stole the savings and property of 6.4 million citizens, made refugees of 20 percent of the population from a nation formerly deluged with immigrants and whose citizens had achieved a higher standard of living than those residing in half of Europe. Che Guevara's regime also shattered—through executions, jailings, mass larceny, and exile—virtually every family on the island of Cuba. Many opponents of the Cuban regime qualify as the longest-suffering political prisoners in modern history, having suffered prison camps, forced labor, and torture chambers for a period *three times* as long in Che Guevara's gulag as Alexander Solzhenitsyn suffered in Stalin's gulag.

Can you guess which A&E show mentioned "hundreds of destroyed lives"?

One week into power the regime Che Guevara cofounded abolished habeas corpus. Guevara commanded his regime's prosecutorial goons to "always interrogate our prisoners at night. A man's resistance is always lower at night." He boasted that, "We execute from revolutionary conviction!" and that "judicial evidence is an archaic bourgeois detail." Edwin Tetlow, Havana correspondent for London's *Daily Telegraph,* reported on a mass "trial" orchestrated by Che Guevara where Tetlow noticed the death sentences posted on a board before the trial had started.

Can you guess which show had "The Great Inquisitor" in the title?

In case you haven't guessed, the answer to all of the above questions is Joe McCarthy's.

One signed his name "Stalin II," professed that "the solutions to the world's problems lie behind the Iron Curtain," and boasted that "if the nuclear missiles had remained we would have fired them against the heart of the United States including New York City." He also professed that the victory of socialism was well worth "millions of atomic victims."

Can you guess which show mentioned, "his idealism will rarely be equaled"?

Immediately upon entering Havana, Che Guevara stole and moved into what was probably the most luxurious mansion in Cuba. The rightful owner fled the country barely ahead of a firing squad, and a reporter who wrote of Che's new house in a Cuban newspaper was himself threatened with the firing squad. A year later, thousands of Cubans were sent to forced-labor camps on Che's orders, based on his whim to fashion "a new man."

Can you guess which show included the phrase "he never abused his power"?

During a 1961 speech in Cuba, Che Guevara denounced the very "spirit of rebellion" as "reprehensible." Earlier he had cheered the Soviet invasion of Hungary and the concurrent slaughter of thousands of Hungarians who resisted Russian imperialism. According to Guevara, these freedom fighters were all "fascists and CIA agents."

Can you guess which show described its subject as "a potent symbol of rebellion, liberation, and resistance to imperialism"?

In case you haven't guessed, the answer to the above questions is Che Guevara's.

As described in greater detail in the previous chapter, on his second-to-last day alive, Che Guevara ordered his guerrilla charges to give no quarter, to fight to the last breath and to the last bullet. With his men doing just that, a slightly wounded Che snuck away from the firefight and surrendered with a full clip in his pistol, while whimpering to his captors: "Don't Shoot! I'm Che! I'm worth more to you alive than dead!" He then groveled shamelessly, desperate to ingratiate himself.

Nonetheless, the History Channel gushed that Guevara "was valiant until his last moment alive."

So far, subjective matters. Now on to more objective ones.

Despite numerous attempts, nobody has managed to locate any record of Ernesto Guevara's medical degree. Shortly after his capture Che admitted to his captor's commander, Captain Gary Prado, that he (Che) was not a doctor but "had some knowledge of medicine."

Nonetheless, the History Channel referred to Ernesto Guevara as a "newly qualified doctor."

It is a matter of historical record that in January 1959 the United States gave diplomatic recognition to the Castro/Che regime *more quickly* than they had recognized Batista's in 1952. State Department records also show that the United States imposed an arms embargo on the Batista government and refused to ship arms the Cuban government had already paid for. The official record also documents that U.S. ambassador Earl T. Smith personally notified Batista that he had no support from the U.S. government, which strongly recommended that he leave Cuba. Batista was then denied political asylum in the United States.

In 2001, while visiting Havana for a conference with Fidel Castro, the CIA's Caribbean Desk's "specialist on the Cuban Revolution" from 1957 to 1960, Robert Reynolds boasted that, "Me and my staff were all Fidelistas."[1]

"Everyone in the CIA and everyone at State were pro-Castro, except ambassador Earl Smith." This statement is from former CIA operative in Santiago, Cuba, Robert Weicha.[2]

Nonetheless, the History Channel reported that "Che Guevara helped overthrow the 'U.S.-*backed*' Cuban dictator, Fulgencio Batista."

"At his (Che's) orders around fifty men were executed," asserted the History Channel.

As mentioned earlier, *The Black Book of Communism,* written by French scholars and published in English by Harvard University Press (neither an outpost of the vast right-wing conspiracy, much less of "Miami maniacs") estimated there were 14,000 firing squad executions in Cuba by the end of the 1960s. "The facts and figures are irrefutable," wrote the *New York Times* (no less!) about *The Black Book of Communism*. Cuban eyewitnesses to the early months of the Che-directed massacre estimate from four hundred to nearly two thousand men were sent to the firing squad on Che's direct orders.

Historically speaking, documenting regime murders while that murderous regime remains in power has proven almost impossible. Yet the Cuba Archive Project headed by Maria Werlau and Dr. Armando Lago has already documented 216 firing squad death warrants signed by Che Guevara, a figure quadrupling the History Channel's. What can possibly account for such a relentless contempt for the truth by the History Channel?

We'll see in a minute.

"He studied the evidence in each case [of the fifty executions] with methodical care. The executed were all torturers and murderers of women and children," asserted the History Channel in their Che biography.

Well, Guevara's judicial methods I've already mentioned, simply by quoting Che Guevara himself. If "judicial evidence is an archaic bourgeois detail," if no defense counsel or witnesses are permitted, then just how did Che determine who is "a torturer and murderer of women and children"? The History Channel provided no clue.

But their main source, Che biographer Jon Lee Anderson who was interviewed and quoted extensively through the "documentary," did. This diligent historian got the figure of fifty executed and the accounts of the sterling judicial procedures preceding the executions from one of the Communist prosecutors himself, Orlando Borrego, who features as a major source in Anderson's book and who is a minister in Cuba's Stalinist government to this day. Indeed, Anderson wrote his book while living in Cuba using ministers of a Stalinist government as primary sources. Other sources such as *Che's*

Diaries were edited and published by Castro's propaganda ministry with the preface written by Fidel Castro himself. Given the subject, perhaps such a thoroughly "revolutionary" form of historiography is fitting. Let's step back for a second and contemplate it.

Adolph Eichmann, Rudolf Hess, Karl Donitz, Baldur von Schirach, and many other Nazi officials were still alive when William Shirer wrote *The Rise and Fall of the Third Reich*. Yet these were not Shirer's primary sources. Therefore, applying contemporary logic as it applies to Cuban history, Shirer's book should be thoroughly discredited. Anything and everything former Nazi officials had to say should have been taken at face value. Instead Shirer relied on sources such as German exile Fritz Thyssen. This man was "embittered," had an obvious "ax to grind" against the Nazi regime, and should have been discounted as biased and not credible by William Shirer and by all right-thinking people.

Robert Conquest was also derelict in using Ukrainian refugees such as Marco Carynnyk as sources for his book *The Great Terror*. From Leonid Brezhnev to Yuri Andropov to Nikita Khrushchev, thousands of Stalin's henchmen were available to Conquest as perfectly reliable sources. For not relying upon them exclusively in his studies of Stalinism, Robert Conquest should be laughed off any lectern. His book consists of nothing but embittered ravings and cheap gossip from people with "an ax to grind."

Simon Wiesenthal, Elie Wiesel, and Anne Frank all had obvious "axes to grind" against the Nazi regime, so nothing they said or wrote should be taken seriously. Alexander Solzhenitsyn, Cardinal Mindszenty, Nathan Scharansky, Vladimir Bukovsky, etc. are all "embittered exiles and cranks" with obvious "axes to grind" against the Soviet regime. So the same applies to them.

The above may sound flippant, but it's precisely the methodology applied in media and "scholarly" circles when it comes to studying Cuban totalitarianism. The normal rules of historiography—and even of decency, logic, and common sense—get turned on their heads, resulting in shows like those on the History Channel.

Meet Cuba's New Boss—Same as Cuba's Old Boss

In 1956 when Fidel Castro's motley band of eighty-two guerrillas were training in Mexico for their "invasion" and "liberation" of Cuba from Batista, a trainee named Calixto Morales, suffering from a recent injury, was forced to briefly hobble away from one particularly strenuous training session.

He was trussed up, dragged in front of what a guerrilla leader called a "court-martial," and quickly sentenced to death by firing squad.

Fortunately the "maximum" guerrilla commander showed up in time and ordered his brother to rescind his hasty death sentence. Morales, after all, had the proper "revolutionary" attitude and had merely suffered an unfortunate accident.

Raul Castro had done the hasty sentencing. His big brother Fidel ordered the pardon.

Two years later the anti-Batista "guerrilla war" (occasional shoot-outs and skirmishes that the Crips and Bloods would shrug off as a slow week) was chiefly centered in Cuba's eastern province of Oriente and consisted of two fronts. One was commanded by Fidel in the Sierra Maestra mountains, the other was commanded by Raul in the Sierra Cristal mountains slightly north of Fidel's group.

One day a teenage rebel soldier named Dariel Alarcon overheard Fidel sputtering complaints to his assistant Celia Sanchez about the northern front. Raul's zeal for firing squad executions of "informers," "spies," "counter-revolutionaries" etc., where he often applied the coup de grâce himself, was hampering progress on what Fidel had always treated as the "war's" primary front.

This primary front, of course, was the media front: the almost effortless bamboozling of the swarms of gaping reporters who queued up to interview him. Thanks to these "gallant crusaders for the truth" (as the Columbia School of Journalism hails its students) the stirring tale of Cuba's Thomas Jefferson/Robin Hood/Richard the Lionhearted/Saint Thomas Aquinas—all in one heroic package, sporting a beard and combat fatigues—was thrilling audiences from New York to Paris.

The *New York Times* ignited the process in February of 1957 with Fidel Castro on its front page. Soon a conflagration raged in both print and video. The stories leaking out regarding the "Revolutionary justice" practiced in Raul's front, though completely ignored by the foreign media throng, were causing a bit of grumbling in the Cuban press. So would Raul please cut down on the firing squad bloodbath, requested Fidel. It could hurt the image Fidel was so expertly crafting, with the eager help of media dupes and acolytes, of their "humanistic rebellion."

Raul's response is what caused Fidel's sputtering to his assistant. "Got your message and will take immediate corrective measures," Raul responded to his brother. "No more bloodbath. From now on we'll start hanging the counter-revolutionaries."[3]

Cuban American scholar Dr. Armando Lago who, with Maria Werlau, runs the Cuba Archive Project that meticulously attempts to document the tally of Castro regime murders have documented 278 executions in Oriente province on Raul's orders within the very first week of the Revolutionary triumph on January 1, 1959. Potential contras lurked from one end of Cuba to the other.

So Raul rolled up his sleeves, spit on his hands, and got to work as eastern Cuba's version of Cheka chief Feliks Dzerzhinski, while his bosom friend Che Guevara handled the matter in western Cuba by converting Havana's La Cabana fortress into a tropical Lubyanka.

Dr. Lago has documented 550 executions on Raul's direct order by mid 1959. Eyewitness defectors report that Raul gleefully administered the coup de grâce to at least seventy-eight of these.[4]

Raul's chum Che Guevara was breathing down his neck in the competition, however. Dr. Lago documented 1,168 executions islandwide by that time. The best man at Che's first wedding in 1955 in Mexico City was Raul Castro. So maybe there was some friendly competition involved.

Stalinist type purges of Cuba's military have continued sporadically for decades. "In one week during 1963 we counted 400 firing squad blasts from our cells," recalls former political prisoner and freedom fighter Roberto Martin Perez. Most of these were junior officers accused of being disloyal to the regime.

Much more highly publicized was the Stalinist show trial, confession, and execution in 1989 of General Arnaldo Ochoa and the attendant purge of any military man even rumored as his friend or supporter.

Arnaldo Ochoa was the Cuban general widely credited with Cuba's victories in both the Angolan civil war and in Ethiopia's early crushing of the Eritrean rebellion. "Every officer in the Cuban armed forces admired Ochoa," according to Cuban defector General Rafael Del Pino, who was close to Ochoa both personally and professionally.

Ochoa was on especially close and friendly terms with Raul Castro, whom the general always affectionately called "jefe."

In the dawn hours of July 13, 1989, General Arnaldo T. Ochoa was executed by a firing squad on Raul's orders. A sickening "trial" and "confession" had preceded his execution, all of it on camera. Cuban defector Alcibiades Hidalgo, who served as Raul Castro's chief of staff, asserted that the prosecution and execution of Ochoa was on Raul Castro's orders and subsequently rubber-stamped by the council, as were all of Raul's orders.[5] Cuban defector Rafael Del Pino, who once headed Cuba's air force, explained that "Ochoa was a pragmatic man who was flexible enough to recognize the sense behind Gorbachev's reforms of the time. Even worse, Ochoa, like many other Cuban military officers, was trained in the Soviet Union and had close ties to the Soviet leaders then involved in the reforms with whom they had served in Africa."

That Glasnost and Perestroika stuff could be contagious, in other words. Yet media and scholarly wizards keep telling us it's the "pragmatic" Raul himself who will inspire a "political opening" in Cuba. Given the mainstream media's favored sources on the Cuban Revolution and their consequent track record on reporting the truth on Cuba, perhaps some skepticism is in order.

NOTES

Introduction

1. "Benicio Del Toro Talks Guevara," EmpireOnline.co.uk, April 3, 2005.
2. "The Legacy of Che Guevara," PBS, November 20, 1997.
3. Luis Ortega, *Yo Soy El Che!*, Mexico: Monroy Padilla, 1970, p. 179.
4. Mona Charen, *Useful Idiots: How Liberals Got It Wrong in the Cold War and Still Blame America First*, Washington, D.C.: Regnery, 2003, p. 186.
5. Ryan Clancy, "Che Guevara Should Be Scorned—Not Worn," *USA Today*, October 30, 2005.
6. Jorge Castañeda, *Compañero: The Life and Death of Che Guevara*, New York: Alfred. A. Knopf, 1997, p. xx.
7. David Kunzle, *Che Guevara: Icon, Myth, and Message*, Los Angeles: University of California Press, 1997.

Chapter 1: New York Fetes the Godfather of Terrorism

1. Homer Bigort, "Bazooka Fired at U.N. as Cuban Speaks," *New York Times*, December 14, 1964.
2. Pedro Corzo, tape of Guevara speech in documentary *Guevara: Anatomia de un Mito*, Miami: Caiman Productions, 2005.
3. Jon Lee Anderson, *Che: A Revolutionary Life*, New York: Grove Press, 1997, p. 617.
4. "Che's Explosive Return," *Newsweek*, December 21, 1964.

5. Anderson, *Che*, p. 618.

6. Laura Berquist, "Our Woman in Havana," *Look*, November 8, 1960.

7. Laura Berquist, "28 Days in Communist Cuba," *Look*, April 9, 1963.

8. Edward V. McCarthy, "Conspiradores en Nueva York Vinculador a Fidel Castro," *Diario de las Americas*, February 18, 1965.

9. "Person of the Year," *Time*, December 31, 2001.

10. Daniel James, *Che Guevara: A Biography*, New York: Stein and Day, 1969, p. 276.

11. "Carlos the Jackal: I'm Proud of Bin Laden," Fox News, September 11, 2002.

12. Humberto Fontova, *Fidel: Hollywood's Favorite Tyrant*, Washington, D.C.: Regnery, 2005, p. 2.

Chapter 2: Jailer of Rockers, Hipsters, and Gays

1. Sean O'Hagan, "Just a Pretty Face," *The Observer*, July 11, 2004.

2. James, *Che Guevara*, p. 305.

3. Ibid., p. 323.

4. Ernesto Guevara, *Que Debe Ser un Joven Comunista*, Secretaria Nacional de Propaganda y Educación Política, FSLN, 1962.

5. Anderson, *Che*, p. 470.

6. Leo Sauvage, *Che Guevara: The Failure of a Revolutionary*, New York: Prentice-Hall, 1973, p. 126.

7. Ibid., p. 258.

8. "The Legacy of Che Guevara," PBS, November 20, 1997.

9. Dariel Alarcon, *Benigno: Memorias de un Soldado Cubano*, Barcelona: Tusquets Editores, 1997, p. 253.

10. Castañeda, *Compañero*, p. 146.

11. Author interview with Carmen Cartaya, February 21, 2006.

12. Víctor Llano, *El Carnicerito de la Cabaña, Libertad Digital*, Madrid, November 22, 2004.

13. Author interview with Henry Gomez, February 22, 2006.

14. Ibid.

15. *Guitar World*, February 1997.

16. *Proceso*, Mexico, October 17, 2004.

17. Marc Cooper, "Che's Grandson: Fidel's an 'Aged Tyrant,'" Marccooper.com, October 19, 2004.

18. Hector Navarro, "Un Viaje a Cuba," ContactoCuba.com, January 22, 2006.

19. Sauvage, *Che Guevara*, p. 70.

20. David Sandison, *Che Guevara*, New York: St. Martin's Griffin, 1998, p. 152.

Chapter 3: Bon Vivant, Mama's Boy, Poser, and Snob

1. Enrique Ros, *Che: Mito y Realidad*, Miami: Ediciones Universal, 2002, p. 35.

2. Marcos Bravo, *La Otra Cara del Che*, Bogota, Columbia: Editorial Solar, 2004, p. 97

3. Ibid.

4. Tito Rodríguez Oltmans, "El Compromiso Sangriento," *Revista Guaracabuya*, February 2006.

5. Ortega, *Yo Soy El Che!*, p. 185.

6. Andres Oppenheimer, "How Latin American Elite View the World," *Miami Herald*, September 25, 2005

7. Martin Ebon, *Che: The Making of a Legend*, New York: Universe Books, 1969, p. 13.

8. Sandison, *Che Guevara*, p. 15.

9. Pedro Corzo, interview with Miguel Sanchez in documentary *Guevara: Anatomia de un Mito*.

10. Ortega, *Yo Soy El Che!*, p. 191.

11. Author interview with Frank Fernandez, January 19, 2006.

12. Antonio Navarro, *Tocayo: A Cuban Resistance Leader's True Story*, Westport, Conn.: Sandown Books, 1981, p. 99.

13. "Franz Kafka's Trial as Symbol in Judicial Opinions," *Legal Studies, Forum*, Vol. 12, No. 1, 1988.

14. Sauvage, *Che Guevara*, p. 112.

15. "We're Number One," Lewrockwell.com, August 11, 2001.

16. Paul Johnson, *Intellectuals*, New York: Weidenfeld & Nicolson, 1988, p. 155.

17. The Guevara Photographer Series, BBC News, August 7, 2000.

18. Johnson, *Intellectuals*.

Chapter 4: From Military Doofus to "Heroic Guerrilla"

1. Bravo, *La Otra Cara del Che*, p. 90.

2. Ibid., p. 97.

3. Ibid.

4. Ibid.

5. Author interview with Carlos Lazo, February 20, 2006.

6. Author interview with Enrigue Enrizo, February 21, 2006.

7. Anderson, *Che*, p. 367.

8. Francisco Rodriguez Tamayo, "Como Ganaron los Rebeldes Cubanos," *El Diario de Nueva York*, June 25, 1959.

9. Author interview with Manuel Cereijo, March 21, 2006.

10. Paul Bethel, *The Losers*, New Rochelle, N.Y.: Arlington House, 1969, p. 51.

11. Bravo, *La Otra Cara del Che*, p. 167.

12. Ortega, *Yo Soy El Che!*, p. 31.

13. Ros, *Che*, p. 194.

14. Anderson, *Che*, p. 368.

15. Pedro Corzo, interview with Jaime Costas in documentary *Guevara: Anatomia de un Mito*.

16. Bethel, *The Losers*, p. 51.

17. Author interview with Julio Cañizarez, February 7, 2004.

18. Ortega, *Yo Soy El Che!*, p. 266.

19. Georgie Ann Geyer, *Guerrilla Prince*, Boston: Little, Brown & Co., 1991, p. 70.

20. Warren Commission, Volume XXVI: CE 3081—FBI Report on Fair Play for Cuba Committee.

21. Castañeda, *Compañero*, p. 110.

22. Anderson, *Che*, p. 553.

23. Juan de Dios Marin, "Estuve en una Escuela de Terrorismo en Cuba," *Reader's Digest*, January 1965.

24. Geyer, *Guerrilla Prince*.

25. Castañeda, *Compañero*, p. 200.

26. Grayston Lynch, *Decision for Disaster*, Washington D.C.: Brassey's, 1998, Dedication, p. 1.

27. Jack Hawkins, "Classified Disaster," *National Review*, December 31, 1996.

28. Lynch, *Decision for Disaster*, p. 112.

29. *Revista Girón: Órgano Oficial de la Asociación de Combatientes de Bahia de Cochinos Brigada* 2506, July 2005.

30. All information in this section is from author interviews with Bay of Pigs Veterans Association members, including President Felix Rodriguez and Vice President Nilo Messer.

31. Author interview with Mario Riveron, February 7, 2006.

32. Pedro Corzo, interview with Huber Matos in documentary *Guevara: Anatomia de un Mito*.

33. Author interview with Bay of Pigs Veterans Association Vice President Nilo Messer, May 30, 2005.

34. Anderson, *Che*, p. 505.

35. Author interview with Jose Castaño, January 18, 2006.

36. All information in this section is from author interviews with Bay of Pigs Veterans Association members, including President Felix Rodriguez and Vice President Nilo Messer.

37. Foreign Relations of the United States 1961–1963, Volume X, Cuba, 1961–1962, Department of State.

38. Author interview with Alberto Quiroga, November 24, 2006.

39. Foreign Relations of the United States 1961–1963, Volume X, Cuba, 1961–1962, Department of State.

40. Fontova, *Fidel*, p. 28.

41. Michael Beschloss, *The Crisis Years: Kennedy & Krushchev 1960–63*, New York: HarperCollins, 1991, p. 538.

42. Bethel, *The Losers*.

43. Peter Schweizer, "Cuban Missile Crisis: Kennedy's Mistakes," History News Network, November 4, 2002.

44. Fontova, *Fidel*, p. 23.

45. William Breuer, *Vendetta! Fidel Castro and the Kennedy Brothers*. New York: John Wiley & Sons, 1998.

46. Fontova, *Fidel*, p. 27.

47. Castañeda, *Compañero*, p. 274.

48. Richard Nixon, "Cuba, Castro, and John F. Kennedy," *Reader's Digest*, November 5, 1964.

Chapter 5: Fidel's Favorite Executioner

1. Ros, *Che*, p. 140.

2. Bravo, *La Otra Cara del Che*, p. 136.

3. Ibid., p. 142.

4. Ros, *Che*, p. 187.

5. Pedro Corzo, interview with Agustin Soberon in documentary *Guevara: Anatomia de un Mito*.

6. Sauvage, *Che Guevara*, p. 157.

7. Ortega, *Yo Soy El Che!*, p. 180.

8. Ros, *Che*, p. 118.

9. "Como Asesinado El Che Guevara," *El Nuevo Herald*, December 28, 1997.

10. Mario Lazo, *Dagger in the Heart: American Policy Failures in Cuba,* New York: Funk & Wagnalls, 1968, p. 180.

11. "A Man Without a Country," *Milwaukee Journal Sentinel,* July 4, 2004.

12. Author interview with Roberto Martin-Perez, February 19, 2006.

13. Mario Lazo, *Daga en el Corazon: Cuba Traicionada,* New York: Minerva, 1972, p. 254.

14. Hiram Gonzalez, interviewed by Enrique Encinosa in documentary *Yo los He Visto Partir,* El Instituto de la Memoria Histórica Cubana Contra el Totalitarismo, 2002.

15. Bethel, *The Losers,* p. 383.

16. Henry Butterfield Ryan, *The Fall of Che Guevara,* New York: Oxford University Press, 1998, p. 5.

Chapter 6: Murderer of Women and Children

All of the assassinations included in this chapter are fully documented, using a minimum of two sources, by Armando Lago, Ph.D., and Maria Werlau, who head the Cuba Archive Project.

1. Lazo, Daga en el Corazon.

2. Fulgencio Batista, *Cuba Betrayed,* New York: Vantage Press, 1962, p. 300.

3. Ruby Hart Phillips, *The Cuban Dilemma,* New York: Ivan Obelensky, 1962, pp. 62–63.

4. Pedro Corzo, interview with Jose Vilasuso in documentary *Guevara: Anatomia de un Mito.*

5. Ortega, *Yo Soy El Che!,* p. 179.

6. Bravo, *La Otra Cara del Che,* p. 194.

7. Armando Valladares, *Contra Toda Esperanza,* Barcelona: Plaza Janes Editores, 1985, p. 17.

8. Anderson, *Che,* p. 386.

9. Ibid.

10. Pedro Corzo, interview with Jose Pujols in documentary *Guevara: Anatomia de un Mito.*

11. Valladares, *Contra Toda Esperanza,* pp. 24–25.

12. Author interview with Miriam Mata, March 4, 2006.

13. Valladares, *Contra Toda Esperanza,* p. 27.

14. Ibid., p. 25.

15. Humberto Fontova, "We Love You Fidel," *Newmax* magazine, November 18, 2002.

16. Ibid.

17. James, *Che Guevara*, p. 113.

18. John Keegan, ed., *HarperCollins Atlas of the Second World War*, New York: HarperCollins, 2001.

19. Castañeda, *Compañero*, p.145.

20. Guevara, *Que Debe Ser un Joven Comunista*, p. 13.

21. Maria Werlau and Dr. Armando Lago, Cuba Archive Project.

22. Bethel, *The Losers*, p. 383.

23. Ibid., p. 384.

24. Eloy Escagedo, "Masacre de Jovenes en Sancti Spiritus," CircuitoSur.com.

25. Sauvage, *Che Guevara*, p. 157.

26. Author interview with ex-rebel Santiago De Juan, January 16, 2006.

27. Anthony Daniels, "The Real Che," *New Criterion*, October 2004.

28. Sauvage, *Che Guevara*, p. 263.

29. Castañeda, *Compañero*, p. 178.

30. Author interview with Emilio Izquierdo, November 24, 2005.

31. Cecilio Lorenzo, interviewed by Pedro Diaz Hernandez, January 23, 2002, for La Voz de Cuba Libre.

32. Bravo, *La Otra Cara del Che*, p. 136.

33. Anderson, *Che*, p. 700.

34. Ibid.

35. Author interview with Margot Menendez, March 16, 2006.

36. Anderson, *Che*.

37. Author interview with Barbara Rangel-Rojas, February 7, 2006.

38. Tanía Díaz Castro, "Por qué fusilaron a mi Papá?" CUBANET.INDE-PENDIENTE, December 4, 2000.

39. Ibid.

Chapter 7: The "Intellectual and Art Lover" as Book Burner and Thief

1. Ebon, *Che*, p. 13.

2. Salvador Diaz-Verson, *One Man, One Battle*, New York: Worldwide, 1980, p. 105.

3. "The Legacy of Che Guevara," PBS, November 20, 1997.

4. Christopher Hitchens, "Goodbye to All That," *New York Review of Books*, July 17, 1997.

5. Ros, *Che*, p. 189

6. Geyer, *Guerrilla Prince*, p. 240.
7. Author interview with Sylvia Diaz-Verson, November 24, 2005.
8. Testimony of Salvador Diaz-Verson, Communist Threat to the United States Through the Caribbean, U.S. Senate Subcommittee to Investigate the Administration of the Internal Security Act and Other Internal Security Laws, of the Committee on the Judiciary, May 6, 1960.
9. Nat Hentoff, "Book Burning in Cuba," *Jewish World Review,* August 18, 2005.
10. Ibid.
11. Fontova, *Fidel,* p. 139.
12. Maritza Beato, "El Saqueo del Patrimonio Cultural Cubano," *El Nuevo Herald,* March 1, 2006.
13. Ibid.
14. Ibid.

Chapter 8: Academia's Rude Surprise

1. "Cuba Salutes 'Che' Guevara," CNN, October 17, 1997.
2. Ibid.
3. I. F. Stone, "Mc Carthy and the Witch Hunt," *Stone's Weekly,* April 4, 1953.
4. "L.A. Symposium Debates Che and Cuban Revolution," *The Militant,* November 24, 1997.
5. Author interview with Hugo Byrne, January 22, 2006.
6. Author interview with Jose Castaño, January 18, 2006.
7. Ibid.

Chapter 9: Brownnoser and Bully

1. Author interview with Marcos Bravo, January 7, 2006.
2. Author interview with Miguel Uria, February 19, 2006.
3. Ortega, *Yo Soy El Che!*
4. Bravo, *La Otra Cara del Che,* p. 196.
5. Ibid, p. 197.
6. Ortega, *Yo Soy El Che!,* p. 122.
7. Bravo, *La Otra Cara del Che,* p. 196.
8. Ibid.

Chapter 10: Guerrilla Terminator

1. Bethel, *The Losers*, p. 372.
2. Enrique Encinosa, interview with Agapito Rivera in documentary *Al Filo del Machete*, El Instituto de la Memoria Histórica Cubana Contra el Totalitarismo, 2002.
3. Author interview with Emilio Izquierdo, November 24, 2005.
4. Author interview with Guillermo Robaina, March 24, 2006.
5. Author interview with Lazaro Piniero, March 24, 2006.
6. Fontova, *Fidel*, p. 107.
7. Enrique Encinosa, *Cuba en Guerra*, The Endowment for Cuban-American Studies, 1994, p. 190.
8. Carlota Guillot Pérez, "Presencia del Che en la Limpia del Escambray," *Las Montañas Son Nuestras*, December 20, 1987.

Chapter 11: "The Brains of the Revolution" as Economic Czar

1. Sauvage, *Che Guevara*, p. 143.
2. Ortega, *Yo Soy El Che!*, p. 207.
3. Bravo, *La Otra Cara del Che*, p. 267.
4. Author interview with Frank Fernandez, Cuban factory worker, January 17, 2006.
5. Rene Dumont, *Cuba Est-Il Socialiste?* Paris: Seuil, 1973.
6. Bravo, *La Otra Cara del Che*, p. 288.
7. Anderson, *Che*, p. 632.
8. Mario Lazo, *Dagger in the Heart*, pp. 82–83.
9. Batista, *Cuba Betrayed*, p. 172.
10. Lazo, *Dagger in the Heart*, p. 82.
11. Anderson, *Che*, p. 438.
12. Kirby Smith and Hugo Llorens, "A Comparison of Socioeconomic Indicators in Pre-Castro and Current-Day Cuba," Proceedings of the Annual Meetings of the Association for the Study of the Cuban Economy (ASCE), University of Texas at Austin, August 1998.
13. Ibid.
14. Alberto Iglesias, "Socio-Economic 'Conquests' of the Communist Experiment on Cuba," Miami: Cuba Free Press, Inc., June 1999.
15. Fontova, *Fidel*, p. 39.
16. Alberto Bustamante, "Notas y Estadisticas Sobre los Grupos Étnicos en

Cuba," *Revista Herencia,* Volumen 10, 2004, Herencia Cultural Cubana, Miami, Florida.

17. Theodore Draper, *Castro's Revolution,* New York: Frederick Praeger, 1962, p. 43.

18. Christopher Ruddy, "Powell and Castro," *Newsmax,* May 14, 2001.

19. Kirby Smith and Hugo Llorens, "A Comparison of Socioeconomic Indicators in Pre-Castro and Current-Day Cuba," Proceedings of the Annual Meetings of the ASCE.

20. Ibid.

21. "El Comandante en Jefe si Tiene Quien le Escriba," *El Nuevo Herald,* January 8, 2006.

22. Humberto Fontova, "Fidel as Business Partner," *Newsmax,* February 20, 2002.

23. Anderson, *Che,* p. 469.

24. Lazo, *Dagger in the Heart,* p. 82.

25. Ibid.

26. United Nations, General Assembly, GA/10417, August 11, 2005.

27. Anderson, *Che,* p. 471.

28. Isane Aparicio Busto, "Viaje Literario," *El Mundo de España,* October 25, 2005.

29. Pascal Fletcher, "Supermodels Impressed by Cuba's Castro," Reuters, February 22, 1998.

30. "Czech Model Helena Houdova Briefly Detained in Cuba," *Prague Daily Monitor,* January 26, 2006.

31. Ibid.

32. "Insider Report: Castro Taped Jack Nicholson, Hollywood Stars," *Newsmax,* April 10, 2005.

33. G. Fernández and M. A. Menéndez, "Castro Graba Intimades de Visitantes," *Revista Guaracabuya,* March 12, 2001.

34. Ibid.

35. Ortega, *Yo Soy El Che!,* p. 57.

36. Julia O'Connell Davidson, "Sex Tourism in Cuba," *Race & Class* 38.1, July–September 1996.

37. Ibid.

38. Ibid.

39. Ibid.

40. Felix Hernandez, "Jineteras en el Paraiso," *La Nueva Cuba,* December 20, 2005.

41. Author interview with Eusebio Peñalver, June 9, 2004.

Chapter 12: Che in Africa

1. Author interview with Ninoska Perez-Castellon, radio hostess, January 17, 2006.
2. Pedro Corzo, interview with Miguel Sanchez in documentary *Guevara: Anatomia de un Mito*.
3. Sam McGowan, "Operation Dragon Rouge," The HistoryNet.com, June 2002.
4. Ros, *Che*, p. 262.
5. Ibid.
6. Bravo, *La Otra Cara del Che*, p. 307.
7. Anderson, *Che*, p. 658.
8. Bravo, *La Otra Cara del Che*.
9. Alarcon, *Benigno*, p. 103.
10. Bravo, *La Otra Cara del Che*, p. 310.
11. Author interview with Gus Ponzoa, February 7, 2005.
12. Ibid.
13. Ibid.

Chapter 13: Che's Final Debacle

1. Castañeda, *Compañero*, p. 332.
2. James, *Che Guevara*, p. 260.
3. Author interview with Mario Riveron, CIA, retired, February 7, 2006.
4. James, *Che Guevara*, p. 247.
5. Author interview with Felix Rodriguez, CIA, retired, February 19, 2006.
6. James, *Che Guevara*, p. 268.
7. Anderson, *Che*, p. 716.
8. James, *Che Guevara*, p. 276.
9. Ibid.
10. Alarcon, *Benigno*, p. 152.
11. Ibid.
12. Ibid.
13. James, *Che Guevara*, p. 229.
14. Bravo, *La Otra Cara del Che*, p. 438.
15. Sauvage, *Che Guevara*, p. 241.
16. Alarcon, *Benigno*, p. 103.
17. James, *Che Guevara*.

18. Anderson, *Che*, p. 549.
19. Alarcon, *Benigno*, p. 181.
20. Castañeda, *Compañero*, p. 399.
21. Ibid.
22. Anderson, *Che*, p. 733.
23. Bravo, *La Otra Cara del Che*, p. 458.
24. Ibid., p. 466.
25. Ibid., p. 450.
26. Castañeda, *Compañero*, p. 404.
27. Colonel Arnaldo Saucedo Parada, *No Disparen Soy El Che*, Santa Cruz de la Sierra, Bolivia: Editorial Oriente, p. 137.
28. Pedro Corzo, interview with Miguel Sanchez in documentary *Guevara: Anatomia de un Mitro*.
29. Parada, *No Disparen Soy El Che*, p. 137.
30. Bravo, *La Otra Cara del Che*, p 487.
31. Ibid., p. 467.
32. Ibid., p. 499.
33. Castañeda, *Compañero*, p. 400.
34. Author interview with Felix Rodriguez, CIA, retired, February 17, 2006.

Epilogue: The History Channel Heralds Che

1. Tim Weiner, "Bay of Pigs Enemies Finally Sit Down Together," *New York Times*, March 23, 2001. Also Fontova, *Fidel: Hollywood's Favorite Tyrant*, Washington, p. 93.
2. Geyer, *Guerrilla Prince*, p. 240.
3. Pedro Corzo, *Perfiles del poder*, Hialeah, Fla.: Instituto de la Memoria Historica Cubana, 2007, p. 89.
4. Ibid, p. 88–89.
5. Ibid. p. 102.

INDEX